CUBA,
CASTRO,
AND THE
UNITED
STATES

CUBA, CASTRO,
AND THE UNITED STATES

Philip W. Bonsal

University of Pittsburgh Press

Library of Congress Catalog Card Number 72–151505
ISBN 0–8229–3225–3

COPYRIGHT © 1971, UNIVERSITY OF PITTSBURGH PRESS
Henry M. Snyder & Co., Inc., London

Manufactured in the United States of America

For Margaret

Contents

Illustrations

Acknowledgments

This book was written with the hope that a record of my two years as American Ambassador in Cuba at the start of Castro's long rule and my analysis of the destruction during those years of the long-standing Cuban American relationship would contribute to an understanding of a sad yet instructive episode in the conduct of American foreign policy.

My wife's patience and encouragement made possible this autumnal project. She listened to and read the manuscript and made valuable suggestions along the way. The scrapbooks she had so faithfully kept during our stay in Cuba were of the greatest assistance.

My old friend and colleague, former Ambassador John C. Dreier, now in charge of Latin American studies at the School of Advanced International Studies of Johns Hopkins University, encouraged me to persevere. His indulgent but penetrating criticism and his cordial faith in the importance of my goal command my deep gratitude. He was prepared to secure financial help for my project either from the School or from a foundation. Though this proved unnecessary, he made it possible for me to procure research and typing assistance at the School. Ann Tonyes, a candidate for an M.A. degree in 1968–1969, carried out a number of investigations and prepared reports at my request; she demonstrated industry and perceptiveness of a high order.

Members of the faculty of the School, including Charles Burton Marshall and Herbert Dinerstein were good enough to read parts of the manuscript and to offer helpful suggestions. My thanks are due them, but, of course, I am solely responsible for the pages now before the reader.

The first draft of my manuscript was read by Daniel Braddock who was the senior member of my staff in Cuba. He made valuable suggestions and saved me from error in a number of cases. I am most grateful to him for his time and trouble. Former Ambassador Robert F. Woodward also read one of the early drafts and made many useful comments. My thanks are due him. But neither of these helpful friends and colleagues is in any way responsible for the opinions and views I have expressed.

I am proud to have been an officer of the Foreign Service of the United States. During my Cuban assignment I had the good fortune to have as my friends and colleagues an exceptionally efficient and loyal staff even by the high standards of the service. I wish I could mention them all by name—and their wives, too. They acquitted themselves magnificently under circumstances often disagreeable and sometimes alarming. I must note the outstanding performances of my deputy, Daniel Braddock, a wise, thoughtful, and vigorous veteran; of Eugene Gilmore, the able and incisive Economic Counselor; of Chester Davis, the Agricultural Attaché with his wide knowledge of the facts and personalities of the Cuban sugar and tobacco industries; of John Topping and William Bowdler, the Embassy's knowledgeable political analysts; and of the late James E. Brown, the Consul General, who wisely guided a devoted staff in its task of meeting an extraordinary burden of emergency visa work on behalf of tens of thousands of Cubans escaping from their homeland. I recall, too, with many thanks the thoughtful and resourceful backstopping of Robert Stevenson, the Cuban desk officer in the Department of State.

Mrs. Bonsal and I share a feeling of affectionate admiration for Viola Keskinen, my efficient, loyal, and knowledgeable secretary and executive assistant. We served together over seven years—in Colombia, Bolivia, Cuba, and Morocco. We were fortunate indeed in enjoying her devoted help, her sound advice, and the inspiration of her buoyant spirits.

CUBA,
CASTRO,
AND THE
UNITED
STATES

Chapter 1

Introduction

THE Cuba into which Castro erupted in January 1959 had long appeared to accept Western political, social, and economic values. The existence in Cuban society, as in other societies, of collective blemishes and shortcomings was uncontested; the prevalent wisdom was that these would be mitigated or removed, when and if the national wealth increased, through the operation and the perfection of the methods of representative democracy. The institution of private property was widely cherished as a major dynamic in the promotion of the general welfare. The prejudicial effect on essential social mobility of traditional social stratification was becoming increasingly, if inadequately, recognized. Most Cubans appeared to believe that they had a right to choose their political leaders and to define the mandate of those leaders through the ballot box. The opposition to Batista was in part fueled by a determination to assert that right.

Castro achieved power because he successfully led a nationwide movement to expel Batista. He had promised to restore Cuban democracy and, in the framework of the violated Constitution of 1940, to carry out a number of the reforms demanded by Cuban nationalist sentiment as it had evolved during the previous two or three decades. He could not have become the leader of the anti-Batista revolt on a platform foreshadowing the policies he later adopted. I do not believe those policies were realistically present in his planning during the fight against Batista. Castro did not then believe that he could evade his promise to hold elections soon after the ejection of Batista. He thus accepted a field of action for the new Cuban government limited by the traditions and habits, the aspirations and prejudices of a political majority of the Cuban people.

Within three years after he had come to power Castro had utterly destroyed the preexisting structure of the Cuban community and had rejected participation by his fellow citizens in the governing process in favor of "Marxism-Leninism" as practiced by his own personal dictatorship. He had virtually eliminated private property and had divested most of what was left of any social function. He had brought about a revolution in the ownership and control of the means of production (including land), in education, in housing, and in employment. He had initiated and had stimulated the chain of developments that severed the traditional ties between Cuba and the United States. He had successfully defied the United States and he had made of Cuba a client of the Soviet Union.

Explanations for Castro's sweeping success belong to two schools. One of these presents a flourishing Cuban society developing along Western lines as the hapless and helpless victim of a diabolical Communist conspiracy engineered by Fidel Castro with a mixture of demagoguery, deceit, and intimidation—a conspiracy which the United States, Cuba's protector, failed to detect and counter. The other school holds that pre-Castro Cuba was a depressed, exploited "colony," dominated and managed by American "imperialists" and their Cuban "lackeys" for selfish profit. The island is said to have been seething with revolutionary hopes and desires brutally held down by Batista with American backing. In this version, Castro, the Cuban Communists, and the Soviet Union appear as liberators from both American and local oppression.

Neither of these theses will be adopted by serious historians. These historians will, however, point out that the Castro-Communist take-over met with a mimimum of resistance from the hundreds of thousands of Cubans whose rights, prospects, and property it blasted. Brave men lost life and liberty fighting Castro after he had abandoned his pretense at democratic rule. But, considering the revolutionary process as a whole, it must be conceded that seldom has so much been taken from so many, in terms of both moral and material goods, in so short a time and with so little opposition.

When I arrived in Havana in February 1959, I shared a widespread belief that the Cuban establishment, including the politicians who had opposed Batista and those citizens (from "capitalists" through "the emerging middle class" to the members of the labor unions) who had enjoyed relative economic stability and security, now had a major role to play. This establishment would, I thought, confine the new government and the leaders from the Sierra Maestra, including Castro, within democratic patterns of behavior. Thus a national program of renewal and progress would eventually be agreed upon and implemented through an orderly political mechanism with roots in the Cuban past.

However, the establishment not only did not provide leadership, it proved lacking even in that capacity for self-defense essential to survival. It failed to move a significant proportion of the Cuban community to react effectively to the loss of the prospect of political freedom Castro had promised when he was in the hills. This was all the more remarkable because until Castro revealed his alleged long-standing and long-hidden Marxism-Leninism to an unbelieving world late in 1961 the Cuban Republic had been ruled by men who, Castro included, paid lip service to representative democracy and some of whom were sincere in their efforts to promote and perfect its politics. Yet Castro soon destroyed any possibility of a return to those politics in spite of the fact that they had absorbed the energies and emotions of major elements of the island population and that many of the prominent figures involved were vigorously and often prosperously alive and available.

Castro himself at once achieved a phenomenal hold on the imaginations of most of his countrymen. That hold was not affected by the Maximum Leader's ideological and policy gyrations, by the nonfulfillment of his multiple promises and by the hardships resulting from his measures. Yet even after making full allowance for this extraordinary charisma, I am still amazed at the ease with which Castro established a thoroughgoing personal dictatorship over a society which seemed long to have worked and hoped for democracy even though it had not, except fleetingly, enjoyed its substance.

Hundreds of thousands of Cubans have indeed expressed their opposition to Castro by abandoning their native land. Other hundreds of thousands are ready to leave Castro's Cuba though departure involves loss of livelihood and personal possessions. But this disaffection of a large fraction of the population does not present the regime with a challenge commensurate with the numbers or with the former status of the dissenters. Nor can it be asserted with any plausibility that Castro's power today rests on the presence or the threat of foreign bayonets as is the case with the rulers of some countries of Eastern Europe.

Years after the end of my Cuban mission, I lunched with a distinguished Cuban friend who had shared the early enthusiasm of most of his compatriots for the Maximum Leader but had later broken with him. To my question as to the reason for Castro's total success and for the lack of effective opposition, he replied: "Very simple! We had no confidence in any possible Cuban leadership of the anti-Castro forces, and we did not believe that you, the United States, would let Castro get away with it." With the benefit of hindsight I accept this as a good, one-sentence answer to my question. It confirms my conviction that a more vigorous American policy, including a less imperfect Bay of Pigs or even an intervention along the lines of that in the Dominican Republic in 1965, would not have replaced Castro with a viable Cuban leadership. The human materials for such a leadership were not available from the Cuban past. They could only have been forged in a purely Cuban struggle against Castro.

After November 1959, when I had given up hope of accommodation with Castro, I believed that Castro and his Revolution would sooner or later be confronted by a democratically oriented opposition. Meanwhile I held that the United States should avoid the use of superior force, military or economic, to overthrow Castro. Our treaty commitments, the absence at that stage of any Cuban alternative to Castro, and the practical difficulties involved in intervening against a leader with such fervent support among the Cuban masses justified a passive policy even in the face of the deliberately provocative slander and calumny that Castro carried to such extremes.

My thinking by no means precluded measured American responses to Castro's aggressions against American interests in Cuba. But I relied for the elimination of Castro on the eventual emergence of a Cuban resistance movement with a new leadership identified with the anti-Batista forces which had carried Castro to power but as uncontaminated as possible with the less savory phases of Cuban political life. Such a movement would have given Castro and his followers a good deal more trouble than either the Washington-sponsored coalition of refugee political figures in early 1961 or the handful of brave patriots landed under American direction at the Bay of Pigs that spring. Even if the movement I envisaged had been at first unsuccessful, it would have sown the seeds of further struggle in a genuinely Cuban context.

The United States abandoned nonintervention in Cuban domestic affairs in March 1960 and thereafter adopted a series of measures which, while stopping short of the use of American armed force in Cuba, were designed to overthrow Castro. Castro's defeat of this American-engineered effort to crush him has been a major bulwark of his regime, comparable in importance with the economic support the Russians perforce have given him and with the continued hold he exercises over so many of his people.

The immediate causes of Castro's success may thus be stated as (1) his ability to fanaticize masses of his fellow Cubans, (2) the disorganization and the leaderlessness of the Cuban classes, (3) the belief of those classes that the United States would bail them out, (4) the failure of the measures taken by the United States to overthrow Castro, and (5) the creation by the American economic sanctions of a situation in which the Russians had no other choice than to come to the rescue of Castro's Revolution.

Behind these immediate causes, however, there were influences that had long eroded (to a degree unsuspected by most observers, including myself) the bond of faith between leaders and followers which is essential if any society is to meet serious challenges to its existence. These influences had undermined the belief of Cubans, particularly those in the establishment, in the possibility of Cuban control of Cuban destinies and, hence, in the power of the Cuban political machinery to produce Cuban governments that would shape those destinies. The pertinent elements in the Cuban experience may be summarized as follows:

1. Wide, sudden, and unpredictable fluctuations in the amount and the value of Cuba's major product, sugar, that is marketable in a given year. Even as late as the fifties sugar represented over 30 percent of the country's gross national product and nine-tenths or more of it was exported. The ups and downs of sugar reflect events and conditions over which the Cuban people and their governments have had little or no control. This major feature in the stage-setting of Cuban national life over the past century and a half had engendered a sense of helplessness leading to passivity and cynicism in evaluating the role of Cuban institutions in the shaping of the Cuban future.

2. The politico-economic tutelage either actually or potentially exercised by the United States government over the actions and the conduct of the Cuban government. That tutelage was first expressed in the Platt Amendment (1902–1934) and then in a *de facto* relationship symbolized by the unilateral nature of the successive United States Sugar Acts on which Cuban welfare so largely depended. It is important here

to distinguish between the influence actually exercised by the United States and that greater and more absolute influence most Cubans believed could be exerted; the latter was the more important factor in terms of its effect on Cuban thinking about Cuban problems.

3. The continuing impact on the Cuban government and on the Cuban political process of extensive American investments in Cuba. American companies were believed, only in part exaggeratedly, to exercise effective pressures not only on the Cuban decision-making process but also on the policy of the government in Washington toward Cuba.

These three influences greatly complicated what for Cuba would in any event have been an arduous task of nation-building. For such a task Cuban society was fully competent. But the existence of factors that diminished the local community's belief in its own power demonstrably drained the local political machinery of the vitality needed for its healthy functioning.

During the modern history of Cuba, sugar has been buffeted by anarchic conditions uncontrollable from Havana. And, ironically enough, the stability achieved in the American market after 1934 was accompanied, because of the unilateral character of American sugar legislation, by a further crippling of the Cuban sense of control over Cuban destinies.

In pre-Castro Cuba, the pervasive American presence in geopolitical terms was a constant reminder of the imperfect nature of Cuban sovereignty. Valued by some as a guarantee of stability and of the maintenance of what was on the whole a satisfactory way of life, it was rejected by others as an intolerable infringement on the independence and dignity of the Cuban people. I suspect that the majority of thinking Cubans regarded it as a fact of life against which it was useless to struggle. It did, after all, bring Cuba a number of apparently irreplaceable economic advantages.

The antiimperialist mythology of which Castro and his men are such devotees has invested this American presence with all the horrors of unbridled oppression and exploitation. Castro's own use of fraudulently fabricated history is too notorious to justify any expenditure of time or space in commenting on his inventions. It was, however, the American presence itself, rather than the use or misuse of the power flowing from it, that shared with the eccentric fluctuations that afflicted sugar the responsibility for the sense of helplessness that robbed the Cuban political mechanism of credibility and made the Cuban masses so receptive to Castro's anti-Americanism. Indeed, from its earliest days, the Castro Revolution was energized by its identification with a reassertion of national independence from real or fancied domination by the United States.

The pages that follow contain my account of relations between the United States and Cuba in 1959 and 1960. I describe the policies our government followed and those in which it should—in my judgment—have persisted during these two critical years. In the last two chapters I touch upon the problem of future relations between Cuba and the United States. A rational relationship is in the interest of both countries, but I do not see it as a possibility as long as Castro remains in power.

Since, however, much of what happened and, above all, of what didn't happen when I was in Cuba has roots in the past, I have added some "Notes on the Cuban Background" to my work. I hope these will prove useful especially to those unfamiliar with such matters as the market for Cuban sugar, Cuban American relations, and the dynamics of Cuban politics since the establishment of the Cuban Republic in 1902.

My narrative is based on published official documents, on press reports and articles, and on personal recollection and opinion. I have read a good many of the available books on Cuba. Some of the works I have studied are listed and described under "Principal Books Consulted."

Chapter 2

Batista Paves the Way
for Castro, 1952-1958

On March 10, 1952, three months before scheduled presidential elections, former Sergeant Fulgencio Batista overthrew the government of Cuba.[1] His swift and bloodless coup ended the twelve years of constitutional politics, to the beginning and the consolidation of which he had contributed in 1940 and 1944. He was correct in his view that the vanished regime would have few active mourners. Many elements in the community, notably among the property-owning classes, welcomed the disappearance of the corruption, gangsterism, and harassment of business interests they believed had characterized the administrations of Ramón Grau-San Martín and Carlos Prío-Socarrás during the previous eight years. But Batista's hope that he would be able to build a broad political consensus that would uphold his new order was not realized.

Instead he soon found that he had inaugurated a period of increasingly violent struggles for power which culminated in his flight from Cuba in the early hours of New Year's Day, 1959, and his replacement as dictator by Fidel Castro. The tragedy of the situation is compounded by the probability that, although the constitutional system had suffered an undeniable loss of prestige, either of the major candidates in the frustrated elections of 1952 (Carlos Hevia for the ruling *Auténticos* and Roberto Agramonte for the opposition *Ortodoxos*) would, if elected, have ruled with unprecedented integrity and dignity.

In evaluating the new military regime in Cuba, the Department of State

10

in Washington soon became convinced that Batista was in full and virtually unopposed control. Neither the ejected politicians nor the disappointed voters posed any threat. The politicians held lively meetings in exile; months later some of them filed a suit in the Cuban Supreme Court challenging the constitutionality of the coup. They lost.[2] Cuban labor rejected a call by the head of the Labor Federation for an anti-Batista general strike. As he had earlier done with the Auténticos when they were in power, their leader, a former Communist, made his peace with Batista. Most of the functionaries on the government payroll adjusted to the new state of affairs, although there were exceptions, including the distinguished Cuban Ambassador in Washington, Luis Machado, as well as Felipe Pazos and Justo Carrillo, the central bankers. The coup was on the whole not unwelcome to Americans with interests in Cuba and to their advisers and associates in Havana.[3]

After seventeen days of pondering these facts—a period that would have been ample to reveal any indication of effective resistance to Batista—Washington recognized the new government. Batista had already broken relations with the Soviet Union. Throughout his rule he was a firm ally of the United States in the cold war then at its height. He was consistently friendly and helpful to American business interests. But he failed to secure the broad popular support that might have legitimized his rape of the constitution.

During these years (1952–1958) when Batista was trying to revive the corpse of Cuban political life which he himself had slain, Cuba was basking in unparalleled prosperity in spite of continued fluctuations in the sugar market. Although Prío in 1952, allegedly for electoral purposes, had permitted what turned out to be an ill-judged production of over seven million Spanish long tons of sugar, a record unmatched until 1970, the resultant surplus had been readily financed. The industry was in good shape. Government revenues were running in excess of three hundred million pesos a year, also a record; the potential of the government in terms of jobs and favors was at an all-time high.

From the very first days of his rule Batista bent his energies to the creation of a political situation that would confer respectability on him and his fellow adventurers. Although he had achieved power with hardly any resistance and had had no trouble staffing the government payroll, he was disappointed by the scarcity of pragmatists willing to play the game of electoral politics under his auspices. He suspended the Congress in favor of an appointed advisory council but continued to pay the congressmen their salaries for the remainder of their elected terms. He allowed freedom of the press until the time of Fidel Castro's assault on the Moncada barracks in Santiago over a year after the coup.

Batista was amazed and frustrated at his inability to persuade the politicians and the parties he had pushed aside in March 1952 to play the political game in accordance with his new rules. The two recent presidential candidates refused to cooperate. Batista was to write pettishly of the "intolerance of the opposition political organizations."[4] He lacked respectable political figures at his side. In the role of political opposition he could do no better than the elderly and tarnished ex-President Grau-San Martín, head of a splinter group of the formerly dominant Auténticos.

Fidel Castro, a graduate lawyer, was twenty-five years old when President Prío's government was overthrown by Batista's coup. He was a member of the opposition Ortodoxo party and a candidate for the lower house of the Cuban Congress. Deciding that the only way to fight force was with force, he organized an unsuccessful attack by his followers on the Moncada barracks in Santiago on July 26, 1953. Over a hundred Cubans on both sides lost their lives, including many of Castro's men butchered by the military after the fight. A period of violent repression ensued. Hundreds of political personalities were arrested, and an unconvincing attempt was made to prove Communist involvement.[5] Castro was eventually arrested, tried, and convicted as the instigator of the attack.

This tragic slaughter and its aftermath were serious setbacks in Batista's progress toward elections that would "legalize" his power. Much of the political opposition began to move from passive abstention to a determination to promote armed insurrection. The party leaders tended more and more to pin their hopes on the prowess of young men willing to risk their lives against the armed forces of the regime.

Elections were finally held on November 1, 1954, thirty months after the coup. Batista, with the weight of the government, the armed forces, and the officeholders behind him and with support from the more conservative and nonpolitical classes, put on an energetic campaign. He was believed to retain the favor of the American government and of American interests in Cuba. Grau, as the leader of the electoral opposition, traveled widely and spoke freely until, just before the end of the campaign, he was led by a flurry of insurrectionary activity and consequent repressive official measures to advise his followers to refrain from voting because of insufficient civic guarantees.

Nevertheless, Batista insisted that the election was legal and that the followers of Grau had voted in spite of their leader's injunction. He held that his coalition had won and that he, Batista, had been duly elected President of the Republic. (The election itself was held in an atmosphere of apathy except insofar as the candidates themselves were concerned. Only half the qualified citizens bothered to vote.)

If the partisans of Grau had in fact voted, their party as the runner-up was legally entitled to eighteen out of the fifty-four seats in the Cuban Senate. The government promptly announced the names of the eighteen candidates so entitled. Lengthy discussions within Grau's party and with the government led to an agreement under which seventeen of the eighteen took their seats. The Constitution of 1940 and the electoral code of 1943 were to be reinstated. The Batista-dominated Congress was promptly to pass an amnesty that would free the regime's political prisoners. Civic guarantees were to be maintained so that the elections due in 1956 could be held freely and without constraint.

Though the partial elections of 1956 were not held, the bargain concerning the amnesty was kept. The necessary law—introduced by a member of the "opposition"—was passed in May 1955 and signed by Batista. Fidel Castro was freed from the prison on the Isle of Pines where he was beginning his fifteen-year term for his part in the slaughter of a hundred of his fellow citizens at the Moncada barracks. He owed his liberty to a deal that he and the other abstentionists had bitterly denounced and Batista had accepted only to promote the legalization of his rule.[6]

Meanwhile Batista had been inaugurated as President with a maximum of ceremony. Over fifty foreign delegations including one from the United States had attended the elaborate function in late February 1955 that was supposed to confer legitimacy on the regime. Some three weeks earlier Batista had been gratified by a visit from Vice President Nixon. This was Mr. Nixon's first stop on a South American tour that included Mexico, the Caribbean, and the Central American republics and ended with his call on Trujillo, the "Benefactor" of the Dominican Republic. While in Havana, Mr. Nixon reinforced the impression that the United States was as pleased with Batista as it had ever been—an impression Batista valued. I was a member of the Vice President's party in Havana and witnessed the atmosphere of intimate cordiality generated by Ambassador Arthur Gardner in his relations with the Cuban President-elect.[7]

After his release from prison in May, Castro returned briefly to a triumphal reception in Havana. Although he was hailed as a hero by some of his old Ortodoxo brethren, he turned his back on them and organized the 26th of July movement with tenets not very different from those of the Ortodoxos but with himself in charge. He soon left Cuba and after some wandering in the United States and in Mexico settled down in the latter country to organize an invasion of Cuba. The Mexican authorities harassed him from time to time, but, according to some accounts, he was saved from crippling difficulties in his enterprise against the Cuban government (with which Mexico maintained friendly relations) by the intercession of powerful influences traceable to the former Mexican President, Lázaro Cárdenas.[8] The financing of the movement, however, came mostly from Cuban sources. It is generally believed that former President Prío furnished the funds with which Castro bought the yacht Granma on which the expedition was to sail.[9]

After the amnesty of May 1955 and prior to the landing of Castro's men in eastern Cuba in December 1956, numerous attempts were made to solve the impasse created by Batista's overthrow of constitutional government and the refusal of a substantial proportion of the organized political elements to accept the façade of a duly elected Congress behind which the Batista dictatorship operated. There were a number of insurrectionary attempts and conspiracies. The atmosphere became increasingly unfavorable for a normal exercise of civic rights.

It is not necessary here to describe all of the political maneuvering during this period; the total effect was to drive the parties further apart and to increase their intransigence. Early in 1956 there took place what was known as the Civic Dialogue. The highly distinguished, but then octogenarian, Cuban statesman, Cosme de la Torriente, led the so-called Friends of the Republic in an endeavor to find, through a confrontation with the regime around a conference table, a formula by means of which institutional normality might be restored. (It is tempting to suggest a parallel with the round table discussions a quarter of a century earlier which had contributed to the fall of Machado. Then, however, the American Ambassador, Sumner Welles, was believed to favor the end of the dictatorship, whereas in this case the friendship and the unconditional admiration of Ambassador Gardner for Batista were known to all concerned.)

The efforts of the Friends of the Republic broke down in the face of

Batista's insistence that elections be conducted under the auspices of his regime and not under those of an interim or caretaker government. That failure marked the point of no return in Castro's progress toward supremacy in the councils of the anti-Batista movement. The intransigence of Batista and his friends was due to their complacency about the economic situation, to their reliance on American goodwill, and to their confidence in the ability of their security apparatus to contain the increasingly numerous and bloody subversive incidents that were taking place.

The conclusion that Batista could be overthrown only by force was more and more fatalistically accepted. Violence became the arbiter of the nation's politics; the gunman, on both sides of the fence, took the place of the politician. On both sides there was a regression to a struggle for power between the activists, while the Cuban public was reduced to the role of mere spectator and object of a conflict between elements whose deeds steadily escalated the climate of savagery into which the country was sinking.

One illustration of the temper of the times should suffice. In October 1956 the head of Batista's military intelligence service was murdered. (Batista accused Prío of having instigated the deed.) The next day General Rafael Salas Cañizares, Chief of the National Police and a longtime crony of Batista's, burst into the Haitian Embassy at the head of his men, violating the diplomatic immunity of the Embassy, and shot down nine Cuban youths who had sought asylum there several weeks earlier. The young men were suspected of terroristic activities. Seven of the nine died on the spot though one of them managed to shoot the General—fatally, as it turned out. The two surviving youths, badly wounded, were taken to a hospital where, according to an employee of the *New York Times* bureau in Havana who claims to have witnessed the deed, an officer on the wounded general's staff shouting "Never mind the doctor!" cut their throats as they were awaiting medical attention on the operating table of the emergency ward.[10]

Within the regime there were defections. In April 1956 a military conspiracy led by Colonel Barquín, an able officer who had been military attaché in Washington, was discovered and the participants jailed. The group had civilian supporters, some of whom sought assistance in Washington with the plea that the elimination of Batista was now in the interest of the United States. Years later a member of the group told me that if the United States had helped a covert plot to free Barquín from the Isle of Pines prison, Castro might have been denied the leadership of the anti-Batista forces.[11]

The progressive degradation of the political process took place against a background of sustained material prosperity and development. The sugar industry operated at relatively high levels of output and income, in spite of the end of the Korean boom and the possible loss to Cuba under the modifications of American sugar legislation in 1956 giving increased access to the American market to other foreign producers. In 1955 the Russians gave the industry and the regime a shot in the arm by buying nearly half a million tons at world market prices; comparable purchases were made in some later years. In 1956 the Suez crisis stimulated demand for Cuban sugar. Government revenues had surged up from three hundred million to four hundred million pesos. A large if reputedly corrupt program of public works was spreading purchasing power over the land. Many substantial private investments were being made. The most important of these projects were the oil refineries and the nickel extraction plants on the northern coast of Oriente province. The business climate and outlook appeared excellent. Long-range commitments were made in the fifties that were to be bitterly regretted in the sixties.

Castro Leads the Fight Against Batista

On December 2, 1956, Castro landed in eastern Cuba with eighty followers and established a guerrilla base of operations in the mountain fastness of the Sierra Maestra—a deed of courage and endurance in the face of heavy odds and cruel losses. Once it was demonstrated that the government forces could not eliminate Castro and his tiny band, Castro's leadership of the "Batista must go" movement in Cuba became uncontested. Neither the leaders in exile nor the protagonists of the bloody and unsuccessful insurrectionary attacks against the dictator could rival the man who was permanently and spectacularly in arms against the government on Cuban soil.

It is sometimes alleged that the aura of legend surrounding Castro and his men was the spurious creation of a number of American journalists, including Herbert Matthews of the New York Times, who visited Castro in the hills. But the Castro story, plain and unvarnished, was a remarkable one. It is in no way diminished if one accepts, as I do, the fact that some of these writers—notably Matthews—became Castro's wholly uncritical admirers and even dabbled somewhat in Cuban politics.[12] They later forfeited their credibility as reporters. Yet the original story was, in the main, a true one with an immense appeal to the imaginations and the enthusiasms of Cubans who had been struggling against Batista under other and not noticeably successful leaderships. As Castro held his ground, the fight against the regime gained a heroic symbol around which it could and did rally.

Castro had plenty of rivals in the early part of 1957. In March a band of youths under the leadership of an Auténtico politician and of members of the student union assaulted the Presidential Palace in Havana and came within an ace of murdering Batista and perhaps of taking over the government. Castro, with his congenital dislike of competition, published an article in the Havana weekly, *Bohemia*, disapproving the venture.[13]

After Castro's establishment of a base in the hills, Washington found it necessary to give serious attention to Cuban developments. The devotion of the Batista government to the free-world side in the cold war and its understanding of the problems of American business in Cuba remained unquestioned. On the other hand, the growing squalor of the situation on the island was causing American public opinion and the policymakers on the banks of the Potomac mounting qualms. The terrorism, the counterterrorism, and now the guerrilla operations in Oriente, plus the feverish self-enrichment at public expense in which Batista and many of his leading henchmen were believed engaged, created for the regime an increasingly unfavorable atmosphere in the United States.

An obvious first step in the deidentification of the United States from the Batista administration was a change of ambassadors. Arthur Gardner was succeeded in mid-1957 by Earl E. T. Smith, a prominent financier, corporate director, and member of the New York Stock Exchange with close friends in both political parties. (Senator John F. Kennedy was to be his houseguest in Havana.) The new Ambassador had made frequent visits to Cuba over the past thirty years. Though he spoke no Spanish he believed, in his own words, that he "had traveled widely and knew Cuba well and I felt I could judge the thoughts and moods of the Cuban people because of the close relationship I had enjoyed on the island for so many years."[14]

The new Ambassador was expected to achieve a posture of neutrality contrasting with Ambassador Gardner's unconditionally pro-Batista stance. He sent the new policy off to a good start when, soon after his arrival in Cuba, he publicly expressed disapproval of the rough handling by the police of some women demonstrators in Santiago—a scene he witnessed. Some of Batista's men talked of declaring the new Ambassador *persona non grata* and having him expelled because of his alleged interference in the internal affairs of Cuba. Secretary of State John Foster Dulles, however, backed the Ambassador; the furor in Cuba quickly died down.[15]

Ambassador Smith soon developed a visceral conviction that Castro was a tool of the Communists and that for him to seize power in Cuba would be contrary to the interests of Cuba, the United States, and the free world. Batista cherished parallel views on the importance of thwarting Castro. Neither Smith nor Batista were able to persuade the government in Washington of the soundness of their conclusions, though that government had before it the evidence with which they buttressed them.

During the early months of Smith's mission there were repeated insurrectionary outbursts. The various formulas designed to secure, under Batista's auspices, a successor government minus Castro could not compete with the determination of Castro and of the wide spectrum of forces then supporting him to accept no solution other than a complete elimination of the Batista regime and the restoration under new management of the Constitution of 1940.

Against the background of the government's bloodthirstiness and corruption, Castro's stature grew steadily. He was now in direct contact with other opposition leaders. His broadcasts from the Sierra Maestra were heard throughout Cuba and in the United States. Cubans "with a stake in the country" began to pour contributions into his treasury—some of them voluntarily and some responding to the kind of pressures the prospect of success made increasingly available to the leaders of the rebellion. In the filibustering tradition, arms were smuggled into the mountains from many sources; the guerrilla fighters captured and even bought weapons from Batista's decaying forces.

In late 1957 a distinguished exile group in Miami including representatives of Castro's own party, the 26th of July movement, suggested several names, among them Felipe Pazos, a member of that movement and an internationally known economist and former head of the National Bank, to be chief executive on the fall of Batista. When Castro heard of this he rejected the suggestions in characteristically vehement and voluble fashion. He castigated all concerned for making decisions behind the backs of the revolutionaries fighting in the hills. But he denounced all forms of autocracy and affirmed that the new government when it took over would "be guided by the Constitution of 1940 and . . . guarantee all rights guaranteed therein and . . . be completely impartial to partisan politics." He announced his own choice for the presidency: Manuel Urrutia, a worthy if obscure and politically inexperienced judge who had courageously maintained the legality of revolution in the face of arbitrary government. The exile group in Florida meekly accepted Castro's dictum; unity was restored on his terms.[16]

The importance of the broad abstentionist-insurrectionary movement that had accepted Castro's leadership may be judged from the signatures on a manifesto it issued from Caracas in July 1958. In addition to Castro's, those signatures included the leaders of the two major parties and of some other political groups; representatives of the prestigious *Montecristi* civilian movement involved in the Barquín conspiracy; a representative of the then apparently powerful Civic Resistance movement; and representatives of the Federation of University Students and of the Labor Confederation.[17] This collection of names seemed at the time to add up to a representation of majority political sentiment. Within two years, except for Castro, the remaining signatories had been proved to be completely impotent to affect the destinies of their country.

Some of the guerrilla skirmishes in the hills have been dignified with the names of battles in the Castro mythology. Batista's army never truly came to grips with the elusive irregulars. Batista's soldiers, demoralized by the general repudiation of the government they served and by the accelerated corruption among their own officers and elsewhere, simply melted away as a fighting force after mid-1958.[18] Much of the money said to have been drawn from Castro's now bulging coffers to buy treachery that would facilitate rebel military movements was simply wasted; there would not have been any serious fighting even if the money had not been spent.

The efforts made by Batista with the encouragement of Ambassador Smith to find an alternative to Castro as Batista's successor must be seen against the backdrop of the crumbling of Batista's army. Ambassador Smith wrote that next to the President of Cuba the most important man on the island was the American Ambassador.[19] He did not perceive that the position of the President had deteriorated to the point that being his runner-up was not what it had been. Batista, for his part, after a moment of initial perplexity, was satisfied with the new Ambassador. His Foreign Minister (Gonzalo Güell) had investigated Smith's antecedents and was able, as reported by Smith, to advise Batista that Smith's "father was a gentleman and well thought of in the United States. Dr. Güell was convinced that I would see things the correct way."[20]

The Elections of 1958

In his effort to block Castro's march to power, Batista relied heavily on the elections to be held under the auspices of his government to choose his successor and to pass judgment on his administration. Ambassador Smith assumed that these elections would be both fair and representative and that they would result in a non-Castro administration acceptable to Batista's opponents. In fact, however, the majority elements of the parties to which Batista had denied the opportunity to obtain the people's verdict in 1952 were adamant in their refusal to participate in elections as long as Batista was in power. These elements had now accepted the leadership of Castro, the former student gangster, for whom Batista had created the conditions which allowed Castro to achieve power.

For the electoral operation on which he was bent, Batista had meager resources. Supporting the government there was his personal party plus fractions of some of the traditional parties that had been identified with him earlier in his career. For an opposition willing to go to the polls he looked to a splinter of the Auténticos under Grau and a splinter of the Ortodoxos led by Carlos Márquez-Sterling. Batista decided to stimulate the formation of more opposition parties so as to enhance the verisimilitude of the forthcoming contest. Malicious gossip in Havana was to the effect that government money and facilities were lavishly made available to all opposition parties that would participate in the elections. Such diverse personalities as José Pardo-Llada, later briefly Castro's Goebbels; Manuel Artime, a leader of the Bay of Pigs Brigade; and a young doctor named Enrique Huertas, currently prominent in exile politics, figured in some of these minor parties.[21]

Meanwhile the Department of State was aware of and shared the growing distaste for a regime increasingly nauseating to most public opinion in the United States and in Latin America. Ever since the days of Prío in 1951 the United States had had a military assistance agreement with Cuba—and with other Latin American republics—predicated on hemispheric defense concepts. Modest shipments of arms had resulted, although they constituted only a fraction of what Cuba bought with its own resources. There were also training missions. When it became evident that the Cuban government was an odious type of dictatorship that might use training, equipment, and arms from the United States to kill Cubans endeavoring to throw off oppression, Washington felt obliged to act.

In the fall of 1957 the United States began to hold up Batista's orders for military hardware. In March 1958 an embargo on the shipment of arms and ammunition to Cuba was declared. Though this measure had no significant effect on the balance of weaponry between Batista's army and Castro's guerrillas, Ambassador Smith was correct when he stated that it had "a moral and psychological effect on the Cuban armed forces that was demoralizing to the nth degree and it built up the morale of the revolutionary forces."[22] The Ambassador was, however, also aware that by the date of the embargo there was already a sense of impending disaster in the Batista entourage and that many identified with him were preparing to scuttle. The absence of the embargo would not have saved Batista.

However, the failure of the revolutionary strike called in April on behalf of the fighters in the hills gave the regime a temporary reprieve. Once again Cuban labor demonstrated that, whether the country was controlled by the Communists, the Auténticos, or Batista, it would abstain from collective action unless specific labor goals were involved. The Communist attitude about the strike was also negative. In fact, it was not until midsummer that the Communists decided to get on the Castro bandwagon to which they were the last additions of any significance.[23]

By the time the Communists made their decision, Batista's fate had been sealed by the breakdown of a last offensive against the rebels. Many efforts were made—by the church, by civic organizations, by politicians—to find a way that would block Castro. Ambassador Smith encouraged these activities in accordance with his stated conviction that "it is incumbent on me to do everything possible within my limits to obtain a peaceful solution, even though I cannot obtain the support of the State Department for any such peaceful solution."[24] The Department of State did not share (nor did most competent observers) the Ambassador's favorable estimate of the political and civic elements willing to cooperate, under Batista's auspices, in a solution in which Castro would have no part.

The Ambassador allowed his chagrin at his inability to persuade the

Department of State that his analysis of the situation was correct to escalate into a belief that the officials of the Department favored Castro and were working for his success. The truth, as I see it, is that these officials as well as the more knowledgeable members of the Embassy staff in Havana shared an antipathy for Batista's regime; so far as Castro was concerned they had no feeling other than a belief that the movement he headed was destined to take over and that the "legal opposition" that so engrossed the Ambassador's attention had no comparable significance.

The Batista-sponsored elections finally took place on November 3, 1958. The voters were subjected to threats and persuasion from Castro and his supporters to stay away from the polls. In the two provinces of Camagüey and Oriente they were, in many places, physically prevented from voting by the rebels. The government announced that Batista's man had won and would take over the presidency in February. Carlos Márquez-Sterling believed his fraction of the "legal opposition" would have won had Batista and Castro between them permitted a fair election. Ambassador Smith sadly concluded that Batista had failed to live up to "his solemn promise to me he would hold free and open elections acceptable to the people."[25]

Soon after the elections the Ambassador was recalled to Washington for consultation so that, in his absence, an unofficial emissary could call on Batista and tell him that our government believed he should leave the country to the rule of a temporary military junta that might serve as a transition to a more normal situation. The unofficial emissary was William D. Pawley, a prominent businessman and sometime diplomat. The mission failed when Batista said he would only follow the advice given him if he could announce that he was doing so at the behest of Washington, a condition Mr. Pawley was unable to accept.[26] Even if he had, the Pawley formula was no longer realistic by December 1958.

Ambassador Smith's position was not a happy one. He had been deceived by Batista as to the fairness of the elections. He had been unable to persuade Washington to accept his view of Castro. And now it was his duty to tell Batista that the United States did not believe "that any of the respected civil and military elements [in Cuba] would associate themselves with the government of the newly elected President."[27] In other words, Washington was not disposed to recognize the result of the elections. Batista was evidently not unaware of the differences between the Ambassador and the Department of State. The Ambassador reports that when he delivered Washington's message, Batista remarked sadly, "You have intervened on behalf of the Castros but I know it was not your doing and that you are only following your instructions."[28]

As 1958 drew to a close the movement headed by Castro enjoyed extensive backing in American public opinion. Accusations of communism and of bitter anti-Americanism against Castro were discounted because of the reactionary reputations of many of those making them and because of a revulsion against the sweeping and unscrupulous use that had been made of anticommunism earlier in the decade. One retired American diplomat-politician was able to find hospitality for his fulminations about Castro only in the pages of the *Police Gazette*.[29] In the antidictator atmosphere that prevailed—Rojas-Pinilla, Perez-Jimenez, and Perón had fallen to the applause of continental public opinion—Castro, with his promise to restore democracy to a Cuban people eager for it, was looked upon most kindly by many in the United States.

Batista now saw all the elements of his power eroded: his large army useless, his political support at home nonexistent, his henchmen looking for the exits, and the Washington backing he had so long enjoyed withdrawn. He abandoned the effort to continue exercising an authority that had been drained of reality. He had already disposed abroad most of the extensive spoils of his years in power; he fled the country he and his friends had plundered in the early morning of New Year's Day, 1959.

That Castro should succeed Batista was inevitable. He was the recognized leader of the forces that had spearheaded the repudiation of a corrupt and bloodstained regime by the people of Cuba. The sequel was to show that all of the other possible sources of political power in Cuba, with the exception of the Communists, had lost whatever vitality they may at one time have possessed. The failure to recognize that fact led to the belief that Castro, whatever his own desires might be, would be controlled by the supposedly vigorous democratic preferences of the Cuban people. This was a major error in the appraisal of the situation; I shared in it.

I am convinced, however, that a realization in early 1959 of the sinister monopoly of power in Cuba which Castro would soon achieve and long retain as well as of the impotence of the traditional leaders of the island society could not have been translated by the American government into a policy that would have denied to Castro the supreme authority he soon exercised. The only possible course of action to implement such a policy would have been an intervention by American armed forces. Such an intervention was inconceivable in the context of then existing public opinion in Cuba, the United States, and Latin America.

Chapter 3

The United States Recognizes Castro and His Revolution

BATISTA vanished from Cuba in the early hours of January 1, 1959. Later that day vain efforts were made to find a "constitutional formula" that would deprive Castro of the political inheritance of the fallen dictator. The futility of those efforts, the last in a series, once more underlined Castro's domination of the forces that had overthrown Batista. The United States government accepted the situation with good grace and recognized the new government within a week of Batista's flight. But the American Ambassador in Cuba, Earl E. T. Smith, had worked openly and vigorously for a non-Castro alternative to Batista and had hoped that the so-called legal opposition might have generated such an alternative. The elections two months earlier had, however, proved a sterile exercise; they were characterized by apathy and hostility toward both the official and the opposition candidates and were further vitiated by intimidation from Castro and fraud by Batista.

A Change of American Ambassadors

Castro's triumph thus made it necessary for President Eisenhower to find a new ambassador to replace the outspokenly anti-Castro Smith. I was the man chosen. The new government in Cuba had been recognized on January 7; a week later my name was proposed to the Cuban Minister of State and, on receipt of the required approval, was submitted by President

Eisenhower to the Senate for its advice and consent on January 22. I was then serving as Ambassador to Bolivia.

I thought of myself as comparatively well qualified for the Cuban assignment. I had some professional assets: long years of service in Latin America in official and business capacities, experience in Washington and in the field with many of the problems of the area, and a fluency in Spanish that was more often useful than not. I had twice lived in Cuba: once for a few months in 1926 as a student trainee with the Cuban Telephone Company, a subsidiary of the International Telephone and Telegraph Corporation, and again for nearly a year from 1938 to 1939 as Vice Consul and Third Secretary on my first Foreign Service assignment. In 1939 and 1940 I was the Cuban desk officer in the Department of State, and, in my years of service in the Department during World War II, I often had occasion to deal with Cuban problems.

Of great importance in giving me a background on Cuba were the wisdom, the reminiscences, and the writings of my father, Stephen Bonsal (1865–1951). He had served in the United States Legation in Madrid in the midnineties and later, as a correspondent, had traveled in and reported on Cuba in the last years of Spanish rule. He had covered the Santiago campaign of 1898 and a dozen years later had written extensively on the Caribbean area, including Cuba. To the end of his life he maintained a perceptive interest in the region.

My current assignment in Bolivia and my earlier record in Colombia (1955–1957) seemed to me to be assets for the Cuban mission. In Bolivia the United States was conducting a program of economic assistance on a scale then unique in the hemisphere. The Bolivian Revolution of 1952 had eliminated the landholding and the mineowning oligarchies in this desperately poor country. The Truman administration had shown courage in following the farseeing recommendation of the then Ambassador in Bolivia, Edward J. Sparks, to the effect that the new Bolivian goverment should have American support. Ambassador Sparks, an able and experienced career diplomat, believed that the revolution represented an irreversible step in the history of Bolivia.

The policy adopted remained for many years a solitary outpost of American thinking in this field. The program of the United States in Bolivia was, however, a pioneer of the programs believed desirable by many realistic and experienced analysts in the field of inter-American relations.

The fact that I had been identified with that program should, I thought, be an asset in dealing with the revolutionary Cuban government.

My experience in Colombia also appeared to enhance my acceptability for the Cuban post. In 1953 a regime in that country which had brought the community to a state of widespread and bloody civil conflict was overthrown by a military coup d'etat led by General Gustavo Rojas-Pinilla. The latter promised to pacify the nation and to restore the normal operation of democratic institutions including the traditional political parties. But the wine of power and the incense of adulation turned the general's head. He decided to force Colombia to a new state of affairs in which an alliance of the army and the masses under his guidance would destroy the old oligarchies and the political parties, which, he charged, had exploited the many for the benefit of the few. He soon found that his estimate of political forces (at that time, at least) was at odds with reality and he was ignominiously expelled from the Presidential Palace in May 1957—one of the many dictators and would-be dictators to be repudiated during those years.

Because I had kept up my long-standing friendships with a number of the political leaders who rejected the Rojas-Pinilla thesis—notably Alberto Lleras-Camargo, a great Colombian and a continental leader—I soon achieved a major entry in the general's black book. His concept of the proper behavior for an American Ambassador in Colombia was as warped as his understanding of the political realities he faced at home. While he was unable, except briefly, to suspend the operation of those realities, he managed to get rid of the American Ambassador. He did not declare me *persona non grata*, but he persuaded the Department of State to send me elsewhere. The fact became well known and gave me something of a reputation as a friend of democracy.[1] This, during the brief period when the restoration of democracy in Cuba was the broadest plank in the Castro platform, should have been helpful to me in my Cuban mission.

My appointment, following the rapidity with which Washington recognized the new government in Cuba, reflected a decision on the part of the President and of the Department of State to endeavor to establish constructive relations with Castro and his associates. The latter enjoyed the support of the overwhelming majority of the Cuban people. In January 1959 no one could with any plausibility claim that what had taken place in Cuba was the work of non-Cuban influences or forces. Allegations that Castro was Communist controlled were at a heavy discount due both to the lack of standing of those who made them (including Batista) and to the then plausible view that Cuban society would control Castro and not the reverse.

Critics of the administration's policy have since alleged that Washington could have thwarted Castro's drive to power but that officials of the Department of State favored the guerrilla leader who turned out to be such a bitter enemy of the United States and eventually took his country into the Communist camp.[2] I can only say that when I was in Washington in early February 1959 to be briefed for my Cuban mission, I was impressed by the reserve with which Castro was viewed by the departmental officers with whom I dealt. They accepted the Cuban reality as it then appeared and were determined to develop productive relations with the new government. They had had no direct relationship with Castro though they had had contacts with representatives of the numerous democratically minded forces that fought Batista under Castro's leadership. Their thinking had been influenced by the sordid and bloody morass into which the regime of Batista had sunk. But they had no enthusiasm for Castro, only a determination to be in the best possible position to deal effectively on behalf of American interests with the new ruler whose people appeared united in idolizing him.

Cuba Seen from Washington, February 1959

My two weeks of concentrated briefings on recent events, personalities, and prospects in Cuba confirmed my impression that the island was entering uncharted seas under a pilot whose skills were unknown and whose course was unrevealed except in the most general terms. The American position may best be defined as one of benevolent, if nervous, watchfulness. Washington recognized that Castro was the leader not only of the activist elements directly responsible for the fall of the dictator but also of most of the potentially dynamic forces in Cuban life—now including those (the labor unions, for example) which had been more or less neutral during the recent struggle.

At that time many believed—as I did—that whatever Castro's political philosophy might be other than the restoration of Cuban democracy to which he was pledged, he was to a large extent bound by the preferences of the community in which he would have to act politically. He might be able to stretch, indeed to modify, the rules of the game of politics as his fellow citizens thought it should be played, but that he would completely abolish the rules and the game as well did not then seem conceivable. In fact, in those early days, Cubans of all classes, especially the wealthy, had climbed on the Castro bandwagon and were reaching for the steering wheel.

There were, of course, disquieting elements in Castro's past. Even those who regarded Castro's presence at the Bogotá uprising in 1948 as purely coincidental, the uprising itself as unplanned, and his participation in that episode as the act of an unstable youth suddenly confronted with a complete breakdown of law and order, could hardly deny his active role over several years in the gangsterism and the killings that had disfigured Cuban student politics or his dedication to violence as a method of political action. Some of his associates, including the then relatively unknown Che Guevara and his own brother Raúl, were unsavory from the point of view of American opinion. But it seemed reasonable to hope that the responsibilities of power and the checks inherent in the community Castro was called upon to lead would keep him within bounds that would make it possible for the United States to deal constructively with the new situation on the island.

There was no evidence of a convincing nature that Castro enjoyed decisive or even effective support from the Communist world. Nor was there, in my judgment, any valid indication that the local Communists would play a significant role in Cuban politics—or at any rate a more significant one than they had played when they had formed part of, but had not dominated, one of the heterogeneous coalitions typical of Cuban politics in the forties. Besides, there was much reason to hope that the Cuban people would relatively soon be given an opportunity at the polls to select their leaders. (In any election held at that time, Castro could have had any office he wished or he could have become the real power behind a façade of elected officeholders, a position which Batista had held in the thirties.)

I shared a belief based on the Cuban American experience of sixty years that the reciprocal economic interests of Cuba and the United States would exercise a stabilizing and a moderating influence on developments in Cuba. Cuba's economic welfare had been, was, and seemed destined to remain bound up with the production and sale of sugar at profitable prices and in large quantities. The United States had been, was, and seemed destined to remain an advantageous market for as much as half of the Cuban sugar crop at prices which normally were substantially in excess of what Cuba could get for its major product in other markets. The constant availability and the proven flexibility of Cuba's sugar production were definite assets for the

United States in the same way that American willingness to pay premium prices for Cuban sugar was a major and, I then thought, an irreplaceable asset for Cuba.

My optimism as I prepared to take up my work in Havana was further nourished by a belief that the evolution of American policy toward the Latin American republics was gradually introducing at least the prospect of an expansion in the means available to the United States to assist the other governments of the hemisphere in their efforts to improve the lot of their peoples. Gone were the rigidities of the earlier part of the decade. Then, with the exception of Bolivia and to a lesser degree Haiti and Guatemala, the only programs on a government-to-government basis were those of technical assistance or Point IV, which were mainly concentrated on the conveyance of American practical know-how in a variety of fields. These programs were useful and educational for all involved including our own technicians but were far from an adequate response to the needs of the times.

Except for Point IV our government's philosophy was that the other American republics should look to the expansion of their trade, to the creation of conditions that would attract and hold foreign private investment, to the development of their own private enterprise potential, and to sound fiscal and monetary policies on a local level as keys to the progress so eagerly and so desperately sought by most of them.[3] We rejected the concept of soft loans, that is, loans for developing countries at low interest rates repayable in local currencies. We had opposed the concept of an inter-American development bank as late as 1954. We generally disapproved of state enterprises for the production of goods and services (even though in many cases such enterprises were the only nonforeign approaches available for the industrialization and the development of these increasingly nationalistic countries). Even those who concurred in the desirability of commodity agreements for the purpose of stabilizing the prices of the raw materials for production and export on which the economies of so many American republics depended were led by their economic philosophies and their interpretation of experience to the conclusion that arrangements of this kind were in all but a very few cases unworkable.

Now in early 1959, although far from evolving with the vigor imparted to them when the threat of Castroism in the hemisphere had become a real one in the eyes of responsible planners, American policies in the area were moving forward, partly in response to Mr. Nixon's unhappy experiences in Peru and Venezuela in the previous year.[4] It was reasonable to envisage continued progress toward effective assistance to Latin America as an element in American foreign policy. Only a few months earlier, in August 1958, at the time of the Lebanon crisis, I had been briefly assigned to the American delegation at the United Nations. Our government, supplementing its relatively favorable reception of the Brazilian initiative for an "Operation Pan America" for developmental cooperation in the Americas, announced its support for the creation of the Inter-American Development Bank, thus reversing its position of opposition only four years earlier. It seemed to me as I prepared to depart for Havana that American policy in the area was becoming constructive.

Castro's Anti-Americanism

Even before I reached Havana, however, I became aware of developments and trends which clouded the relatively hopeful prospect. I do not refer here to such sensational but intrinsically minor incidents as the provocative and impromptu answer Castro gave to a provocative question as to what would happen if American Marines invaded Cuba.[5] It was rather that on certain matters Castro and his propagandists were becoming rapidly, systematically, and virulently hostile to the United States, its government, and the past relations of the two countries.

From the very beginning of his rule Castro and his sycophants bitterly and sweepingly attacked the relations of the United States government with Batista and his regime. The record was vulnerable on some points. Ambassador Gardner and certain of our military men had displayed an unnecessarily florid and spectacular cordiality to Batista and his officials. This was unfortunate since, although Batista was reputed to have a cooperative understanding of the American position in the cold war and of the problems of American business on the island, his administration had become increasingly discredited because of its corruption, its despotic nature, its bloodthirsty repression, and its savage counterterrorism. On balance, however, Washington's policies and attitudes had reflected the concept of nonintervention and had been distasteful to the Batista government particularly after Castro's landing in Cuba in December 1956.

It was ridiculous and fraudulent of Castro and his propagandists to attribute any significant part of the limited success the Cuban army had had in fighting Castro and his men to equipment and training supplied by the United States. Yet Castro's magic was such that he could unblushingly tell his people that the victory of his men had been won over American trained and equipped forces.[6]

Prior to the Castro regime, the United States was not in the counter-insurgency business. Arms and training supplied to the Cuban army by the United States government were designed to meet the somewhat nebulous requirements of hemispheric defense against an external aggression. The arms furnished were an infinitesimal fraction of the arms acquired by the Batista regime with its own funds for purposes of national defense and internal security. Only a small part of the arms available to the Cuban military were ever used against Castro and his men. The distintegration of the Cuban armed forces was not hastened by the lack of well-equipped manpower but by lack of morale and the will to fight.

In the fall of 1957 the United States government began holding up shipments of weapons and munitions to Cuba. An arms embargo was publicly announced in March 1958; it indicated the distaste of the government and people of the United States for conditions on the island.[7] It was a heavy blow to the already decaying morale of Batista's armed forces and of the regime as a whole. Washington had not only withdrawn the support for Batista symbolized by Ambassador Gardner, it had also rejected the policies advocated by Ambassador Smith and by Batista designed to bar Castro from power. Nevertheless, Castro harped incessantly on the alleged partiality of the American government and its agents for the Batista administration.

It was further alleged that this partiality for Batista and his followers continued after January 1, 1959. Much poisonous nonsense was poured forth to the effect that the United States was officially harboring and protecting the "war criminals" of the fallen regime. It was even alleged that they were being helped in their conspiracies against their successful opponents. No evidence was adduced to support these charges. Indeed, if the United States had wished at that time to overthrow Castro, the least efficient tools it could have selected would have been the representatives of the hated regime just expelled to the applause of an overwhelming majority of the Cuban people.

So far as the prominent Batistianos who had found refuge in the United States before the first of January were concerned (few if any were admitted after that date), it was hardly to be expected that, on learning that some of them had been designated war criminals in the course of one of Castro's orations or in his press, the American authorities should arrest them and ship them to Cuba. After all, the Castro people were executing their prisoners by the hundreds after judicial proceedings of questionable repute or without any proceedings. Castro and his followers were familiar with the policy the United States has traditionally followed toward political refugees; many of them had benefited from that policy. Yet the Castro claim about the war criminals in the United States was insistently broadcast over the airwaves and in the press in Cuba in a manner obviously designed to produce misunderstanding and lack of confidence in the integrity of the government of the United States and in its goodwill toward the new and immensely popular regime in Cuba.[8]

This fraudulent hate propaganda went far beyond the relations of the United States and the Batista dictatorship. It embraced the common history of the two countries in all its aspects since the Spanish war. It attempted to rewrite that history so as to achieve a maximum of odium for a crudely imperialistic United States and its Cuban "lackeys" and of indignant sympathy for a noble, virtuous, and constantly oppressed Cuban people.

Popular views of Cuban American relations have belonged to two main schools, the *traditional* and the *revisionist*. People with a serious interest in the subject have based their conclusions on a careful selection of elements derived from both schools. Both, in the manner of conventional wisdoms, have taken to themselves a fair number of myths, fallacies, and misconceptions. The traditional view holds that the United States has consistently played a benevolent role in its dealings with Cuba and has showered moral and material benefits on a sometimes unappreciative, ungrateful, and occasionally badly behaved small neighbor. It praises American policy especially in the earlier years of the relationship as extraordinarily enlightened in comparison with the colonial policy of the leading European powers. To the revisionists, on the other hand, Cuba has been during much of its history and particularly since 1898 the hapless victim of materialistic exploitation by the Colossus of the North.

The versions of the elimination of Spanish rule in Cuba cherished by the two schools are revealing. In the traditional view the United States victory over Spain was the deciding factor in the independence of Cuba. At a sizable cost in blood and treasure, the United States freed an oppressed and mistreated people from a harsh, backward tyranny and set it on the road to self-government, a road it followed imperfectly and falteringly through no fault of the United States. American policies, furthermore, created the conditions for a tremendous development of Cuba's economy.

In contrast, a favorite thesis of the revisionists is that the Cuban uprising of 1895 was the final episode in a purely Cuban struggle for independence begun nearly thirty years earlier. Not until the triumph of the insurgents appeared both certain and imminent did the United States intervene militarily thus snatching the rewards of victory from the Cuban patriots; then, after a four-year military occupation, the United States engineered the transfer of power to reactionary groups. Called by the American authorities the "better elements," most of these groups had cooperated with the Spanish rulers and were now disposed to cooperate with the United States in saddling Cuba with a semicolonial status, in exploiting its people, and in denying them the conditions under which they might have created a politically democratic, economically diversified, and nationally responsive society.

In like manner other major episodes in the relations between the two countries were contrastingly interpreted. The revisionist school grew in acceptance with the surge in nationalist sentiment and with the desire for increased freedom from the tutelage of the northern neighbor. A revisionist literature of great quantity developed. Ironically, four ponderous tomes of pseudoscholarly, elaborately footnoted, emotional pamphleteering on the subject of the relations between Cuba, Spain, and the United States were produced with the help of a grant from an American foundation.[9] This work and others like it were a rich mine from which Castro and his followers extracted the raw material for their vicious distortions of facts and of American motivations.

With the advent of Castro the history of Cuban American relations was subjected to a revision of an intensity and cynicism which left earlier efforts in the shade. When I reached Cuba this campaign was beginning. Its purpose was to alienate the people of the island from the traditional version of their past relations with the United States and to promote a version in which the monopoly of virtue was held by the oppressed Cubans and that of evil by the Americans. The conclusion to be drawn was that the Americans had no rights in Cuba which the Cubans were bound to respect unless forced to do so by superior strength.

These manifestations of a fraudulent and excessive anti-Americanism were distasteful and alarming to those responsible for seeking an understanding with the new Cuba. Much of what was written and said could, however, be attributed to excesses stimulated by a heady freedom from the repressions of the Batista days. After all, Batista had been conspicuously pro-American; a conscientious revolutionary would feel he had to take the opposite position. I shared the hope of many observers that all this would be abandoned and forgotten as both governments faced the realities of the relationships which geography and history seemed to impose on them. I expected that Cubans conscious of these realities would express themselves so that matters would once more come into a rational focus.

There were indeed elements in the relations between the United States and Cuba that denied to Cuba the exercise of the responsibility for Cuban destinies that would have developed the self-confidence and the vitality of the Cuban community and thus have rendered it less susceptible to the sick fantasies we were hearing and reading in such abundance. The relationship could have been modified in ways I was prepared to explore. It was only months later that I was forced to conclude that Castro himself had aimed, through his unscrupulous campaign of historical revision, to create a climate in which diplomacy could not operate.

In February, however, as I prepared for my Cuban mission a hopeful element in the situation was the fact that several prominent officials in the new Cuban government were responsibly identified both with the overthrow of Batista and with Cuba's past. Their presence seemed to promise a realistic and democratic approach to the desirable changes to be anticipated from the current enthusiasm for renovation. Although the reputable and confidence-inspiring José Miró-Cardona had just been replaced as Prime Minister by Castro himself, the Cabinet included Roberto Agramonte as Foreign Minister, an eminent exponent and practitioner of political democracy, and Rufo López-Fresquet heading the Treasury Department, a man well known to the business community and believed to be a man whose reforming zeal would not prove intolerably destructive. The Minister of Social Affairs was Elena Mederos with many friends and admirers in American circles; an injection of New Deal social consciousness might be expected from this able and charming woman. Felipe Pazos brought his international reputation among Western economists and central bankers to the presidency of the National Bank. Justo Carrillo, a man of energy, drive, and private-enterprise convictions had a major post in the development planning and financing institutions expected to be crucial in the programs of the new government. There were other ministers and officeholders about whom less was known but who were described as more evolutionary than revolutionary.

"Operation Truth"

Castro's concept of himself as the spokesman of the righteous infallibility of the Cuban people (except for those who had collaborated with Batista or with the imperialists) led him to demand from the United States government, the mass media, and other organs of American public opinion respectful applause for his every action and pronouncement. When this expectation was disappointed, as it was in the case of the executions of those allegedly guilty of committing war crimes under Batista, his reaction was severe and hostile. The example is an instructive one.

The Cuban public had been fed the legend that Batista's army and his security apparatus had slaughtered twenty thousand men and women in the course of the savage counterterrorism of which the regime was guilty. This was a gross exaggeration but the truth was bad enough. Thousands of Cubans felt entitled to revenge for the murder of family or friends. Thirty years earlier, the hirelings of the Machado regime deemed guilty of similar crimes were simply ferreted out by the mob and killed. The Castro procedure of setting up special tribunals to try the cases of people who, on the basis of the Nuremberg principles, were accused of serious crimes could have been an improvement over the earlier method.

On the other hand, there was reason to believe that shortly after the Castro triumph some seventy prisoners were mowed down by rebel soldiers at the command of Raúl Castro and bulldozed under ground without any semblance whatever of a trial. Castro himself, in one notorious case involving a number of Batista's airmen, overruled his own court's verdict of acquittal and had the accused retried and sentenced to thirty years' confinement. Presumably there were other less publicized cases of directed verdicts. These special courts were subject to all sorts of pressures including those generated by the circuslike atmosphere in which many of them were conducted. In some cases private or ideological motivations rather than the guilt of the accused appear to have brought about capital sentences.

As might be expected these executions caused some unfavorable comment in the United States. A number of Senators expressed themselves critically and some—by no means all—of the press gave the matter an aura of barbarous arbitrariness. Castro was furious. He mounted an elaborate exercise known as "Operation Truth" with free trips to Cuba for journalists from all over the hemisphere. He said that the fact that the judical processes of the Revolution were being criticized while the atrocities of the Batista regime had met with silence or with approval in the United States—a statement entirely contrary to fact—was proof positive that the United States was hostile to the Revolution and to all the hope it held out for the welfare of the Cuban people and of Latin America. This episode was a foretaste of what became the real Castro.

Chapter 4

Cuba Seen from the American Embassy, February 1959

When Mrs. Bonsal and I landed at the Havana airport on the rainy evening of February 19, 1959, we were cordially received by old and new friends. The official who greeted us had been a member of the protocol establishment twenty years before when we had been in Havana on our first Foreign Service assignment. I had a friendly chat with a bearded rebel soldier symbolizing the new state of affairs. My words of pleasure at being in Cuba again and of enthusiasm and faith as to my mission were well received.

On the night of my arrival I had the first of many exchanges of views with my principal Embassy associates. They at all times gave me loyal support and helpful advice; I am proud to have been associated with each of them. Beginning with Daniel Braddock, the able veteran professional who was my deputy, these men knew Cuba well; they had lived with and analyzed the developments leading to the fall of Batista and his replacement by Castro. I wish I could give each one of them by name the tribute of praise and gratitude to which they are individually and collectively entitled.

Our cordial exchanges on that first evening in the Embassy residence were interrupted by an opportunity to hear Castro on television. Part of his lengthy address was devoted to an extreme version of the revisionist thesis on the relations between Cuba and the United States at the turn of the century—a thesis that feeds the Cuban ego while it wounds American pride and self-esteem. I then resisted the idea that Castro had planned his remarks with my arrival in mind or that his expression of views on a long-dead past, views which he knew would be distasteful to me and to my compatriots, reflected a negative attitude toward the current possibilities of Cuban American relations.

Although I was at once caught up in the time-consuming official and social activities essential to my establishment as part of the local scene, I thought hard and, I believed, realistically about the problems of my mission. After lengthy consultations with the members of my staff, I concluded that the following were the major features of the situation with which I would have to deal:

1. The most important: supreme authority over the affairs of Cuba had been turned over to Fidel Castro. Early in February a constitutional decree had been issued concentrating legislative as well as executive power in the Cabinet. Castro had become Prime Minister. It could still be hoped that he would exercise his authority after hearing the Cabinet, the membership of which included a number of persons competent to give forward-looking but realistic guidance to the new Cuba. Nevertheless, the first steps in the implementation of the Cuban Revolution would now come before rather than after the Cuban people had been given the opportunity promised them when Castro was in the hills to elect their representatives and to express majority and minority views as to the courses open to the nation. Elections which had earlier been announced as imminent were put off for as much as four years. In one of his public appearances in March, Castro generated an audience reaction of hostility to having elections at all.

2. Notwithstanding Castro's supremacy at the moment, the people of Cuba, even if denied the early exercise of their democratic rights, were in a position to influence and to modify the direction of the Revolution. Freedom of expression had not been suppressed. The democratic preferences, the devotion to the so-called middle-class social and economic values, and the individualism and conservatism inherent in what had been the dominant elements of Cuban society all supported what then seemed a reasonable assumption: if Castro tried to ride roughshod over these people and threatened to deprive them of their rights, their status, and their properties, he would be effectively opposed.

3. American policy toward Cuba must conform to the inter-American doctrine of nonintervention to which the United States was pledged by solemn treaty. Possible exceptions to this binding commitment did

not seem to apply. There was no serious evidence of effective Communist influence upon the new Cuban government either from the local Communist party or from abroad. I assumed that if the United States became convinced that Moscow or Peking were financing and arming Castro to establish a Communist satellite in the Western Hemisphere against the will and behind the back of the Cuban people and if the United States was unable to persuade its fellow members of the Organization of American States to join in remedial action, the United States would have been justified, on grounds of self-defense, in trying to extirpate the regime. But there was no such evidence. Such adverse information as there was against Castro and some of his companions, even if given the evaluation of the most imaginative of the cold-war warriors in our own government, was much less substantive than that on which the CIA's Guatemalan adventure of 1954 had been justified. Nor had the elimination of Arbenz and his replacement by Castillo-Armas produced results in Guatemala or in Latin America that encouraged lighthearted recourse to the method used.

4. The major asset of both nations in working toward an improvement in their relations consisted in the mutual advantage inherent in their existing political and economic ties and in the nonavailability to either partner of an alternative relationship with equivalent advantages. At the time, Cuba belonged to an area where the economic and political influence of the United States was dominant; it seemed desirable for both countries that this continue to be the case. Furthermore, it was reasonable to hope that the bulk of the Cuban people understood and supported the efforts and the sacrifices the United States had made and was continuing to make for the preservation of the integrity of the community of nations of which Cuba was a member and the values of which it then seemed to share.

With these four assumptions in mind I envisaged my task as one of convincing the new Cuban leaders of the important role the American relationship might continue to play in the improvement of the welfare of the Cuban people as well as of the receptivity I believed the United States government and private American interests would wish to show toward reasoned Cuban proposals for alterations in the relationship. American recognition of the regime had, of course, been based on the new government's assertion that Cuba would continue to observe its international obligations including the treaties to which it was a party bilaterally and multilaterally. These included the Rio Treaty, the Charter of the Organization of American States, and the other agreements that defined the rights and duties of the inter-American community. I assumed that Cuba would wish to remain a member of that community though, of course, exercising the right of every member to advocate changes in an evolving regional system.

In this framework I assumed that the treaty under which the United States held the Guantanamo naval base would remain in force. It was, nevertheless, my hope (which I kept to myself) that it might be possible eventually in view of the changing nature of our own defense requirements to achieve a modification of the status of Guantanamo that would give Cuba a participation in its operation similar to that enjoyed by our NATO allies in the American bases on their soil. But unfortunately the Cuban American alliance was to be destroyed, not modified.

I believed that my major opportunity for constructive dealing with the new Cuban government would be in the economic field. I was aware of a number of long-held Cuban aspirations unsuccessfully advanced in negotiations with the United States three or four years earlier. In view of the evolution of our Latin American policies I hoped it would be possible now to arrive at some useful and equitable agreements that would demonstrate American flexibility and understanding of Cuban needs.

A major promising possibility was a new tariff arrangement along lines the previous Cuban government had requested. This would have permitted the Cubans to increase and to change the nature of some of their duties in order to stimulate the industrialization and the agricultural diversification so important to the country's development. Such an arrangement would, ideally, have included the Cuban sugar quota which would thus have been removed from periodical determination by the United States Congress in the midst of competitive lobbying. A new tariff agreement, even though it merely involved putting the sugar we would allow Cuba to send to the United States on the same contractual basis as the American rice Cuba would admit, would not have been easy to negotiate. But the success of the effort could have had a stabilizing effect on the whole relationship.

I knew that another major Cuban aspiration was for a greatly increased quota for Cuban sugar in the United States. This was demanded not only by Cuban sugar interests but notably by the urgent need to increase Cuban export earnings if the country was to continue to finance the development programs its expanding population with its growing needs demanded. I must confess that I saw little in the sugar picture at home or in the countries that had become Cuba's serious competitors for a share in the American market to warrant any optimism on this score.

A reforming Cuban government would wish to transfer from foreign to national ownership some property now in American private hands. The extensive cane lands of the United Fruit Company were especially in my mind. Even though that company and others like it had early in the century converted waste lands into economic assets, the issue of foreign—and domestic—latifundios ("large landholdings") had become a major one in Cuba. The holdings in question would be affected by the land-reform program we knew was coming. Then, too, there was the possibility of the nationalization of the American-owned public utilities, a measure Castro had at times advocated. The terms offered as well as the capacity to pay and the ability of the Cuban government to create credit instruments which would make possible adequate and prompt compensation would be affected by the attitude adopted by the American government. To find through "quiet diplomacy" formulas that would be equitable and would not interrupt the flow into Cuba of private capital for many much-needed purposes seemed to me a promising possibility in those hopeful early days.

Finally, there was another area in which I thought the American government could be helpful to the new Cuban regime. It was generally believed that the departed Batista administration had left Cuban finances in deplorable shape and had looted the treasury. It was alleged that foreign-exchange reserves were below the danger point, that the balance of payments was precarious, and that the budget was in serious deficit. A friendly attitude on the part of United States officials would have a favorable impact on any decisions the International Monetary Fund might be asked to make to tide over the Cuban emergency. Conversations were in fact held between representatives of the Monetary Fund and the Cuban government but were inconclusive in spite of the goodwill shown by all concerned at the Washington end.

The Private American Stake in Cuba

In any appraisal of the prospects for Cuban American relations under Castro the extensive private American interests in Cuba were of major significance. A brief description of those interests seems to me indispensable in order to convey an understanding of the role they played in Cuban and in American thinking.

Since the large Hershey properties had been sold to Julio Lobo, a major Cuban sugar operator, American mills no longer dominated sugar production. The American third of the total production came mostly from the more modern mills and was believed to represent the most profitable operation though according to Castro's Minister of Finance the tax evasion practices of the Cuban millowners made of sworn taxable profits per unit of production an imperfect guide to relative efficiency.

These American sugar interests, in alliance with seaboard sugar refining companies in the United States, played a major role in the wide ranging strategy of defending the Cuban sugar quota from the attacks of its enemies, foreign and domestic. Prestigious law firms in New York and a most competent lobbying organization in Washington spearheaded an influence which, until Castro came along, had been listened to with deference and respect by the government in Havana. American exporters to Cuba were also enlisted in the struggle to defend Cuba's purchasing power by protecting its sugar quota. Indeed all American investors in Cuba had a stake in the defense of that quota.

Some American sugar interests, notably the United Fruit Company mentioned earlier, owned large tracts of Cuban cane land, parts of which were held in reserve and out of production. A clause in the Cuban Constitution of 1940 had established as national policy a restriction in the size of landholdings and the separate ownership of mills and plantations, but no implementing legislation had been passed to give effect to the national aspiration for the elimination of foreign and domestic *latifundios*.

In spite of the relatively high levels of sugar production since World War II, the sugar industry in Cuba did not reflect the progressive and enlightened competitiveness ideally associated with the private-enterprise system. No new mill had been built in over thirty years. The industry, in its production quotas, prices for cane, wages and employment, the introduction of laborsaving devices and methods, and so on, was most carefully regulated in a manner designed to maintain the structure arrived at in the depression of the thirties. The reasons for this were of a politico-social nature and reflected the importance of each separate unit of the sugar industry to the local community in which that unit operated. Inefficient mills received higher benefits from the regulatory legislation than did the more modern and progressive ones. Increases or decreases in the market for Cuban sugar were reflected in the production quota of each unit in the industry. The fact that a mill or plantation had a quota was a measure of its value, a value which depended on the prospects for sugar and on the legally established quota rights of the unit in question.[1]

Most politically sensitive of the American interests in Cuba were the two major utilities: the electric light and power company and the telephone company. They piled foreign ownership on top of the public relations problems inherent in this type of operation. They labored under the onus of a widespread belief that some previous governments had unduly favored them and that they had engaged in practices contrary to the public interest. In spite of the efficiency and goodwill displayed in many ways by the managements of these companies, there was sufficient basis for this belief to warrant the establishment of effective regulatory machinery of a continuing character. In view of the fact that both of these enterprises had been foreign owned for several decades, the possibility of nationalization was one to which the Cuban government would probably give consideration.

The importation and the refining of crude oil and the marketing of refined products including gasoline and diesel oil were in the hands of two American and one Anglo-Dutch company. The refining industry in Cuba was a recent growth; it had been established beginning in 1954 thanks to special inducements offered by the now repudiated Batista government. It was easy to convince people that the refiners who imported their crude oil from their own wells in Venezuela enjoyed a monopoly position and that if they had been obliged to buy competitively in world markets (including the Soviet market) and to distribute competitively as well the Cuban public would have benefited.

For many years foreign companies, largely American, had been exploring for petroleum in Cuba without significant success. (It does not appear that the Russians have as yet been luckier in spite of occasional reports of notable finds.) It was not difficult for extremists to transform the pre-1959 failures into ingenious plots designed to keep the Cuban people from the enjoyment of their own natural resources while permitting the "imperialists" the exploitation of a quasi-monopoly of refining and distribution.

Americans also controlled Cuba's extensive nickel resources (one of these operations was the property of the United States government) and presumably had an inside track in the next phase of Cuban metallurgical development, that is, in the promising prospects of extracting the iron from Cuba's extensive deposits of laterite ore once the stubborn metallurgical problem was solved, commercially speaking, of separating the iron completely from the ore in question.

There was an important American-owned railroad. The cement plant that supplied the booming construction industry of Havana was American owned and operated. Americans were identified with much manufacturing and some merchandising. They were developing a promising, modern cattle industry. American durable consumer goods including automobiles, televisions, and household appliances were widely distributed.

American institutions were still prominent in banking, though Cuban banking had made a notable and aggressive comeback since the debacle of 1921 when the Cuban banks had almost all failed and had to be replaced largely by branches of American and Canadian banks. Many of the hotels were American owned and managed. American operators were prominent in the flourishing gambling casinos. American participation in drug smuggling and peddling and other vice was suspected.

Most of the American interests mentioned above were constructive. They had contributed substantially to the economic and social development of the country. They had pioneered many concepts of employee and worker welfare. Yet taken as a whole the impact of these interests, both in themselves and because of the protection they were supposed to enjoy from the overall Cuban American relationship, was irritating and frustrating to the Cuban sense of nationalism and to the Cuban desire to be master in Cuba's own house. American private interests in Cuba, in spite of the capricious harassment and demagogic abuse some of them received from time to time, did not appear to be subject to the sort of public scrutiny, control, and regulation developed in the United States, especially since the great depression of the early thirties.

Above and beyond these specific American interests there was the all-pervasive presence of American culture in its multiple aspects. With the exception of baseball which the Cubans embraced enthusiastically and enriched, the cultural invasion from across the Florida Straits was displeasing to those seeking an affirmation of national values and traditions.

I had some appreciation of the emotions of Cuban nationalists on all these matters. I hoped that arrangements could be worked out that would diminish the Cuban sense of inferiority in dealing with questions where the corporate interest of American enterprises might be or appear to be in conflict with the interests of the Cuban people. I did not then realize to what extent hatred for all things American dominated Castro's spirit, how grossly he was to exaggerate the alleged misdeeds and motivations of the "imperialists," and how determined he was to reject any idea of rectification and reform in order to bring about a complete break with the United States.

The Telephone Company "Intervened"

Within two weeks of my arrival in Cuba I was furnished with the first of many examples of the policy the new Cuban government was to follow with respect to private American interests. Early in March the authorities "intervened" the Cuban Telephone Company, that is, took over its management "temporarily," lowered its rates to the level that had prevailed before Batista raised them in 1957, and announced a thoroughgoing investigation of the company's affairs. Some said that the action had been timed to coincide with the presentation of my credentials to President Urrutia and thus defiantly to demonstrate the reduced stature of the American Ambassador in a country where he was said often to have operated in proconsular fashion. However that may be, I was face-to-face with an opportunity to establish my approach to my dealings with the Cuban government.

I had spent nine years in the telephone business including a few months with the Cuban company in 1926 when I was twenty-three. I also had had some practical experience in the telephone rate regulation process in the United States (1935–1937) and in the factors involved on the public-interest side of these questions. I knew that the concession of the Cuban Telephone Company (the name had never been nationalized) had been granted in 1909 by President José Miguel Gómez and had through the years, perhaps unfairly, achieved in nationalist circles some of the ill repute attached to many of the actions of that free and easy administration. I knew that the local rates which produced the bulk of the company's revenues had remained unchanged from 1909 to 1957, a period of forty-eight years during which price levels, costs, and general conditions had varied widely. I remembered from my own days with the International Telephone and Telegraph system that the Cuban company had at one time been considered the most profitable

of the operating subsidiaries and, indeed, a bulwark of solvency in a finan-
cially stormy era. I knew that the acquisition by the Cuban company of
equipment and supplies from system-owned manufacturers without benefit
of competitive bidding could have resulted in an inequitable inflation of the
company's rate base. I accepted the possibility that there might be other
aspects of the relations between the Cuban company and the parent corporation that could be considered unfair to the Cuban users of the service.

I was familiar with the fact that due to the increase in price levels after
World War II the Cuban company had held that its return on its investment had sunk to a level too low to permit it to find financing for the large
additions to the plant and the facilities needed to meet public demand in an
era of expansion and prosperity. I knew that the company, with the support
of the Embassy and with the prospect of a substantial loan from the Export-
Import Bank if rates could be raised, had obtained a rate increase of over
20 percent from the Batista administration. The increase had been angrily
received in Cuban public opinion. (I was told by a company official that
one of the government's conditions for the rate action had been a contribution to the government's slush fund for subsidizing the mass communications media, a principal ingredient in Batista's thought-control mechanism.)

Finally, I was aware that the American Ambassador had accompanied
company officials to the Presidential Palace in March 1957 in order to present Batista with a gold telephone in recognition of his understanding of
the company's problems. The presentation took place on the day after Batista had almost been the victim of an attempt on his life by a group of young
men whose blood still stained the walls and floors of the Palace. These
youths were now regarded as heroes of the Revolution—though Castro at
the time had disapproved of their venture.

Under the circumstances it was hardly to be expected that the revolutionary government would refrain from restoring the rates to the level
from which Batista had raised them or from instituting an investigation of
the company's affairs. I did not see why the management of the company
had to be assumed by the government, but I did not believe that I, as American Ambassador, should take any official notice of the intervention. I received no instructions from Washington to do so.

In view, however, of the almost total lack of professionally competent
personnel in the field of telephone rate regulation in the Ministry of Com-

munications, I hoped that an offer of help on the technical level would be welcome. I proceeded on the assumption that the government was pursuing equity for the capital, management, and labor engaged in rendering telephone service and for the public using that service. I was convinced that in the United States the regulation of public-utility rates in the interest of the people as a whole had made great strides in the direction of accuracy and fairness. I hoped I could convince the youthful Minister of Communications that these procedures in the United States were indeed arm's-length affairs as between public authority and private company. I offered the Minister, and he accepted on behalf of himself and his associates, an opportunity to visit with American regulatory officials at the federal and the state levels.

I hoped that these Cubans would pick up ideas, methods, and procedures which would help them in their investigation of the Cuban Telephone Company. Some officials did go to Washington where they were cordially received and given all the opportunities and facilities they were willing to absorb. But long before their investigation was completed, if indeed it ever was, Castro had demonstrated that he had no interest whatever in the fair treatment of American investment in Cuba.

Neither the lowering of telephone rates and the intervention of the company nor a Castro decree drastically reducing rents was calculated to stimulate the confidence of the business community. The latter measure killed the building boom which had been so important an element in the maintenance of employment over the past few years. Yet both these measures, in addition to promoting unconditional popular support for the Revolution, increased the purchasing power of the people as a whole. They did not discourage efforts on the part of the propertied class to cooperate with the government and, if possible, share in its direction.

Those who had contributed to the Castro war chest thought they should have an inside track with the new regime. These and other personalities representing what in Spanish are called the "live forces," that is, those identified with the leadership of society primarily but not exclusively on the economic side, camped on Castro's peripatetic doorstep. They often spent hours waiting for the unpunctual great man and then, instead of having their views listened to, were more often than not fobbed off with long-winded harangues only tenuously related to what they had come to discuss.

These leaders of the establishment did not give way to frustration largely because of the presence in the government of the reputable Cubans earlier mentioned. The pronouncements and the attitudes of the Ministers of Foreign Affairs and the Treasury and of the President of the National Bank gave reason to hope that the Revolution would be one to which the existing social and economic structures might adapt. In their determination to show what would be regarded by Castro as a spirit of cooperation with the new regime, many leading firms and individuals, including some American enterprises, paid their taxes long before they were due to help alleviate the cash shortage bequeathed by the departed Batistianos.

For its part, the regime showed what seemed to be an understanding and a conciliatory attitude toward the taxpayers. Tax evasion and the suborning of revenue collectors had been notorious. The scale on which these practices were conducted was a serious blemish on Cuban society and a dramatic demonstration of a widespread lack of civic responsibility. If the Castro government had wished to discredit and to ruin the numerous individuals and corporations guilty of defrauding the treasury over many years, it could have readily done so to the tune of popular applause. Instead, the Minister of the Treasury, Rufo López-Fresquet, devised an ingenious formula which, whatever its relevance to the facts of the situation, appeared to reflect a desire to make the transition to a state of fiscal integrity one of minimum discomfort for those who had cheated the Republic in the past.

This formula, incorporated into what was known as Law Number 40, assumed that the taxpayer, responsive to the era of probity and of strict law enforcement now being inaugurated, would file his current return in accordance with the facts of his situation.[2] He would thus reveal sources of income which he had not seen fit to report in previous years. A demand that he should now pay what he should have paid as far back as his legal liability ran would have meant ruin for many and would thus have caused a serious disruption in the private sector—something the government did not at *that* time desire. So the law provided a scale of partial payments through which the taxpayer's liability could be fully discharged and he could become an honest man at a tolerable cost to himself. The law also provided a pleasing moral poultice for delinquent taxpayers, though one that was unearned in most cases: it assumed that tax evasion during the Batista years implied a patriotic refusal to contribute to the support of a dictatorial and corrupt regime. The law brought in over one hundred million pesos in back taxes at a time when the peso was at par with the dollar. It was interpreted to mean that the government looked benevolently on the incorporation of the private sector, or at least of a large part of it, into the economic structure envisaged by the new rulers.

Chapter 5

First Contacts
with Castro

DURING my first weeks in Havana I endeavored through as many channels as possible to convey goodwill and a readiness to enter into serious negotiations on any matters the regime might wish to raise. I took the unusual step of making publicized calls on each of the ministers in Castro's Cabinet. I tried to develop with each one of them a relationship of cordial confidence and to instill in them a belief that the government of the United States was prepared to give the most sympathetic and constructive consideration to any proposals of the new Cuban government in the field of relations between the two countries. I emphasized to these men and women, many of whom were new to official responsibility, the elements of mutual and reciprocal advantage inherent in the existing relationship between Cuba and the United States. I made every effort to avoid the attitude of thinly disguised paternalism which these people had been taught to believe had characterized some of my predecessors. These calls, as well as those I made on the directors of the mass media, including those set up by the new regime but excluding the Communist organ *Hoy* which Castro had allowed to reappear, were designed to and, I believe, did help to create an atmosphere of cordiality toward me and my mission.

It was evident to all of us at the Embassy that Castro himself would be the main channel for any real progress in substantive matters. This was also the view of Dr. Roberto Agramonte, the Minister of State (Foreign Affairs) with whom I at once entered into a close and friendly contact. The Minister was an internationally famed professor of sociology. With Eddy Chibás, a passionate, single-tracked anticorruptionist, Dr. Agramonte had founded in 1947 the Ortodoxo party, a splintering off from the ruling Auténticos. He had become the party's leader when Chibás, in order to underline the vehemence and the sincerity of his views, shot himself fatally as he was ending one of his highly popular broadcasts. Agramonte was the Ortodoxo candidate for the presidency in the elections scheduled in 1952 but never held because of Batista's coup.

In 1959 it was the accepted wisdom that the Agramonte ticket would have won seven years earlier if the elections had been held; this judgment may have reflected in part the fact that Castro had been a member of Agramonte's party and a candidate for a seat in the lower house in 1952. In any case Agramonte had an aura of real if dated popular support. He had played an active part in the fight against Batista and had succumbed to none of the latter's blandishments. His inclusion in the Cabinet, even though Castro had long abjured his Ortodoxo ties in order to put himself at the head of a movement that recognized only one leader, was considered an indication that the Revolution intended to rule the country with the help of personalities significant in the politics subverted by Batista.

Agramonte was a scholar, a patriot, and a man of maturity, integrity, and intellectual achievement. But he was not the man for the times, not the man to influence Castro and the young men around him. Agramonte's knowledge and his reasoned approach to the problems of the day prevented him from achieving that reputation for revolutionary dynamism so much more important to Castro than mastery of specific subjects. Agramonte's incompatibility with the Castro circle soon became as evident as the touching faith he then had in Castro and in the Revolution that had overthrown the tyranny of Batista.

My Introduction to the Maximum Leader

Agramonte and I were agreed as to the urgency of my initiating an exchange of views with Castro. My first interview with the Maximum Leader —as he became known—took place early in March, a day after I had presented my credentials to President Urrutia. It was arranged by Agramonte who was present and was held at the suburban villa in Cojímar where Castro then and later spent portions of many of his days and nights.

The occasion was, as I had anticipated, more in the nature of a public event than of a serious conversation about current affairs. I endeavored to convey to Castro the goodwill and the hopefulness with which my government envisaged the relations between our two countries. We cordially noted the generation gap between us: I had come to Cuba for the first time as a young trainee with the telephone company a couple of weeks prior to Castro's birth in August 1926. After our private talk we emerged to confront the reporters and the photographers. As we chatted informally with the newsmen, we conveyed the impression of being pleased with each other and hopeful for the future. I was encouraged to believe that we could establish a working relationship that would be advantageous to both our countries. Castro had gone out of his way to express a warm desire for frequent meetings with me. He appeared gratified to find that my Spanish was adequate for rapid and colloquial conversation. The next day on television he spoke favorably of our first meeting.[1]

A few days later Agramonte gave a lunch for Castro at which Ernesto Dihigo, the newly appointed Cuban Ambassador in Washington, and I were present. On the sincere assumption that his largely unannounced plans for the welfare of his people would turn out to be rational and practical, I tried to convey to Castro my own conviction that the Cuban American relationship and American interests in Cuba could play a constructive part in those plans. I described the realities of the relationship and of the interests as I saw them and endeavored to combat some of the slanders and calumnies of which he was so willing a victim. I avoided anything Castro might regard as paternalistic and offered no advice except in reply to specific questions.

I saw Castro on other occasions of a social nature. But conditions were unfavorable to the conduct of any serious business with him or with Agramonte either for that matter. The disorganization of the administration had to be experienced to be believed. Castro was functioning primarily as the mouthpiece and the stimulant of a popular enthusiasm with his own glorification as its objective. The separate ministries, with the exception of the treasury (the government had to have money), were paralyzed by lack of direction from the Prime Minister or the Cabinet and by fear that any initiative might draw down upon them the displeasure of their whimsical chief. There was a sense of waiting, of expectancy, of inaction.

The grotesque incident in late March involving José (Pepe) Figueres of Costa Rica illustrated Castro's extreme sensitivity to advice even from a friendly source. Figueres was a former President of his country (elected again in 1970) with a record as a fighter against dictatorship and communism. In the inter-American world he was highly respected both as an exponent and as an exemplar of the virtues of democracy. In the United States he was admired by many people who thought of him as belonging in the same category as Rómulo Betancourt of Venezuela and Luis Muñoz-Marín of Puerto Rico.

Figueres came to Cuba at the Cuban government's invitation and was asked to address a mass meeting in Havana. He appeared on the platform wearing the overseas cap and the khaki shirt and trousers in which he had fought the forces of tyranny in the backlands of his own country. He was greeted with an ovation. In the course of his remarks he said that in the struggle between the United States and the Soviet Union there could be only one place—at the side of the United States. He made the mistake of advising his Cuban hosts to take that side. David Salvador, then the leader of Cuban labor (currently in a Cuban prison), interrupted the speaker after which Castro called Figueres down publicly and rudely. The scene was a painful one. The conclusion we then drew was not so much that Castro did not intend to continue the Cuban foreign policy of support for the Western cause—his public statements up to that time had been reasonably satisfactory—as that he resented any attempt by anybody to tell him what to do and that his resentment would be particularly explosive if the advice was delivered in public.

By the end of March, though I had been unable in my conversations with Castro to come to grips with specifics or to obtain any idea of his programs, I believed that I had conveyed to him the goodwill and the flexibility that would inform American policy toward his government. I hoped that my words had been reinforced and my sincerity confirmed by the course I had followed with respect to the intervention of the telephone company. I had responded affirmatively to a request from Castro's Minister of Justice for an opportunity for some of his men to visit with the Department of Justice in Washington to familiarize themselves with certain law-enforcement techniques. I noted with satisfaction that the Communist daily Hoy, which Castro had allowed to reappear in the context of a short-lived policy of freedom of the press, was increasingly concerned at evidences of cordiality and understanding between the United States and Cuba; it attacked Doctor Agramonte as a plattista, that is, as one who, in spite of the abrogation of the Platt Amendment a generation earlier, thought and acted as though the Amendment, which gave ultimate authority in Cuba to the United States, was still in force. (Though the charge against Agramonte was unjustified, I was to appreciate in the months to come what an enduring and negative a factor was the *plattista* mentality.)

Castro in Retrospect

My narrative will, I hope, prove less baffling to the reader than the experience was to me if I insert at this point some notes on Castro as I eventually came to understand him, recalling, however, that in the spring of 1959 he was far from having fully discovered himself. Castro's major motivation since adolescence has been his drive for absolute personal power. He cannot endure any sharing of authority, any subjection of his will to that of any other individual or body of people. This drive for power is a far more constant element in his makeup than is the philosophy behind any particular revolutionary panacea he may be peddling. Castro has now attained his goal. Everything in Cuba hinges on him. He is subordinate to no legal or institutional structure. He holds his job at his own pleasure.

I did not achieve any intimacy or friendship with Castro. I do not believe he has any friends in the commonly accepted meaning of that word. My definition of friendship does not cover the master-servant relationship that exists between him and the men and women in his personal entourage. He is not lacking in charm or versatility of personality. His mental and physical gifts are phenomenal. He was, in my time, a vigorous practitioner of such normal sensual pursuits as eating, smoking, drinking, and sex. But he seemed to derive from these activities none of the human sociability that usually accompanies them. Castro achieves intimacy only when he addresses the masses in the Plaza de la República or over television. It is only then when he experiences that flow of ideas and sentiments characteristic of real personal ties between human beings.

Castro's major talent—and it is a major one indeed—is manifest in the dialogue he has carried on over the years with hundreds of thousands of Cubans. I use the word *dialogue* advisedly though only Castro speaks. His speeches represent a process, emotional much more than intellectual, in which his hearers participate. These speeches do not give the impression of having been prepared in any serious sense; neither advance copies nor even summaries are made available. Castro seems rather to be reacting emotionally and vocally to ideas, facts, and notions of facts in a process in which the minds and hearts of his hearers participate. His impact is not vitiated by the repetitiousness, the fallacy, the inconsistency, and often the hatefulness of what he says. Each hearer, particularly if he belongs to the masses, shares an experience with Castro in which Castro's chain of emotion-thought becomes his chain of emotion-thought. He reaches the Castro conclusions simultaneously with Castro and not through an absorption of what Castro has said and the subsequent application of his own powers of reasoning and analysis. Popular faith in the Castro "dialogue" is immense; it is unrelated to the success or failure of whatever Castro may be advocating at the moment from cane-cutting machines to artificial insemination to the subversion of Latin American governments. This is magic of a high order!

This sorcery becomes all the more miraculous when viewed in the context of the political mood of the bulk of the Cuban people pre-Castro: ironical, cynical, and apathetic. If any one had prophesied as late as the mid-fifties that from 1959 on millions of Cuban people would be absorbed for three or four hours at a time (often beginning well after midnight) in the words of one of their number and that they would develop a fanatical enthusiasm for the man that would erase their own powers of judgment, most competent observers of the Cuban scene would have been highly skeptical.

I have come to reject the condemnation of Castro as the conscious betrayer of the various revolutions he has from time to time propounded, though the evidence in favor of such a condemnation is strong. Castro has delighted his followers by picturing himself as the crafty deceiver of people who deserved to be deceived. Yet such a role would imply his possession of intellectual and moral powers and failings comparable to those of other men. I do not believe he has them. He is not a thinker or a planner; such plotting as he does is in the narrow field of personalities. He is rather the vehicle of a mysterious force that drives him on to his goal of personal power. He is endowed with a mystique, a charisma, that relieves him from the demands of doctrine and consistency that to some extent govern most politicians.

Castro has an intuitive faculty that reveals to him the weakness or the strength of the obstacles with which he may be confronted at any particular time. His forward movement is comparable to that of a flow of lava or of a torrential stream in full spate. His course, too, is governed by the lay of the land and the nature of the obstacles encountered rather than by a directing human conscience. In Castro's case the obstacles proved weak; there was little that could not be destroyed.

In the short space of two years Castro preached the restoration of Cuban democracy under the Constitution of 1940 with elections and respect for private property and then a vague "humanism" that would avoid both the terror the Maximum Leader then associated with communism and the insecurity and hunger which he regarded as the fruits of capitalism. At the end of the third year he became a high priest of Marxism-Leninism, giving lessons in the true faith to the pundits in Moscow and to Communist leaders everywhere.

The key to Fidel Castro is not to be found in the domain of theoretical politics but in that of the tactics of power. The irresponsible myths of the antiimperialists which Castro so eagerly absorbed produced the Castro conviction that the major barrier to his own ambition was not so much the desire of his countrymen for that participation in the political process denied them by Batista as it was the role of the United States and of American interests in the Cuban decision-making machinery. He found that his personal magic readily overwhelmed the none too self-confident aspirations of his fellow Cubans for the share of power he had promised them. It followed that the one constant in all his gyrations was a determination to free Cuba from that American presence he regarded as his own major competitor. He swallowed the gospel of the antiimperialists because he sensed that that American presence was inimical to his own drive for absolute power. In attaining his objective he has, ironically enough, subjected his country to dependence on the Soviet Union.

Early in 1959 the masses from whom Castro drew his strength looked to him as the guarantor of long-desired social and economic reforms. Beginning with the restoration of the political processes contemplated in the Constitution of 1940, these reforms included the full implementation of that constitution. They embraced land reform, tax reform, administrative reform, perhaps the nationalization of the public utilities, a stimulation of industrialization and of agricultural diversification, a serious attack on the structural and seasonal unemployment that was such a blight on the community, the elimination of the corruption that had so disfigured the civic life of the Republic, and a dilution of the American presence. But as Castro began to weave his spells, the specifics of the desired reforms became blurred. Castro received a blank check to proceed as he wished with the assurance of mass support for his every action. No sooner had the Cuban masses achieved a prospect of asserting their own responsibilities for their destinies than they abjured that prospect and turned over the control of their fate to a relatively unknown young man with an extraordinary television presence.

A Meeting of American Ambassadors

The perceptions of Castro which I have just outlined were not those I entertained in late March 1959; my education in *Fidelismo* was just beginning.[2] At the time I had the impression that I had established the basis for useful diplomacy whenever the programs of the Cuban government were defined. My opportunities for substantive discussions with Castro were now to be interrupted for several weeks. I was occupied with a meeting of American ambassadors in San Salvador beginning April 8. Castro's trip to the United States and to Latin America, beginning in mid-April and ending on May 8, prolonged the interruption of our contacts.

Meetings of American ambassadors on a regional basis have been held for a number of years. They serve useful and agreeable purposes. Normally they attract little or no public attention. But this meeting in the capital of El Salvador was poorly timed. It could not fail to encourage the view that it was designed to work out ways and means whereby the United States might cope with the revolutionary ferment personified by Castro's triumph in Cuba. Policy in this delicate context could have been evolved more effectively and less obtrusively without such a gathering.

The meeting was attended by the American Ambassadors accredited to the three island republics of the Caribbean, the five republics of Central America, Mexico, Panama, Venezuela, and Colombia together with our Ambassador to the Organization of American States. The Deputy Under Secretary of State for Administration, Loy Henderson, a highly respected and greatly admired veteran of the Foreign Service, and Richard Rubottom, the Assistant Secretary for Inter-American Affairs, a man of understanding and experience, were the principal Washington representatives. The proceedings were off the record. Yet members of the press had been attracted to San Salvador, including Paul Kennedy of the *New York Times*, an able and reliable correspondent, and a young man from a minor Cuban newspaper who would soon join *Prensa Latina*, the propaganda organ in Latin America of the Cuban government.

Cuba was obviously the star attraction. I made a presentation of the situation there and urged continuance of the policy of hopeful and watchful "wait and see" which the American government had been pursuing. Though what I said was on my own responsibility, it reflected the views and the staff work of my principal associates in Havana. I stressed the degree to which Castro had captured the imagination and the passionate loyalty of the immense majority of the Cuban people. I said that our policy toward Castro should march with that of Cuban public opinion as long as that opinion remained, as it was then, relatively free to express itself. I confirmed the presence in Castro's entourage of undesirable influences but pointed out that the Cuban people, so far as I could judge, were fundamentally anti-Communist.

I said that the United States would be making a serious mistake, even if it believed Cuban public opinion to be wholly misled and misinformed as to Castro's intentions—which I did not at the time—to take a hostile position before the Cuban people accepted the evidence some of us—not I— believed justified such a position. My views seemed acceptable to most of my colleagues and were, generally speaking, those to which the Department of State adhered at the time.

Robert Hill, the American Ambassador to Mexico, dissented and two years later testified that he had advocated a submittal by the United States to the Organization of American States of the evidence that had convinced him that Castro was then and had long been a tool of Moscow and Peking. This would have been an entirely futile and indeed damaging proceeding in view of contemporary American and Latin American opinion even if Ambassador Hill had been able to convince our government that his evaluation of the intelligence on which he based his recommendation was sound. His proposal had, again according to Ambassador Hill's testimony before a senatorial committee, little support from his colleagues at the meeting. Before this same committee he described me as "the chief architect of the Cuban Disaster."[3]

I have a vivid recollection of an incident involving Ambassador Hill at San Salvador. An innocuous communiqué was submitted by Assistant Secretary Rubottom for the pro forma approval of those present. Ambassador Hill took the position that his approval could be granted only if there were added a hard-nosed paragraph he had drafted. He said that if the meeting did not agree to his suggestion he would make a minority report to the press.

I commented that I thought he should resign if he could not be a team player; he had had a full opportunity to develop his views and they had been rejected by his colleagues. The cogent remonstrances of Under Secretary Henderson and Mr. Rubottom reduced him to a state of emotional contrition. Later it was revealed in the press that, on the previous evening, Ambassador Hill had confided to a correspondent the position he planned to take and from which he had now receded![4]

The accounts of the meeting and the reports that filtered back to Havana by word of mouth were useful to me in my dealings with the Cuban government and increased my acceptability to the Cuban public. I appeared as one who had expressed views to his ambassadorial and departmental colleagues that were more or less in line with dominant Cuban opinion. In those days that opinion held that to accuse Castro of communism was primarily an almost blasphemous tactic of those in Cuba and in the United States wishing to defend their properties and their privileges from the reforms—as yet largely undefined—on which the Cuban Revolution was bent.

Ambassador Hill's belief in Castro's covert communism and his alarm at the threat this posed for Cuba and for the United States were shared by others. For example, my immediate predecessors in Cuba—Arthur Gardner who had embarrassed Batista with his praise and Earl Smith who had favored a variety of schemes designed to deny power to Castro—generally agreed with Ambassador Hill. There were others who, both before and after Castro's assumption of power, denounced his alleged pro-Communist leanings and entanglements. They advocated stern measures including American intervention if the inter-American system could not rid the hemisphere of the bearded leader.

Batista, too, had strenuously if not convincingly endeavored to pin the Communist label on Castro. When the ex-sergeant fled Cuba, repudiated by most of his fellow citizens, some of his supporters with hopes for a future in Cuban politics found it more promising to denounce Castro and his inner circle as Communists than to defend the fallen regime.

I was then and I remain convinced that these Cubans and Americans had insufficient evidence for the views they expressed in the winter and spring of 1959. Nevertheless they have been proven right about Castro: by the end of 1961 the latter had proclaimed himself a Marxist-Leninist. The unheeded prophets have naturally not been backward with their "I told you so's." Also some of those who were trying to climb on the Castro bandwagon in 1959 have revised their records so as to place themselves in the ranks of the allegedly clearheaded analysts and advocates of strong action.

At the time, however, those who preached the Castro-Communist menace were plagued not only by the scarcity of respectable evidence with which to buttress their views, but they were handicapped as well by their own rigidly conservative positions on social and economic matters. They were plausibly believed to be conditioned to brand as communistic any threat of change. In this they ran the risk of convincing people that change was possible only through communism. In the United States many of them had been identified with the anticommunism exemplified by Senator Joe McCarthy and with unscrupulous and irresponsible accusations impugning the patriotism and the integrity of such eminent servants of the American people as President Truman, Dean Acheson, and General George Marshall. Particularly among those with a continuing familiarity with foreign affairs— the press and the career Foreign Service, for example—these people in the spring of 1959 no longer enjoyed much credibility or influence. I hope this narrative will demonstrate that these people were right about Castro for the wrong reasons.

The real failure of judgment at this particular juncture was not in the determination of what Castro had been, was, or would be. The primary error—one in which I participated—was the belief that the nature, the will for democracy, and the strength of a Cuban society released by its own efforts from the dictatorship of Batista would be the dominant factors in determining the character and the measures of the new Cuban government rather than the notions of a power-mad Fidel Castro. Castro almost certainly shared in this error; it was not until months later that he sensed the extreme weakness and the reliance on outside help to defend its interests with which the traditional leadership of the community was afflicted.

Chapter 6

Castro Visits the United States, April 1959

My return to Havana from the ambassadors' meeting in San Salvador coincided with the last days of feverish preparations for Castro's trip to the United States. He had received an invitation from an association of American editors to address their annual meeting in Washington on April 17. An eventual Castro visit to the United States, perhaps in conjunction with a reciprocal one by the President of the United States to Cuba, could have been a useful personification of the establishment of cordial and understanding relations with the new Cuba. But the time for such visits was still distant when the editors, so far as I know without consulting any responsible American official, issued their invitation to the Cuban Prime Minister, and the latter accepted it without giving any official of the country to which he, the Prime Minister of Cuba, was planning to travel the courtesy of advance notification of his intention.

The Department of State wisely decided to overlook the aberration of the editors and the inexperience of the Prime Minister, especially since to accomplish what he had been invited to do Castro could have left Havana in the morning, made his speech at the lunch in Washington, and been back home that night. But the insatiable hunger for sensation of many elements in the United States and the equally insatiable Castro ego made such an expeditious handling of the matter out of the question. The trip and its complications expanded daily as invitations and suggestions for appearances poured in. Nevertheless, Washington held to its willingness to be helpful and to welcome any indication that Castro wished to use his unofficial visit to further relations between the two governments.

Such an indication appeared to have been given when Castro announced that among the hundred or so persons who would travel with him to the United States would be the Ministers of the Treasury and of Economy, the President of the National Bank, and one or two of the prominent businessmen who had financed Castro when he was struggling to achieve power. It hardly seemed possible that so many competent and busy people were being taken along just for the ride or to serve as a claque for the speech to the editors. I concluded that Castro envisaged preliminary conversations with officials of the American government and possibly with representatives of American private enterprise. I suggested, and Foreign Minister Agramonte arranged, a meeting attended by Castro, by some of the economic advisers who were to accompany him to the United States, and by myself and members of the Embassy staff. My purpose was to find out if the Embassy could be helpful in making preparations for the Prime Minister and the high officials accompanying him. The meeting, though cordial, was absolutely unproductive. I put this down at the time to the chaotic conditions known to prevail at what should have been the coordinating level of the regime and to absence of time for constructive planning.

It happened that on the day of Castro's departure for the United States (April 14) his Finance Minister and I, in compliance with invitations we had received weeks earlier, addressed the annual luncheon banquet of the Cuban-American Chamber of Commerce. This was a most useful and influential organization with a binational membership. At the end of my speech, I inserted the following:

> And now before I close a word about an event which I know is very much in all our minds. I refer to the trip to the United States of Prime Minister Fidel Castro. I know that you join with me in the confident expectation that this highly welcome informal visit, in the course of which Dr. Castro will be received by our people with the same warm hospitality all of us have experienced from our Cuban friends, will help toward mutual understanding and will strengthen the ties of affection and solidarity between our two nations. Such mutual understanding

*and affection are needed if both countries are to continue to reap the
advantages to which their geographical situation, their historical bonds,
their common ideals and their complementary economies entitle them.*

That afternoon together with thousands of others I spent four hours at
the airport waiting for Castro to leave on his flight to Washington. The
number of hours wearily lost on account of his unpunctuality was astronom-
ical. When he finally appeared the only reference he made to the purpose
of his trip was a cryptic statement about recovering the lost sugar quotas.
Whether he alluded to the relatively minor loss Cuba had suffered at the
hands of the American Congress in 1956 or to the more profound sense of
grievance that Cuban nationalists (even those who regard sugar as a symbol
of colonial bondage) have long felt at the treatment Cuba received during
the Great Depression of the thirties was never revealed.[1] Castro did not raise
the matter in Washington. In fact, he and his fellow voyagers made no use
whatever of the opportunities arranged for them to discuss the practical
aspects of Cuban American relations or to explore the assistance our government might provide to help meet pressing Cuban requirements.

Castro and company's expedition was a picturesque, disorderly, and
apparently pointless affair. Under the circumstances people in Washington
did all and more than the most ardent partisan of the bearded leader might
reasonably have expected. The Acting Secretary of State (Mr. Herter)
hosted a lunch in Castro's honor; he was cordially received by Vice President
Nixon and by a number of Senators and Representatives on Capitol Hill.
President Eisenhower was out of town and, quite properly in my opinion,
did not arrange to see the man who had expressed himself so unfavorably
in public about the United States and was not in the United States officially.
But the Vice President conferred with Castro at length and stressed the
perils to which the machinations of international communism could expose
the naive leader of a popular revolution. Castro's reaction to this interview
was unfavorable and Mr. Nixon's was pessimistic.

Castro's need to be warned of the menace of international Communist
plots and conspiracies was not neglected by the Central Intelligence Agency.
A friendly, persuasive, and fluently Spanish-speaking representative of the
agency who had an opportunity of talking to the Cuban Prime Minister for
over an hour emerged in a state of ecstasy about Castro's receptivity, responsiveness, and understanding.[2] A channel was established through which

Castro might be kept up to date as to the intentions and deeds of Moscow and Peking. (The channel dried up almost immediately and was never effectively used; Castro's interest in what the United States could tell him about the Communist world proved no more than a flash in the pan.)

At the editors' lunch, on television, and in other public appearances Castro had ample opportunities to make those reassuring statements that gave so erroneous a notion of the economic and political philosophies he was to pursue and of his devotion to freedom of the press.³ That star of the American newspaper world, May Craig, pushed him rather harder on the sensitive subject of communism than his admirers thought proper; the "old woman with the cherries on her hat," as she was called from the bonnet she wore on the program in question, was a nine days' object of obloquy in Havana for even having raised the subject.

It seems to me that on balance Castro was more the victim of the self-deception he inflicted upon himself in the course of his American jaunt than he was the successful perpetrator of deceit upon the American people. He was exposed under varying and wide-ranging circumstances to the eager and friendly curiosity with which Americans tend to favor anything picturesque that comes over their horizon. He deceived himself—at least this is my speculation—as to the significance of the cheers and the applause he harvested at the universities and in the cities which he visited. His domination over his own people led him astray as to his impact in the United States. He misinterpreted the active and cheerful sensation-hunting of the crowds he drew and the cordial politeness of the intellectuals and others with whom he conversed.

By and large the impression produced in Cuba by Castro's American junketings was in the direction of increased cordiality in the relations between the two countries. This pleased some and alarmed others. I hoped the trip had been moderately helpful and that it would do something to dispel the notions put in Castro's head by some of the antiimperialist demonologists to whom he was exposed in Cuba. But I am afraid that the final verdict must be that the trip strengthened his preconceptions about the inevitability, if not the immediacy, of changes in the United States along the sweeping lines he was beginning to meditate for Cuba. He thought of himself as riding a wave that would engulf the future in Cuba, the United States, and Latin America. He saw himself as the heroic pioneer of that future.

What had started out as a one-day dash to the District of Columbia for the purpose of making a speech expanded to include several of our states, Canada, and certain countries of South America. At Buenos Aires, Castro made his famous speech demanding billions in assistance from the United States for Latin America, one of the early indications of that sense of continental mission in the response to which he has been so grievously disappointed. During his absence some of his followers mounted a comic-opera expedition from Cuba to overthrow the government of Panama; the failure was complete and the damage slight. Castro's disclaimer of personal responsibility was probably truthful though if the venture had been successful he would have taken credit for it.

Castro Returns to Havana

Castro returned to Havana on May 7. I met him at the airport and proposed an early interview to discuss the relations between our two countries. He agreed cordially and was emphatic as to the desirability of our meeting frequently. Over a month elapsed before I had any serious conversation with him.

In spite of his promise, my repeated requests for an interview elicited no response from Castro. I saw him casually at social affairs as well as at a briefing for some touring United States War College students. He was friendly, charming, and apologetic about the delay in scheduling the conversation in which he claimed to be most interested. But nothing happened in spite of Dr. Agramonte's best efforts.

What was Castro's own thinking about the United States during these spring weeks? I hoped and perhaps flattered myself that my endeavor to develop a basis for understanding and for negotiation promised constructive results. The officers of the Embassy engaged in political reporting and in intelligence work shared my anxiety to be informed of Castro's real sentiments and purposes and of the views he expressed in private. Little enlightenment was obtained in spite of the energy and ingenuity expended. In any event, the man was so loquacious and self-contradictory in public and in private that he furnished material for the most varied and mutually exclusive theories as to his intentions.

With the benefit of hindsight I have come to the conclusion that in the spring of 1959 Castro believed it probable that the Cuban Revolution as he envisaged it would sooner rather than later come into irreconcilable conflict with American interests on the island and that the United States government would respond with a full-scale invasion of Cuba. Under this hypothesis he expected the Marines to occupy the principal cities. Castro and his followers would for a time play the role assigned to the Nicaraguan Sandino and his band in antiimperialist folklore. The invasion and the long-drawn-out guerrilla struggle which Castro would mount against the invaders and against their Cuban "puppets" would eventually produce such a revulsion of feeling in the United States and in Latin America that the American government would be forced to recognize that it had embarked on an enterprise both wrongly conceived and beyond its power to carry to a successful conclusion. Castro's Minister of the Treasury, Rufo López-Fresquet, has written that Castro's thinking was predicated on the probability of an American invasion.[4]

Castro's initial attitude toward the arming of his followers had been negative but his question, "¿Armas para qué?" ("Arms—what for?") reflected, as did so many of his utterances, only a fleeting mood.[5] By May he was desperately trying to buy small arms and ammunition in Europe. He had decided to arm his supporters against possible local opposition, to equip groups of Cubans and exiles for the invasion of other countries in the area and to bolster his own forces for the American invasion he believed probable. His dream was to emerge from a long struggle as the conqueror of the United States and the liberator of Latin America from "imperialism," just as Bolívar had defeated the Spanish rulers and freed the continent from colonialism.

I am convinced that Castro's scenario at this time did not contemplate the massive help in the form of economic aid and weapons that he later received from the Soviet Union. His thrust in 1959 was radically and exclusively nationalistic; it became oriented toward dependence on the Soviet Union only when the United States, by its actions in the spring and summer of 1960 (see chapter 16), gave the Russians no choice other than to come to Castro's rescue.

During May 1959, however, Castro seemed anxious to dispel any impression that the Communists were gaining in influence in his regime. His attitude caused serious concern to the Cuban Communists who were having their troubles with the labor unions.[6] These troubles reflected a widespread belief that Castro was not an admirer of the Cuban Communist party with all it had to live down in the past politics of Cuba, including its reluctance to support Castro until the summer of 1958.

On the other hand, the issue of communism was beginning to take on the aspect that was to characterize it in the coming weeks. When Castro came to Havana in January, those who suspected his regime of being actually or potentially Communist dominated were few and uninfluential; many of them were tarred with the Batista brush. But as the measures the Revolution took, or was believed to be contemplating, adversely affected more and more interests and as the possibility of a consultation of the electorate receded, the number of those who saw the sinister hand of communism in the government naturally increased and became more vocal. Castro bitterly resented the anticommunism that seemed to him to function simply as the guardian of the *status quo*. The next development in his thinking was to consider as an enemy of his Revolution anyone who described a revolutionary measure or personality as having Communist aspects.

Perhaps in part to take care of this issue Castro developed his doctrine of "humanism." It appeared as palatable to his devoted audiences as the democratic freedoms about which he had been so emphatic a few weeks before. Humanism, according to Castro, was supposed to guarantee bread to the people without the insecurities inherent in the capitalist system and without the terror characteristic of communism in power. He described his humanism as neither to the right nor to the left but one step ahead of both communism and capitalism. What this meant—if anything—seemed not to trouble his hearers. That they listened so enthusiastically and uncritically was another measure of the Castro magic.

Another of Castro's straws in the wind during the month of May was the playing down (on May 20) of the anniversary celebration of the Cuban Republic's inauguration in 1902. In the past this had been a major Cuban holiday and the occasion for amiable official courtesies about American participation in the liberation of the island from Spanish tyranny. This year it was practically neglected by higher officials; Castro and some of the people around him stressed the theme that Cuba's independence was not fully achieved under the Republic of 1902 and that true independence was only now being realized. This was part of a campaign to discredit much of Cuba's past and the role played by the United States in that past.

Another indication of things to come was more immediately disquieting. Castro was passionately upholding the doctrine of nonintervention so far as any attempt to interfere with the Cuban Revolution was concerned. At the same time he was welcoming, training, and arming numerous exiles and refugees from the Dominican Republic, Nicaragua, Guatemala, and other Latin American countries. He had already begun to send arms and supplies to guerrilla bands in some of these countries and was maturing the plans and preparations for the expeditions that were to cause him such bloody setbacks in June.

Chapter 7

Land Reform at Home and Intervention Abroad

Whatever Castro's long-range concerns may have been in May 1959, his energies in the domestic field were devoted to the formulation of his land-reform program. The major changes advocated over the years by forward-looking Cubans (for example, the limitation of the size of landholdings and the separation of the ownership of sugar mills and plantations as provided in the Constitution of 1940) had not been legislatively implemented at an earlier date because of the opposition of local vested interests—both Cuban and American. A good deal had, however, been achieved during the previous generation, particularly in the matter of giving security of tenure ("permanencia") to tenants and even to squatters in the sugar sector. The eviction of persons actually cultivating the land they occupied had largely become a thing of the past.

Castro himself, in an early version of his famous speech "History Will Absolve Me," said to have been delivered at his trial in 1953 (but often since revised), had a concept of land reform that was close to the liberal thought of Cuba in the early fifties. In synthesis, the lot of tenants and squatters was to be improved further by making many of those who cultivated the land into its owners, the *latifundios* of Cubans and foreigners were to be severely limited, and the land thus taken, together with state-owned lands, was to be distributed to the rural landless. Compensation was to be paid to former owners, and ways and means were to be devised whereby the small land-owners, especially those created by the reform, might be given access to modern machinery and modern techniques through the formation of farmers' cooperatives and through increased state assistance in agricultural education.

Nothing that Castro had said, nothing contained in the agrarian reform statute Castro had signed when he was fighting in the hills in October 1958, and nothing in the law that was promulgated in the *Official Gazette* of June 3, 1959, warranted the belief that within two years a wholesale conversion of Cuban agricultural land to state ownership would take place. Such a notion then would have been inconsistent with many of the Castro pronouncements, including the thesis of a peasant revolution and the Castro pledges to the landless throughout the nation. Today most of those who expected to become independent farmers or members of cooperatives in the operation of which they would have a voice are laborers on the state payroll.

The new law was drawn up most secretively and indeed was disapproved by the Minister of Agriculture (Humberto Sorí-Marín—executed at Castro's orders in March 1961). The Cabinet members were given no opportunity of discussing it or even of reading it carefully. They were flown to a remote point in the Sierra Maestra where, in order to stress the Revolution's obligations to the peasants of the area, the document was signed. (The method used in the case of this Castro land-reform project contrasted with that followed by the Minister of the Treasury in drawing up his project of tax reform which became law at about the same time; López-Fresquet had gathered together respected experts, had published drafts, had welcomed suggestions and criticisms from all quarters, including foreigners, and had made many changes in consequence.)

This Land Reform Law was the first of the revolutionary measures that seriously affected multiple American interests in Cuba. Since, however, it was never applied by the Cuban authorities, there is little to be gained here by any detailed analysis of its terms. In brief, it contemplated continued private ownership of land. It established maximum and minimum landholdings and provided a method of valuation and compensation for the benefit of those whose land was to be taken from them. It created the National Institute of Agrarian Reform (INRA) with broad and ill-defined powers—powers which in practice and under Castro's personal direction became unlimited and eclipsed those of the other agencies of government in both the executive-legislative and the judicial branches. The law made clear that large amounts of land would be taken from the present owners, that many efficient agricultural operations would be broken up—this applied especially to sugar and to cattle—and that the debt the government would incur even under the proposed method of valuation, one not slanted in favor of the landowners to be dispossessed, would exceed its ability to finance. But since an implementation of the law was never really started, all this is academic.

The preparation and the publication of the Land Reform Law added to my sense of the urgency of my now long-delayed meeting with the Prime Minister. The approach to Cuban American relations which I had endeavored to communicate to Castro, to his colleagues in the Cabinet, and to public opinion in general seemed to me to indicate that it would have been judicious for Castro to have seen me without delay and to have discussed with me a law which was drastically to affect many American interests on the island—interests the constructive potential of which Castro had cordially admitted in our earlier conversations. These interests, in common with similar Cuban interests, had been rigorously excluded from any opportunity of a hearing during the preparation of the law.

In my frame of mind then I thought Castro would have liked to hear from me that the government of the United States was sympathetic to a carefully considered and executed land reform and had been identified with the successful execution of such a reform in Japan. I thought Castro would have liked to know that American interests in Cuba which had in the past, according to some Cubans, relied unduly on the American Embassy to exercise on their behalf a leverage superior to that available to similar Cuban interests would find that before their government would even consider their claims of unfair treatment, much less pass upon those claims with a view to possible diplomatic action, the allegedly injured party would have to exhaust all of the remedies available to him in the Cuban administrative and judicial process.

These American interests were extensive and long-standing. The Cuban government had now issued a measure that would vitally affect them. I believed both countries would have profited if the Cuban government had given the concerned Americans in Cuba a hearing before decisions were reached on such an important matter. I also thought that informal discussions at a high official level would have contributed to an understanding by the United States government of the intent of the Cuban government and would have enlightened the latter as to some possible repercussions of the action it proposed to take. I did not necessarily assume that such exchanges would have modified the measures of the Cuban government, but I hoped they would create the best possible atmosphere for the working out of whatever problems might arise from the implementation of Castro's decree.

These views had been conveyed to Foreign Minister Agramonte in Havana and to Ambassador Dihigo in Washington. Both these men concurred in the importance of their being transmitted personally by me to the Prime Minister. The latter's failure to see me after repeated promises seemed both unwise and discourteous even after allowing for the extreme disorganization and the impromptu character of the Maximum Leader's way of life.

Under the circumstances and at the State Department's instructions, I sent a note to the Foreign Minister on June 11, formalizing the American position and gave its text to the press.[1] This action reflected a belief that, in view of the known fact that there was no contact between myself and the master of the Cuban government and very little between the latter and his Foreign Minister, public opinion in Cuba and in the United States as well as the interests directly concerned was entitled to an authoritative statement of the position of the United States government. The note expressed sympathy for the objectives of land reform and, of course, recognized the right of expropriation. It referred to the generally accepted obligation of prompt, adequate, and effective compensation. It expressed concern as to the provisions for compensation in the case of the United States citizens who would be affected, and it proposed further exchanges of views on the subject.[2]

That same evening, in a development which I have no reason to believe was related to the note described above, Dr. Agramonte, the Foreign Minister, and the Ministers of Health, Agriculture, Interior, and Social Welfare were peremptorily dismissed from the Cabinet. The shakeup, a reflection of Castro's own whim of the moment, came as a surprise to the victims who attended the late-night Cabinet meeting at which it was announced by the Prime Minister. Dr. Agramonte, who had dined with me that evening, did not appear aware of his impending dismissal. I was sorry to see him go. I liked, admired, and trusted him though I realized that his effectiveness with Castro had declined to the vanishing point. The pleasure of dealing with a man whom I respected and who in turn respected the goodwill and the high purpose, if not the infallibility, of the United States was one denied me during the rest of my mission in Cuba.

The next day, June 12, probably as a consequence of my published note,

I received a summons to call on Castro at his suburban home. I was accompanied by my deputy, Dan Braddock. Before the Prime Minister's arrival, I gathered that my note had produced some disappointment in Castro's entourage where anything less than praise for his every word and action was considered to reflect a hostile attitude.

When Castro arrived he was cordial. He expressed regret at his failure to see me earlier as I had requested. He stressed the vital importance of land reform for Cuba. I rehearsed for him some of our previous conversations when I had emphasized the goodwill and the desire for accommodation of the United States in the face of the situations arising from the new state of affairs in Cuba. I told the Prime Minister that the close proximity of our two countries and the intimate relationship of their economies rendered imperative frequent and thorough exchanges of views at effective levels especially in the circumstances of the times. The note I had sent the Foreign Minister had in part been occasioned by the lack of opportunity for such an exchange, one which I had eagerly sought for the past five weeks. I added that it was generally agreed that American enterprise in Cuba had contributed to the development and progress of the country and that on that score it deserved considerate treatment especially from those bent upon changes in the legal structure within which it had operated in good faith. I then asked him whether it was still his thought, as it had been when we talked in April, that these interests had a role to play in the future development of the country as that development was envisaged by the revolutionary government. His answer was an emphatic affirmative.

Later that day, in answer to a question from the press, Castro decried the notion that my note and my approach to him had reflected what in the idiom of some revolutionaries was described as a proconsular attitude. He said that I had been "cordial and respectful." The Cuban reply to my note came a few days later. While it stressed sovereignty and the imperative nature of agrarian reform as decreed by the revolutionary government, it admitted that it should be possible to have discussions with the United States on related matters of common interest. I was pleased to note that the newly appointed Cuban Foreign Minister, Dr. Raúl Roa, who had been serving in Washington as Cuban representative to the Organization of American States, requested and received assurances from Assistant Secretary Rubottom of full cooperation in returning the problems of Cuban American relations to normal, nonpublic channels. I hoped this meant that these channels would be made available to me and that there would be an end to the almost complete absence of any meaningful exchanges that had prevailed during the five weeks after the Prime Minister's return from his travels early in May.

Years later Castro remarked to an American newspaperman that "the American reaction to the agrarian reform of May 1959 made me realize that there was no chance of an accommodation with the United States."[3] This is far from a unique example of the manner in which the Maximum Leader's flexible memory permits him statements contrary to the truth of the event he is recalling.

As a matter of fact all of the American interests affected by the Land Reform Law immediately adopted a posture of compliance. They began at once to prepare the voluminous documents required to identify their properties, to permit the government to decide what it would take, and to initiate the procedures provided in the law. The Embassy engaged in conversations with Cuban officials concerning compensation with particular reference to long-term bonds that would be marketable and would be payable in dollars if desired. Castro, for his part, at once launched attacks against the private landowners throughout Cuba in ways for which there was no authority in his own law. He unleashed a crew of zealous incompetents who soon did great damage to the production of the properties they tried to manage. Three American cattle ranches were "intervened," that is, removed from the control of their owners during June.

The Cuban masses' reaction to the agrarian reform was one of emotional support of anything that had Castro's backing and of a determination that not a comma should be abated from a text few had read. Every word in the document seemed somehow to have become a fragment of the national sovereignty not to be altered without loss of national honor. On the other hand, both the Association of Tobacco Planters and the Association of Cattle Ranchers passed resolutions opposing the law. The latter organization stated that the law "would cause the most harm to the people it claims to benefit."

On the evening of June 12, Antonio ("Tony") Varona, who had been Prime Minister in the administration of President Prío seven or eight years earlier, spoke out courageously on a national television program. He said, "I do not believe the Revolution should remain in power without a popular mandate beyond the time necessary to normalize the country and to convoke free and democratic elections so that the people may give themselves the rulers they desire." Turning to land reform he noted that the projected National Institute of Agrarian Reform (INRA) had been given more power than the President and the Council of Ministers. He concluded that a duly elected Cuban Congress would be capable of legislating suitable land reform.

Five days later ex-President Carlos Prío came into town from his palatial country estate to appear on the same program. He guaranteed the non-Communist character of the Revolution. He expressed sweeping support for the Land Reform Law and for Castro. He dissented from the views advanced by Varona. He said that the Auténtico party, which had ruled Cuba from 1944 to March 1952 and of which he was the titular head, agreed fully with Castro. He announced his own retirement from active politics.[4] Shortly afterward he embarked on a three-month, de luxe tour of Europe. The last freely elected chief executive of Cuba had spoken. That was the end of any serious public debate on the topic of land reform in Castro's Cuba.

Castro's Bay of Pigs

On June 13, the day following my interview with him on land reform, Castro launched the first of three expeditions designed to converge on the Dominican Republic and to overthrow Trujillo. The genius for guerrilla warfare which Castro had persuaded himself had eliminated Batista was to be exported. The result was a complete and bloody failure. Trujillo's peasant militia hunted out and massacred or captured the invaders who escaped from Trujillo's regulars. The Castro-sponsored expedition against Nicaragua met a similar fate though there was less loss of life. A Castro-backed descent on the coasts of Haiti ended in death or dispersal for its protagonists. These violations of the cherished dogma of nonintervention aroused serious concern in the foreign offices of the hemisphere—a concern tempered by the fact that the regimes against which Castro had intervened were unpopular while Castro himself was at a peak of popularity in many of the countries of Latin America. After much soul-searching it was agreed to convene a meeting of Foreign Ministers at Santiago, Chile, in August to consider the situation.

At this meeting the Cuban and the Dominican delegations set new records of unparliamentary language. A resolution was finally passed defining the democratic ideal for membership in the Organization of American

States.[5] Cuba as well as the Dominican Republic were notorious violators of most of the specifications of the resolution. Not all of the other members would have obtained passing grades from even the most lenient of examiners. Since, however, the resolution did not mention any country by name and did not involve any findings of violations or provide for effective investigation, it passed, and the meeting ended as satisfactorily as could have been expected. Provision was made for an OAS presence, in the form of a committee, to reduce tensions in the Caribbean area. Castro's failures, rather than the disapproval of the other American republics, deterred him for a few years from further interventions.

Chapter 8

July and August of 1959

CASTRO had rammed his own conception of land reform down the throats of his people and was now engaged in demonstrating to them that even the law he himself had issued was not binding on him or on his officials at INRA. He had ordered the crudest of interventions against other countries in complete defiance of the international commitments he invoked to protect his own Revolution from outside interference. Yet I did not abandon hope of a rational relationship with the Cuban government. Castro would, I then thought, soon incur opposition from his own countrymen, especially if the Cuban reaction to what he was doing was not distracted by an activist American policy.

Castro himself did not attend the Fourth of July reception at the Embassy; he sent an elaborate floral arrangement and his brother Raúl. The latter behaved quite amiably, paid a visit to the kitchen, had his picture taken with our spaniel, and generally handled himself in the affable fashion of a visiting politician. But in Miami, on the same day, there had been an unfortunate incident. So far as I was able later to ascertain the facts, the newly appointed Cuban Consul General there shared overgenerously in the hospitality with which the local authorities celebrated the holiday. In a mood of enthusiasm he proceeded to the sidewalk in front of the home of some Cuban activists of the Batista era. He launched a defiant tirade at the house. The inmates swarmed out and, before the Miami police could break things up, the Consul General had been soundly beaten. The Castro-oriented Havana press played the matter up as an outrage perpetrated thanks to the negligence—some went so far as to insinuate with the connivance—of the Miami officials. The description of the police as "blond gumchewing janissaries" will give an idea of the tone of the comment.

Optimism, Anticommunism, Propaganda, and Plots

Meanwhile there seemed to be constructive activity in at least one area not favored with Castro's immediate personal interest. The Minister of the Treasury was busy with the implementation of his tax-reform measure.[1] He was getting cooperation and support from the business community. The spirit of that community, while apprehensive in some respects, was still, on the whole, hopeful. The increase in mass-purchasing power produced by some of Castro's measures, notably the reduction of rents and the increase in the minimum wage of government employees, had had a stimulating effect. The notion that the regime intended to eliminate private business entirely occurred to few. Che Guevara was out of the country as a result, hopefully, of a dimming of his star and a loss of the favor he enjoyed with Castro. Investments in new industries that had been started under Batista were, in many cases, continued.[2] The important Moa Bay nickel project was being hastened to completion. An adventurous young Chicagoan secured a concession for the exploitation of the bat droppings, or guano, said to be abundant in many of the limestone caves with which the island is honeycombed and to possess near miraculous properties as a fertilizer for American gardens and window boxes. As late as the end of August the business community got together on a dinner in honor of Castro and his Ministers.[3]

Representative of the spirit of the times was the attitude of a prominent local lawyer for American corporations. He proudly showed me and others a letter he had written to a mass-circulation enterprise in the United States urging it not to pursue its allegedly unjustified denigration of Castro and his government.

During these summer months most Cubans believed that attempts to tie the Communist label on the Castro regime were designed to block needed reforms. The dismissal of the head of the rebel air force, Major Pedro Díaz-Lanz, because of his anti-Communist stand would not in itself have caused much comment. The major was not a political figure; he was an adventurous flier who had smuggled weapons to the Castro forces in the hills. But when Díaz-Lanz was interrogated in Washington by a subcommittee of the United States Senate Judiciary Committee, the uproar in Havana was considerable and was not confined to those with a predisposition to hostility toward the United States. This episode seemed to many Cubans to be a direct interference in the domestic affairs of Cuba by an organ of the United States government. (Neither the doctrine of the separation of powers nor the relative standing of congressional committees are widely understood outside our borders.) Such was the storm of protest that President Eisenhower felt obliged to state at one of his press conferences that the government of the United States had not accused the government of Cuba of being communistic.[4]

The Díaz-Lanz accusations themselves made little impression on Cuban opinion. At the most it was thought the activities he had denounced, notably Communist indoctrination in some sectors of the army, were a reflection of the disorganization and lack of coordination to be expected in the new government and that when these activities came to the attention of Fidel they would be suppressed. This touching faith that all would be set right "if the ruler only knew" has a long tradition in Cuba and is still alive in the current difficult conditions on the island.

Castro's elimination of President Urrutia was also related to the Communist issue and was politically more serious than the Díaz-Lanz affair. Since the February constitutional decree depriving him of real authority, Urrutia had receded into the background. He seldom attended Cabinet meetings. In a television interview on July 10, he said that he had always been in the fullest agreement with Castro and that he was a dedicated supporter of the Land Reform Law and an opponent of any interference from abroad in its operation. He added, however, that he thought the local Communists were doing untold harm to the Revolution (the Communist daily *Hoy* had been attacking Urrutia most harshly).

A few days later Castro stunned the nation by announcing that he was resigning as Prime Minister because of his difficulties with President Urrutia over the Communist issue and over many other issues.[5] He reaffirmed the non-Communist character of the Cuban Revolution. His television harangue that night included many petty and sordid accusations as well as a challenge to Urrutia to form a Cabinet of his own without Castro: Urrutia would doubtless be able to find "American agents" who would serve him. The discourse was interrupted from time to time by messages demanding the President's resignation including one from a justice of the Supreme Court on behalf of himself and a number of his colleagues. Menacing and hardly spontaneous mobs led by Castroite thugs began to form around the Presidential Palace. No one lifted a finger on behalf of Urrutia. Finally the President resigned and, under heavy escort, retired to the home of a relative.

This crushing of a decent, inoffensive, patriotic Cuban by his own erstwhile sponsor was cowardly and repulsive. I wrongly thought it would produce a significant drop in Castro's popularity. Castro was indignant at any criticism of this or of any other action of his. He bitterly denounced a press comment comparing his rejection of Urrutia to the action of a petulant restaurant patron calling on the waiter for a clean spoon to replace a dirty one. Osvaldo Dórticos was the "clean spoon" the Cabinet supplied Castro at the latter's behest.

Dórticos, a lawyer from Cienfuegos, had taken part in the fight against Batista. After he was appointed President it was revealed that he had once accepted a sinecure from the fallen dictator. Only later did it come out that he had had Communist entanglements in his youth. His selection to be their chief executive did not then offend the anti-Communist sentiments of the Cuban people.

The extent to which the Communist issue was considered to be a sinister fabrication of selfish, especially American, interests opposed to Castro and his generous Revolution is illustrated by the following anecdote. I attended a ceremony in honor of Bolívar in one of the Havana parks. Among those present was Emilio Roig de Leuchsenring, a prominent antiimperialist and for many years the official historian of the Havana Municipality. He asked me whether I did not think it dreadful that American newsmen were persuading the innocent Cuban peasants, flocking to Havana for the celebration of the July 26th anniversary of Castro's assault on the Moncada barracks, to pose with clenched fists raised so that their pictures could be published as evidence of Communist penetration of the Revolution. I told him I thought it outrageous that any one would listen to, much less circulate, such a story which I was sure lacked any foundation.

The allegation of Communist penetration in the Castro administration was countered in many ways during these weeks of July and August. As reported above, President Eisenhower had stated that the United States government was not accusing the Cuban government of being communistic. Herbert Matthews of the *New York Times* was assuring his public that there was no Communist influence in the Castro administration and was confiding to the American Ambassador in Havana that Castro would, given time and favorable circumstances, proceed to smash the Cuban Communists.[6] Castro himself had said that the Cuban people in the exercise of the sovereign infallibility he had revealed to them knew their government was not communistic. In early September Vasco Leitao da Cunha, the Brazilian Ambassador, generally conceded to be one of the most knowledgeable of foreign observers, made a reassuring public statement denying Communist influence in the Castro entourage.[7] So great was the indignation that Castro and his men should be suspected of communism that even a moderately sophisticated observer could be excused for concluding that any Communist attempt to infiltrate the regime would be sternly rejected.

Nevertheless, Castro and his public relations men were making an increasingly crucial issue of the allegedly hostile treatment in the American press, radio, and television, not only of the Communist aspect but of all other aspects of the Cuban Revolution. Long stretches of Castro's orations were devoted to fulminations against the news agencies and the popular news and picture weeklies in the United States. The significant body of influential American opinion which at that time viewed the Cuban Revolution with hope and sympathy was completely neglected in these monologues. Castro concentrated his attention on those who found sinister or comic aspects to what was going on in Cuba. His reaction then appeared neither rational nor balanced though his goal has now become clear. He affected to be convinced that the American press was slavishly at the service of "imperialist interests."

I had the pleasure of meeting with many representatives of the American news media including both those stationed in Havana and those who came in on special assignments. Some of them I saw frequently. I most admired Ruby Hart Phillips of the New York Times.[8] She had been in Cuba over thirty years and was courageous, indefatigable, factual, and a good writer —the ideal reporter, even though I didn't always agree with her deductions and opinions. Most of these journalists were men and women of energy and integrity with widely varying philosophies and capacities. I was amused at how often and for what different reasons I was told by them that the Cuban story had been badly or inadequately covered by certain of their colleagues.

Some American reporters may have been influenced by the necessity of serving up stories that accorded with the views and prejudices of the moment of their owners and editors. Some of them tended to stress unduly the freakish or the Communist-potential angles of the Revolution. Their bosses themselves in most cases were engaged in a highly competitive business— that of revealing to their mass readerships or viewers what those readerships or viewers really wanted to read or see and supplying it in greater quantity and quality than their rivals. But when all that can fairly be said on this point has been said, the coverage of Cuba in the American press was vastly superior to that of the United States in the Cuban press especially as the latter became more and more subject to official inspiration. Since Castro's take-over the American people have had a far better break on Cuba in their press and on television than does the Cuban public on the United States in their mass media.

During this period Senator Fulbright made a statement advocating a policy of patience and restraint toward Castro; Castro took no notice of it. If he had he would have said that it was an intolerable indignity to suggest that his conduct had been or ever could be such as to require the display of these virtues. Admiral Burke, however, when he made a remark about the alleged presence in Cuban waters of unidentified submarines was roundly denounced by the revolutionary elements.[9]

After the arrival in Havana in mid-July of the newly appointed Foreign Minister, Dr. Raúl Roa, I became engaged in a series of conversations that led to an exchange of views with the Prime Minister in early September. I have thought it best to treat my contacts with Roa and what turned out to be my final interview with Castro in the next chapter. Progress toward the latter encounter was delayed by a number of developments.

First there was the celebration of the July 26 anniversary of the assault on the Moncada barracks. This involved bringing to Havana hundreds of thousands of peasants or *guajiros*, those who in the fleeting propaganda of the day had made the Revolution and were now, by becoming the owners of their own plots of land, to be the principal beneficiaries of the Land Reform Law. Who then would have thought that the conversion of city office workers into occasional cutters of sugar cane was to be a major Castro contribution to the solution of the problems of tropical agriculture! Later Roa was absorbed for some weeks with the preparations for, and his attendance at, the meeting of Foreign Ministers in Chile. Nor was Castro without his troubles. The month of August saw the first signs of active opposition to him.

The first of these anti-Castro plots was said to be the work of the head of the Cuban Association of Cattle Ranchers and to reflect distaste for Castro's land reform. Many of the conspirators were arrested at a Havana house which had for some time been known as their headquarters. There was a high degree of government penetration of this enterprise which was condemned by many of those who later became victims of the Revolution. An attempt was made to induce one of the young men on my staff to visit with the conspirators shortly before they were caught. What a coup it would have been for Castro had his net drawn an American Embassy official! He was obliged, however, to be satisfied with innuendo.

Another of the conspiracies was backed by Trujillo of the Dominican Republic—a riposte to the invasion attempt Castro had launched in June. In this operation there was a double agent, an American soldier of fortune named William Morgan. He persuaded the Dominican "Benefactor" that he would personally eliminate Castro. He reported every detail of the proposed operation to Castro, and the tiny expedition was ambushed by a greatly superior force when it landed at an airport on the south coast of Cuba. Its members were captured and exhibited on a Castro television spectacular. Morgan achieved such exaggerated confidence in his talents for deception that within two years he was led before a Castro firing squad. In the summer of 1959, however, he was a hero in Cuba and in some American circles. The Embassy received many indignant letters when he lost his United States citizenship because he had joined the Cuban armed forces.

One of my major worries during this period and later was for the safety of resident Americans because of the possible impact of the Castro tirades about the evil intentions of the United States and of American interests toward the Cuban Revolution. It seemed to me that a situation could develop where the mobs would consider they had the sanction or even the mandate of their leader to kill Americans and to loot and burn their homes and their places of business. I am glad to report that these fears proved unfounded and that, in spite of a considerable amount of implicit incitement, there were no serious mob incidents involving Americans during my time on the island.

Another of my nightmares was that Castro might be assassinated under circumstances where the guilt for the assassination could be pinned on the

United States or on an American citizen by the extremely unscrupulous information services of the regime. The idolatry with which the man was viewed in Cuba combined with the viciously venomous nature of the anti-American propaganda to which Castro himself and many of his followers were addicted could, if the murder had taken place, have resulted in mob atrocities against Americans on the island, and there were thousands of them—men, women, and children.

In the welter of rumors and the atmosphere of tension which government propaganda and actual conspiracies were building up, I could hardly expect to remain personally uninvolved. One day when I called at the Foreign Office, the acting Minister in Roa's absence, Armando Hart, a pleasant youth of then enthusiastic democratic sentiments though he has become a pillar of Marxism-Leninism as it is practiced in Cuba, informed me that the government had become aware of a plot to murder the American Ambassador and thus to discredit the regime to which the victim was accredited!

Chapter 9

A New Foreign Minister and an Interview with Castro

I FIRST met Castro's new Foreign Minister, Dr. Raúl Roa, in mid-July 1959. He was in his early fifties—a slight, round-shouldered man with a nervous temperament and an incapacity for immobility. (An unkind Latin American reporter dubbed him *el mico eléctrico* ["the electric monkey"].)[1] He was an intellectual and a fluent writer in prose and verse as well as an exuberant orator. He had been active in the masterminding rather than in the street-fighting of the student movement in the early thirties. In spite of, or perhaps because of, his facility with pen and tongue he had not achieved a first-rate reputation either in politics or in literature. During the latter years of Spanish rule his grandfather had taken a position denounced by the great José Martí as antirevolutionary and treacherous—a fact the grandson was seldom allowed to forget.[2] Prior to the rise of Castro, the highest post this ambitious, frustrated, and embittered man had achieved was that of Director of Culture in the administration of Carlos Prío a decade earlier.

Roa was now embarking on a career that has lasted more than a decade. His major talent, that for vituperation, has been given full play by the requirements of the foreign policy of which he has been the faithful mouth-piece. An early sample of the elegance and elevation of his official style was furnished when he described the President of Argentina, Arturo Frondizi, as "the viscous concretion of all human excrescences."[3] In his frequent appearances at the United Nations, Dr. Roa has maintained his reputation in this department.

86

At my first interview with him Dr. Roa made a point of telling me that Batista, who detected communism in most of his enemies, had been unable to find in Roa even the tiniest tinge of red. Though he has now become as much of a Marxist-Leninist as his chief, he was then a stalwart upholder of democracy and human freedom. He was a bitter critic of Stalin and of Khrushchev. As late as October 1959 he published a collection of his articles in which he identified himself with the democratic left in Latin America and especially with Rómulo Gallegos, the great novelist who was briefly President of Venezuela.[4] In one of these articles he described Jacobo Arbenz, the Communist-oriented President of Guatemala eliminated in 1954 by a coup generally believed to be the responsibility of the CIA, as a "two-bit Cossack who gives himself the airs of a Lenin."[5] (Arbenz was soon to become a favored guest of Castro's and to appear on his platforms as a noble victim of American imperialism.)

During our first conversation Dr. Roa told me how favorably Castro and he had been impressed with the spirit in which I had begun my mission. He said he looked forward to working with me to improve Cuban American relations and to dispel existing misunderstandings. He did not then consider the relationship existing between our two countries to be incompatible with the goals of the Cuban Revolution. I said that the greatest immediate obstacle to what I conceived to be our common purpose was the virulent and unfounded slander and calumny about the United States in which certain officials of the Cuban government and the government-oriented press had been indulging. The impact of these utterances had been thoroughly and justifiably unfavorable so far as American public opinion was concerned. I was careful not to quote any of Castro's own offensive pronouncements or to make an issue of them. To have done so would greatly have diminished Roa's ability to bring to bear whatever influence he may have had to remedy the situation. But we both knew that Castro himself had been the major offender. Roa's attitude was sympathetic.

I discussed with Roa some of the situations confronting American landowners in Cuba who had been the victims of purely arbitrary actions by INRA agents. I emphasized that the Americans affected by the law were complying with its requirements so far as they could interpret them in marked contrast to the INRA officials who were every day demonstrating that they considered themselves to be above the law. He promised to look into these situations.

While not questioning the determinations of the Cuban government with regard to the two American-owned public utilities, I expressed concern about the hostile atmosphere in which these two situations were developing. The telephone company had been intervened since early March; it seemed to have no prospect of being soon returned to its owners. Dr. Roa was favorably aware of what I had done to be of assistance to the Ministry of Communications in the technical aspects of public utility regulation. I told the Minister that the electric light and power company had not been informed of the results of the investigation into its affairs being conducted by the government without its participation but added that the Minister of Economy (Regino Boti—at last account in disgrace with Castro) had volunteered to me that he had assured the company representatives that before any action was taken with respect to the company's rates they would be given an opportunity for full discussion of the government's findings. (This assurance was crassly disregarded—within less than a month of my talk with Roa the rates of the company were cut by about 30 percent on the basis of findings that were made known to the company only after the rate cut had been decreed.)

Though Roa claimed to know little about these matters, he gave me the clear and cordial impression that he conceived of the relationship between us and between the two governments as affording a promising framework for negotiation. He added that he looked forward to playing a positive role in the solution of the problems that had arisen.

Roa and his distinguished predecessor (Roberto Agramonte) differed in almost every way in which one human being can differ from another. Yet they had one view in common. Both were firmly of the opinion that it was of the highest importance for me to see Castro as soon and as often as possible. Roa told me that the Prime Minister was deeply regretful that we had seen each other so seldom. But many things happened to postpone our meeting which did not take place until the third of September.

During much of August, Roa was in Chile attending the meeting of the Foreign Ministers of the American Republics and exchanging bitter words with the representative of the Dominican Republic. While in Santiago he assured Secretary of State Herter and Assistant Secretary Rubottom of the Cuban government's anxiety for harmony with the government of the United States and of the high opinion Castro and he had formed of the American Ambassador in Havana.

An Evening with Castro

My interview with Castro on September 3 took place at Dr. and Mrs. Roa's apartment. After an excellent dinner Mrs. Roa retired. Castro, Roa, and myself were together for six hours; we did not break up until after two in the morning.

At Castro's invitation I made a lengthy exposition of the state of Cuban American relations as I saw it. Castro listened quietly and interrupted me seldom. I covered the ground already covered with Roa, stressing the favorable and hopeful reaction of the American government and of an influential sector of American public opinion to the new situation in Cuba. After endeavoring to make clear to Castro the nature of the relations between press and government in the United States, I turned to the problem of hostile official and government-oriented statements about the United States in Cuba and the bearing of these statements and the attitude they reflected upon the effort to build mutual confidence and respect between the two countries. I cited a number of examples avoiding mention of any afforded by Castro himself. I cited some of the remarks attributed to Che Guevara in the course of his current world tour. In Djakarta he was reported to have observed that Cuba had nothing to fear from Communist penetration, the real threat being aggression from the United States because of the Land Reform Law. In Ceylon, a few days later, Guevara had grossly insulted President Eisenhower in a public statement. (I learned later on good authority that Castro had been irritated by my references to Guevara.)

In reply to my observations Castro said that he appreciated my concerns but that perhaps I was being too sensitive to the exuberances of young and inexperienced revolutionaries and that as time passed a settling down on their part could be anticipated. He gave me the impression that this was his own approach to the problem. I hoped that he would exercise some control over his own tongue, and, indeed, in the following two or three weeks I persuaded myself that there had been some improvement, perhaps in part due to my talk with Castro. But the improvement turned out to be temporary. A perfidious, menacing United States was an essential element in the scenario on which Castro relied more and more for the justification of the dictatorial government he imposed on his people.

In my discussion of the status of American private interests in Cuba,

I noted that all of the Americans affected by the Land Reform Law had turned in their required statements to the Cuban government within the legal deadline and were awaiting the further steps the government was to take under the law. I told Castro that these American interests were seriously concerned at the arbitrary actions of Cuban government agents—actions which appeared to have no authority in the law. I cited a number of examples. I referred to the problems of the telephone company and of the electric light and power company. I expressed the hope that both these enterprises would be given an opportunity to participate in discussions as to their situations and to comment on the findings on the basis of which their rates had been reduced.

A remark by Castro enabled me to deny a story which Castro apparently believed to the effect that the Moa Bay nickel concession to a subsidiary of the Freeport Sulphur Company had been granted by Batista because Ambassador Smith had had a financial interest in it and had agreed, as a quid pro quo for the concession, to assume an attitude of support for the Batista regime.[6] I said that the Ambassador had been a public servant of integrity and that the concession in question, one which offered promise of a notable increase in the wealth of Cuba, had been granted prior to his arrival in Cuba. Castro admitted the possibility that he might have been misinformed. (But I am afraid he kept to his original opinion; the story involved the sort of behavior he had taught himself was characteristic of the "imperialists.")

I endeavored, unsuccessfully, to interest Castro in the world problems with which the United States was concerned at the time. I was proud to be able to recall to him that since World War II the United States, notably through the Marshall Plan, the Truman Doctrine, and the defense of Korea, had done much to rebuild the economic and the political strength of many countries. I said that the attitude and the policies of the United States had increased the area of choice of the smaller nations as to the sort of institutions they wished to live under and had expanded the degree to which they were becoming masters of their own destinies. I hoped that Castro, the leader of a country trying to enlarge the area of its own freedom of choice, might be, indeed I believed that he should be, interested in the story of some of the things that were going on in the world and in which the United States was actively engaged on the side of peace and resistance to aggression. But he did not respond to my discussions of these matters.

Castro made no commitments on the specific questions I brought to his attention. Both he and Roa exuded goodwill toward me and toward the United States. I had reason to assume that Castro was disposed to take a closer look at the problems I had raised and to continue to discuss them with me. When we parted he said that he would see me any time on twenty-four-hours' notice. Whether he meant it or not I don't know. I thought that on balance the meeting had been useful. Roa agreed.

In my opinion my bearing toward Castro and toward his government had been what it should have been considering his susceptibilities and my own desire to achieve a relationship of mutual confidence and respect with this unpredictable young man. Admittedly the interview was inconclusive yet I had the impression I had been given a hearing by a responsible person interested in what I had to say and with sufficient consideration for my country, my government, and myself to give my statements his constructive attention. He had appeared to regard the positions I had outlined as representing the sincere convictions of my government and of myself.

I was aware that Castro's reasonable and friendly attitude at our interview might contain elements of deceit. But I then believed that the detection of the "real Castro" was in the first instance the responsibility of the Cuban people. They were, at that time, in a position to discharge that responsibility.

Castro had spoken favorably of me in public and had given the impression that he and I were on a friendly footing, based on mutual respect for each other and for each other's country. Even in the government newspaper *Revolución*, increasingly anti-American in tone, I was given credit for having abandoned the proconsular style alleged to have been characteristic of a number of my predecessors. Yet a few years later in the course of a lengthy interview granted an American journalist and published in the United States, Castro is quoted as having remarked: "I well remember that when the American Ambassador arrived in Cuba, shortly after the victory of the Revolution, he came with the demeanor of a proconsul. I remember his words, his imposing attitude, and how our reactionary press received him almost as if the Savior had come!"[7]

Chapter 10

An Uncertain Interlude

On September 3, the day of my interview with Castro, Carlos Prío, the last constitutionally elected President of Cuba, returned to Havana after a three-month holiday in Europe. He assured the reporters who greeted him that the Cuban Revolution under the guidance of Fidel Castro was an example for all the world.[1] He then withdrew to his palatial country home. He made no more public statements that I can recollect, though his smiling appearances on platforms from which Castro addressed his increasingly fanaticized followers continued for several months. Prío showed no public concern about the course of events or about the dimming prospects of democracy in Cuba. Because he was the titular leader of one of the major political parties, his smiles and his silences during the latter months of 1959 and the first half of 1960 were symbolic of the lack of vitality of Cuba's democratic politics.

During the days immediately following my talk with Castro, there were developments that seemed to indicate a favorable trend. On September 17 Castro made a speech with passages pleasing to orthodox economists and to the business community. His words reflected the indoctrination on Cuba's balance-of-payments problems he had been receiving at the National Bank where for most of the summer he had been spending one full day a week.[2] What he now said in public reproduced words of wisdom absorbed from Felipe Pazos, the President of the Bank, in the course of many briefings. A few days later Castro made a statement that was interpreted to mean that he was not an enemy of private investment and planned to put no obstacles in its way.[3]

Consultation in Washington

I, also, had been having regular meetings with Felipe Pazos and with the Ministers of Economy and of the Treasury. I was in frequent contact with Cuban and American businessmen and bankers. The general impression was still one of restrained optimism. Pazos, in particular, seemed to believe that orthodox fiscal and monetary policies and the private-enterprise concept were due to win out in the struggle with the more radical tendencies of some of those around Castro. All of us derived comfort from the polemic that was taking place between the Castro and the 26th of July organ *Revolución* and the Communist daily *Hoy* on matters of revolutionary doctrine; the language used seemed to indicate a truly bitter fight, with Castro on the side opposed to the Communists.

Two weeks after my talk with Castro I was called home for a few days of consultation in Washington where the atmosphere was one of growing impatience and puzzlement. The denouncing of the United States and the ill-treatment of American interests in a country where friendship had been the order of the day were disconcerting innovations with possible repercussions in other countries of the hemisphere. The spirit of toleration for the young revolutionaries was wearing thin. In some quarters, at both ends of Pennsylvania Avenue, sentiment was increasing for a more "hard-nosed" attitude toward Castro.

In the Department of State there were as yet no concrete plans as to what might be done. On balance there was a disposition to continue a policy of patience or, as some put it, to give Castro more rope. The notion that developments in Cuba could become such as to warrant direct United States armed interference was not seriously raised. The covert training and arming of Cuban opponents of the Revolution was already in the minds of some. Richard Nixon, then Vice President, has stated that as early as the middle of 1959 he was a member of a minority that advocated instructions to the Central Intelligence Agency "to provide arms, ammunition and training for Cubans who had fled the Castro regime and were now in exile in the United States and various Latin American countries."[4] The opposition to Castro in the early fall of 1959, however, was not significant in Cuban terms, and

Mr. Nixon's view did not become the prevailing one until March 1960.

My Washington consultations did not produce any decisions. But I was made fully aware of the mounting concern in the highest circles of our government. While I was in Washington, I, among others, conveyed that concern in the most emphatic terms to the Cuban Ambassador there, Ernesto Dihigo, a man of integrity and patriotism. I hoped that the Ambassador would transmit a realistic view of Washington thinking to his chief in Havana and to his friends in influential circles on the island so that revolutionary pronouncements and actions might be reassessed by Cubans who valued good relations with the United States.

Discussions on Land Reform

In the relatively hopeful atmosphere engendered by Roa's apparent goodwill and by my meeting with Castro, my staff and I were continuously engaged in conversations with Cuban officials on a wide range of subjects. I then believed that both Castro and Roa accepted the existence of American rights subject to discussion and negotiations between technically competent representatives of the two governments. Questions derived from the capricious application of the Land Reform Law were high on our agenda.

In these discussions I had to assume that the intent of the revolutionary government was reflected in the terms of the law it had promulgated; that proved to be an assumption contrary to fact. I conceived the role of the Embassy as being active but not prominent. I endeavored to promote the idea that the bonds to be issued to Americans in compensation for expropriated lands should be payable in dollars. I drew the attention of the Cuban government to cases where Americans seemed to have been the victims of actions on the part of local authorities which had no justification in the law. These cases were rapidly increasing in numbers and in flagrancy.

In general I held that the United States should intervene formally in particular cases only when it was the considered opinion of the government of the United States that the American interest in question had exhausted its legal remedies and had been a victim of a denial of justice. I did not believe that the penalty for the Cuban government's failure in the first instance to do justice should be an immediate diplomatic claim but should be rather the eventual impact of the action on Cuban and American public opinion and the erosion of the credit of the Cuban government.

There was, however, growing evidence that the activities of the National Institute of Agrarian Reform were in no way coordinated with those of other agencies of the Cuban government, whether in the administrative or the judicial departments. I hoped that the relaxed and friendly conversations in which Embassy officers were engaged with the Foreign Ministry and with other agencies, including the National Bank, would serve to underline the unfavorable bearing of these INRA activities on the goal of improved Cuban American relations which both Castro and Roa had claimed to be pursuing. The Embassy made some attempts (not successful) to get on talking terms with INRA officials.

No demands were made by American representatives on the Cuban government for any particular method or procedure of valuation or compensation. The story that the United States insisted on cash payments and on the acceptance of a type of valuation that would have crippled the land reform on which the Cuban government said it had embarked is completely devoid of foundation. In fact, in September and October 1959, a number of proposals were advanced from the Cuban side in conversation with American officials or representatives of American interests showing a spirit of compromise and a belief in the possibility of accommodation. But the people making these proposals were eliminated from the government in the critical shakeup in November, the shakeup that finally closed the door on the possibility of negotiations with Castro's government on land reform or, indeed, on any other major topic.

Cheers at a Baseball Game

Shortly after my return from the Washington visit I have mentioned, there occurred a heartwarming incident demonstrating that my hopes for understanding and continued friendship between Cuba and the United States were then widely shared in Cuba. Since the incident occurred at a baseball game, I will allow myself a brief digression on the place of our national game on the island. Among all of the manifestations of American popular culture that invaded Cuba after 1898, baseball is in a class by itself. Not only was it adopted enthusiastically by players and general public alike, it was enriched by the Cubans. They added to it in many ways. The game with its skills, its demands for quick-thinking, and its dramatic potential fitted the temper of the Cuban people. The baseball crowds in Havana were more knowledgeable than most American crowds. The number of Cubans in the ranks of successful professional players in the United States was a source of pride to the people of the island. American major league teams regularly sent scouts to look over the crop of Cuban talent. My good friend, the late Joe Cambria of the old Washington Senators (now the Minnesota Twins), discovered and encouraged many of the best of the Cuban players.

The conversion of baseball into something essentially Cuban, even to the vocabulary, explains why Castro, in spite of his passionate anti-Americanism, was a baseball player and, after he became the ruler of his country, continued to be an enthusiastic patron of the game. The spectacle of the Prime Minister, alleged by his admirers to have been a promising pitcher of big league caliber, throwing a few curves to Major Camilo Cienfuegos, a former minor-leaguer, and generally clowning about on the diamond was a feature of the pregame show of many important contests.

Castro's mastery of the crowds at the ball park as everywhere else was total. Baseballs were imported from the United States. The Cuban balance of trade was said to be in trouble. Castro persuaded the Havana fans that when a ball was batted into the stands it should be thrown back on to the field and no longer be kept as a treasured souvenir by the lucky spectator who retrieved it!

I was a frequent attendant at the Cerro Stadium. One evening, early in October, I was in the overflow crowd at a game in the "Little World Series" pitting the Cuban Sugar Kings representing Havana in the International League against the Minneapolis Millers of the American Association. Although patriotic emotion had been aroused, the Cubans behaved throughout with exemplary sportsmanship. When I arrived Castro had not yet made his formal entrance into the park. He was in the bleachers mingling with the spectators preparatory to the march in from the outfield to the grandstand which gave the crowd an opportunity to applaud him after which it would enjoy his baseball act.

As the stadium was filling up for the critical contest the arrival of the "personalities" as they took their seats was announced over the loudspeaker. When my name was reached the crowd rose and gave me a prolonged ovation. I was truly moved by this tribute to my country and, I hoped, to the efforts which its representatives in Washington and in Havana had made to demonstrate that between the United States and revolutionary Cuba harmony and mutual confidence could be established. I treasure the memory of that experience.

A few minutes later Castro made his entrance from the center-field bleachers and was greeted with the customary raptures. There had not been in the cheers for me that aura of counterrevolution which was no doubt an element in the applause accorded my picture when it flashed on the screen at movie houses in the wealthier parts of town. Nevertheless, I heard later that when Castro was asked by a friend what he thought of the ovation accorded the American Ambassador, he was jarred into a unique economy of words and replied, "*¡Excesiva!*" ("Excessive!"). He was not pleased.

Gloomy Omens

Unfortunately, optimism as to the prospect of rational relationships between the United States and Castro's Cuba was dampened by a number of unfavorable developments. At the United Nations General Assembly that fall, Roa removed Cuba from its position as a stalwart member of the free-world bloc and placed his country—briefly—in the ranks of the neutralists. In pursuance of this policy change Cuba abstained on the vote to seat Communist China in the United Nations instead of voting firmly in the negative as had been its practice.

On the third of October the Cuban government seized the records of all the foreign companies that had been prospecting for oil in Cuba. There were many of these enterprises and most of them were American. The seizures reflected a misguided nationalist view that these foreign interests, for sinister reasons of their own, were concealing or holding back the large quantities of oil they had discovered in Cuba because it did not suit either their corporate interests or the "imperial" interests of their governments to develop the oil resources of the Cuban people. The actions taken were arbitrary and unsound. During their ten years of responsibility for oil exploration in Cuba and their possession of the data taken from the former concessionaires, the Russians have made no significant finds. Cuba remains as dependent as ever on crude oil imports.

Also at this time the Cuban authorities began taking steps to reduce Cuban dependence on imports from the United States. Exchange controls were established and manipulated with this object in view. The concept was to cut down all luxury imports, to reduce imports from the United States, and, simultaneously, to promote imports from countries which might increase their takings of Cuban sugar, giving preference to goods significant in the inchoate development-industrialization program. The actions of the Cuban government in pursuance of this policy—ostensibly necessitated by balance-of-payments requirements—were taken without any consultation with the United States, Cuba's major trading partner.

At the end of September and early in October a number of minor terroristic incidents took place. They consisted mainly in the dropping of explosives from small planes on remote sugar mills. Damage was slight. Some of the planes could conceivably have come across the Florida Straits. Equally plausibly they could have been of local origin; there were plenty of planes on the island (such as those used in crop-dusting) that could have been used. Nor were the controls then in use by the rebel air force stringent enough to preclude the use of an official plane by a disgruntled airman.

The incidents themselves were trivial except to the extent that they indicated there were people who did not think all was for the best in the best of all possible Cubas. Castro, however, blew them up into evidence of a determination of the American authorities to destroy him; to this end he devoted his major powers as a persuader and the talents of the propagandists in his official stable. The reasonable notion, that if the United States had declared clandestine warfare against Castro it would bring to bear resources far more effective that the ones employed, was not one for which an audience could be found in Cuba. But the uproar in these cases was minor compared to what awaited us as a result of the so-called "bombing" of Havana on October 21.

In mid-October an untoward and unnecessary episode related to the American arms embargo, still applicable to the entire Caribbean region, occupied the attention of the two governments. There had been no reason to change United States policy after the fall of Batista, once it had become clear that Castro's policies and actions toward his neighbors were inimical to peace in the area. Not only did the United States maintain the embargo; it tried to secure the cooperation of its allies in Europe. These efforts were not uniformly or even generally successful. The Belgians, for example, leapt at the opportunity to sell large amounts of small arms and ammunition to Castro.

Of particular interest to the United States was Castro's attempt to get some jet planes from the British. The United States considered that these planes would add to Castro's offensive capabilities while Castro alleged they were essential to the defense of the island (against whom?). The United States tried discreetly to discourage the deal. The fact was made known to the press in mid-October by an official of the State Department itself, thus proving once more that the spirit of Laurel and Hardy rather than that of Machiavelli sometimes presides over our great bureaucracies.[5] The official responsible excused his action on the basis that if the United States had not publicly announced its opposition to the sale, the British would have gone ahead with it. It could with greater logic have been argued that the British were less likely to yield to pressure publicly applied than otherwise. At any rate the planes were not supplied.

On the morning when the public statement in question was made, I received a message from Roa—he was at home recuperating from the flu— to the effect that this development was truly damaging to the effort on which he and I had been engaged to improve the climate of relations between the two countries. The more moderate of the revolutionaries took the statement as an illustration of the insincerity of American professions of friendship for Cuba while the more extreme interpreted it as proof positive that the United States was planning an invasion of Cuba and wished to see the island as defenseless as possible.

If the incident had been isolated, it might have been quickly forgotten. After all Castro had attacked his neighbors and was ready to do so again when the opportunity offered. The refusal of the United States to help him breach the peace and the American attempts to get its friends to cooperate in that refusal were logical under the circumstances and would have caused little friction had they been conducted with normal discretion. Besides, Castro was encountering no real difficulty in acquiring arms he was ready to pay for. But within a week of the departmental leak I have described, there began the chain of events that dashed all hope of accommodation between Castro's Cuba and the United States.

Chapter 11

The Arrest of Matos and the "Bombing of Havana"

Until the week of October 19 I did not give up hope that Castro would eventually find it expedient to cooperate with me in establishing a rational relationship between Cuba and the United States. Such a course seemed prescribed by the force of circumstances and by the thinking of many of Castro's principal advisers. By the end of the week in question, I had lost any illusions on this score. Within the next month the regime had been purged of anyone likely to stand in Castro's way or to oppose his unscrupulous presentation of the United States to his people as THE ENEMY and the justification of his own absolute power and of the sacrifices he demanded of his fellow citizens.

The decisive week of October 19 began with the inauguration in Havana of the convention of the American Society of Travel Agents (ASTA). That organization, with its great prestige and influence in the dynamic tourist industry, had decided many months earlier to hold its annual meeting in Havana, a decision enthusiastically welcomed by officials of the Cuban government. Castro himself had promised to greet the delegates and to participate in the festivities arranged for them.[1]

As the date for the meeting approached, however, the organizers began to experience second thoughts because of the rising tide of official anti-Americanism. They consulted me. I advised them, though I shared their misgivings, to go ahead as planned. I believed that reciprocal tourism could, and should, continue to serve the interests of both countries. (Under normal

100

conditions the expenditures of Americans in Cuba had contributed significantly to the clearing of accounts between Cuba and the United States though Cubans spent far more in the United States than Americans in Cuba.)

The Cuban extremist-nationalistic view was that American tourism was undesirable because Americans were attracted to Cuba by the wide-open facilities for gambling, prostitution, and drugs. A familiar cliché was that of the poor Cuban country girl destined, because of the poverty of her wretched family ground under the heel of the exploiting "imperialists," to end up in a Havana brothel frequented by blond, gumchewing barbarians from the north. The bulk of American tourists in Cuba, however, came because of the island's well-known attractions in the way of climate, fishing, hunting, sports, historical monuments, beaches, scenery, and so forth. The tourist industry was as worthy of the official support of both governments as any other legitimate business that contributed to mutual prosperity and development. The pandering to the vices of the tourist was no more pronounced in Havana than in many other cities.

On the morning of Monday, October 19, Castro formally opened the ASTA convention. He appeared in the sunniest of moods, exuding cordiality toward his American guests and most eager to stimulate tourist traffic from the United States. He charmed the delegates with his fractured English and with his attitude of warm friendship and interest in their concerns. I said, in my own remarks, that I believed the delegates would find proof during their stay in Cuba of this warm friendship and of the failure of the efforts of those who had wished to impair it.

That same evening in an address to a labor group Castro demonstrated that his morning mood of love for all mankind—including Americans—had, indeed, been a fleeting one. His attitude was dour and menacing as he castigated a wide range of his favorite whipping boys, including the American news agencies. It was clear that something had happened seriously to disturb him. That something was a letter from Huber Matos, the major commanding the important Camagüey province, asking Castro to accept his resignation and raising the Communist issue in a way the Maximum Leader found intolerable.[2]

Huber Matos was a well-known guerrilla officer. He had profited, as had the Castro brothers, Guevara, and Camilo Cienfuegos, from the myth that the overthrow of Batista had been due to the invincible tactics and strategy of Castro and his men. Matos was identified with a number of the operations that formed a part of the legend. He had been given the important post of military and civil head of the province of Camagüey where the work of agrarian reform had been conducted in the most arbitrary and radical fashion by the young men of INRA. Matos, as Castro's loyal follower, had backed these zealous youths, though with misgivings. His own attitude seems to have been nonrevolutionary in such matters as property rights. His democratic leanings were incompatible with the regime as it was being shaped.

According to one source, Matos had persuaded himself that Fidel was in danger from a Communist-oriented conspiracy led by brother Raúl.[3] If Matos really had this notion he was extremely naive. It is inconceivable that Raúl Castro, or even Guevara, would have entertained the idea of overthrowing Castro; the Maximum Leader was, and is, the activator of the Revolution. His major followers' place in the scheme of things depended, and still depends, on Castro. Without him they would again be nobodies. Che Guevara was the only possible exception to this rule.

Matos became worried at the influence it appeared to him the Communists were achieving in the government. He became increasingly perplexed at the contrast between the actions of the young men of INRA and the terms of the law they were supposed to be enforcing. He became alarmed at some of the appointments in the armed forces and in the governmental structure. But he maintained for some time the hope that Castro, if he realized the state of affairs or was informed about it by his old comrades-in-arms, would change the course of his government and pursue what many of his friends still thought was his goal, the establishment of a democratic and popular regime in Cuba.

When he abandoned this hope Matos sent in his resignation through regular channels and wrote Castro a letter setting forth his reasons for his decision. This letter, dated Monday, October 19, the day of the inauguration of the ASTA convention, made clear that Matos was retiring because it was impossible even to discuss with Castro the problem of Communist infiltration in the government.[4] Matos wrote as Castro's follower through the most difficult times of the Revolution who wished to be allowed quietly to withdraw in the face of a situation with which he no longer sympathized and which he no longer understood. He accused Castro of having been unjust with some of his supporters. He pleaded for an atmosphere in which it would be possible seriously to examine the multiple problems of the Revolution. The reasonable, friendly tone of the letter did not avert the wrath of the dictator or the indictment of the writer as a traitor to the Revolution.

Castro's reply to the Matos letter is dated the following day (October 20). Castro wrote that Matos's action put Matos in the same class as Trujillo, the supporters of Batista, and the reactionary press. He described the fear of communism which Díaz-Lanz, Urrutia, and now Matos had expressed as a symptom of immorality and ambition. He rejected the charge of communism as both false and insidious. He was harsh and arbitrary with one who had been a loyal and effective subordinate in war and peace. He appointed Camilo Cienfuegos as Matos's successor. (The designation of such a leading hero of the Revolution was an indication of the seriousness with which Castro regarded the Matos defection.) Castro ended his letter with the statement that the course Matos had adopted could only harm the Revolution and that Matos knew that very well.

Matos received Castro's letter the same day—October 20—toward evening. He spent a part of the night preparing a message explaining his position for public broadcast. He rejected the charge of treason. He revealed that Castro had sent forces from Havana to take over the radio stations and the airport in Camagüey on the apparent assumption that a rebellion was in progress. He denied that any of his troops would fire on those forces. He called on Castro not to permit the Revolution he had made to be destroyed. His message would have had popular appeal had he been permitted to deliver it.

Camilo Cienfuegos arrived in Camagüey at eight in the morning of Wednesday, the 21st, to take over command of the province from Matos. Two hours later Castro landed at the Camagüey airport. He did not go to the barracks or to the headquarters of the provincial government. He proceeded to the INRA offices to confer with the officials of that agency; he was their direct boss. The agrarian reformers fueled Castro's own vigorous animosity against his comrade of the days in the hills. They also confirmed the reports Castro had received to the effect that Matos's officers were loyal to their immediate chief. Castro decided, in the face of a threat of a real division among the forces identified with the Revolution, to resort to the mobilization of the masses gambit of which he was such a master.

With the most blatant sort of mob appeal, with the most shameless flattery of the *pueblo* as the real artificer of the Revolution, he blasted Matos as an ingrate and a traitor. He accused Matos of trying to raise himself up as a popular idol (something permitted only to Fidel). In his denunciation of Matos, the educated traitor, he (a doctor of laws) appealed to the un-lettered mob and to prejudice against pretensions based on education or intellect. He told the mob that its revolutionary merit was independent of the education it did not have. He accused Matos of having been seduced by counterrevolutionaries and of having worked with them. Castro said Matos had smeared him with communism in order to gain the support of reactionary forces within the country and of "foreign embassies." He de-nounced Matos for preparing a barracks revolt. He concluded that he, rely-ing on his faithful *pueblo*, had come to Camagüey "to my barracks which is the public square, to my barracks which is the city!" While a threatening mob activated by Castroite thugs looked on, Matos was taken prisoner; he offered not the slightest resistance. With him nearly forty officers of the rebel army were taken to Havana and to jail. (Matos was condemned to twenty years in prison after a sensational trial in the course of which Castro made a speech that lasted seven hours.)

Castro's "Pearl Harbor"

On the evening of Wednesday, October 21, the day of Matos's arrest, the former head of the rebel air force, Captain Díaz-Lanz flew over Havana and dropped a quantity of virulently anti-Castro leaflets.[5] His flight origi-nated in Florida and represented, therefore, a failure by American authorities to prevent an international flight in violation of American law. The Cuban authorities, led by Fidel Castro, later described it as a bombardment of Ha-vana done at the instigation and with the connivance of the American au-thorities—an action allegedly similar to the attack of the Japanese on Pearl Harbor.

What had actually happened was this: Díaz-Lanz obtained a B-25 bomber converted for use as a cargo carrier, packed it with propaganda leaf-lets against Castro, took off from an abandoned airfield in Florida north of Miami, flew over Havana at dusk, dropped his leaflets, was fired at by anti-aircraft batteries on the outskirts of the city, was perhaps fired at or pursued by one or more Cuban air force planes and then returned to Florida where he and his plane were taken into custody. Some of the fragments of the projectiles fired at his plane fell into crowded Havana streets, killing three people and wounding over forty.

I do not know how Díaz-Lanz acquired the plane in question. There were plenty of wealthy Cuban enemies of Castro who could have helped him. I cannot suppose that at this stage of the game any American government agency would have involved itself in a project of this kind. The flight was a most regrettable one and one which, even without the fraudulent account Castro foisted on the Cuban public, was bad from the point of view of a United States government trying sincerely to find a reasonable basis of relations with the Cuban government. It could benefit only those endeavoring to sow hatred and distrust of the United States in Cuba, that is, Castro and the people who were increasingly dominant in his councils. Untroubled by any considerations of truth or good faith, the Cuban authorities distorted the facts of the matter and accused the United States of a responsibility going far beyond negligence.

The proceedings of those authorities are instructive. The first report on the same evening of the flight was issued by the rebel army's press and radio service in order to counter rumors that some of the military establishments had been bombed; it made clear that antiaircraft machine-gun bullets fired at the "pirate plane" which was dropping leaflets were the cause of the death of one man and the wounding of others. Later on a report was issued by another government agency to the effect that terrorists had taken advantage of the confusion caused by the leaflet plane to attack innocent people so as to panic the citizenry. It was not until two days later that the bombing thesis was elaborated, "witnesses" arranged to prove it, and the propaganda campaign launched against the United States.

I called on the Acting Foreign Minister—Roa was not available—the morning after the incident. I expressed regret at the loss of life that had taken place and a willingness to investigate the possibility that the plane might have come from the United States. I asked to be furnished with such information as might be available to the Cuban authorities as to its time of arrival and departure, its description and markings, if any, the course it followed over Cuba, and its actions so far as the Cuban government had knowledge of them. My call and its purpose were made known to the press. Later the Cuban propaganda apparatus was most emphatic to the effect that I had been two-faced even to ask for information. And, since the Cuban "history" of the matter was being so drastically rewritten, I can understand that my request, while not unreasonable from the American point of view, might well have been embarrassing from that of the Cubans. This type of incident was indeed so welcome to Castro for his purposes that I was not surprised when at a later date a somewhat similar flight was actually engineered by Cuban secret agents in Florida.[6]

Meanwhile the ASTA convention had ended on a note of, to say the least, uncertainty. The violence with which Castro had handled himself in relation to the Huber Matos matter and his castigation of the United States after the Díaz-Lanz "bombing" had countered the effect of his welcome to the convention. As the travel agents took their departure, they were hardly in an optimistic mood as to future bookings. They were convinced that it would be a waste of time to promote tourism by Americans to Cuba, though the business of helping Cubans to leave their homeland was judged to have fine prospects. It was not, however, until the following Monday, October 26, that the full extent of the fabricated hate propaganda Castro planned to extract from the leaflet incident was made clear.

On that day Castro addressed a vast throng of his fellow citizens. He described the Díaz-Lanz flight as an attempt to bomb the Cuban Revolution into submission. He said he had a report that other planes were even then on their way from Florida to bomb Havana (none appeared). He shook his fist, roared defiance at the northern sky, foamed at the mouth, and in every way comported himself in a manner reminiscent of Hitler at his most hysterical and most odious. There was the same blatant disregard for truth, the same pathological extremes of expression, gesticulation, and movement. Castro seemed indeed to have taken leave of his senses.[7]

During this speech, with the "bombing" as a pretext, Castro promised to rearm the country so as to be able to beat off any assailant. He called for public contributions to that end. He announced the creation of a popular militia. (This relieved him of reliance on the rebel army in the ranks of which there was much latent sympathy for Huber Matos as well as sentiment for a more rational pursuit of revolutionary aims and a more reasonable approach to relations with the United States.) He asked the crowd if it wished the revolutionary tribunals restored for the expeditious trial of traitors. The answer was a roared affirmative mingled with shouts of "¡Paredon! ¡Paredon!" ("To the execution wall with them!"). It was a repulsive spectacle of mass hatred inspired by the man wholly and knowingly responsible for the lies used to arouse mob passions.

In my judgment, Castro's behavior at this time was not a reflection of a long-range plan for the communization of Cuba. I believe that the fortuitous combination of the Matos matter with the Díaz-Lanz episode not only permitted him but in fact obliged him, in accordance with the ethics of his behavior, to react as he did. The "bombing" came as a providential diversion from the potentially very serious Matos affair; it enabled him to electrify his mobs with what was then the completely fraudulent issue of an external aggression designed to crush their Revolution. If he had had only Matos to worry about, even he would have been unable to explain away the issues raised by Matos in such a way as to create anything like the mass reaction in his favor he extracted from the phony bombing.

In order to complete the account of events during the critical ten days at the end of October, mention must be made of the disappearance of Camilo Cienfuegos, one of the most popular of the revolutionary fighters. The plane on which he was supposed to be returning from Camagüey on October 28 vanished. Cienfuegos's personal popularity had often been demonstrated in ways that were possibly galling to other revolutionary chieftains, especially Raúl Castro. Cienfuegos was ideologically an unknown quantity. It is difficult to conceive of him as a fanatic of any set of ideas though his personal loyalty to Fidel was unquestioned. His closeness to his chief probably won him some enemies. Cienfuegos was gay and forthcoming. He had proved himself as a leader of men but he did not have any irresistible urge to the exercise of power. He liked the fleshpots, the gay life. He may have had a penchant for friendships and associations deemed undesirable by some of his more austere revolutionary comrades.

My belief, when Cienfuegos vanished, was that he had paid the price for his recklessness in flying in a plane of doubtful airworthiness with a semiskilled pilot late in the evening and under unfavorable weather conditions. I offered the cooperation of American planes in the wide-ranging search that was at once undertaken and that lasted for several days. The Cuban authorities assigned an area to the American fliers in which it was almost inconceivable the Cienfuegos plane could have been. In his report to the Cuban people on the efforts to find Cienfuegos, Castro made no mention of American assistance. Rumors soon spread that Camilo had been the victim of foul play and that Raúl Castro was guilty. I never took much stock in this. Cienfuegos was no threat to any one.

I made a number of unsuccessful attempts to get a retraction or an apology from the Foreign Office for its pamphlet comparing the Díaz-Lanz incident to the Japanese attack on Pearl Harbor. The officials with whom

I discussed the matter had no discretion in dealing with it; the wretched fiction was Castro's. In November my old friend, General Carlos Rómulo, Philippine Ambassador to the United States and also accredited to Cuba, came to Havana on a visit. I gave a dinner in his honor attended by the Cuban Foreign Minister and by other officials and diplomats with their wives. In toasting my guest, I laid particular stress on his loyal and courageous behavior at the time of Pearl Harbor. I described that black day in sufficient detail implicitly to convey to my Cuban hearers the enormity of comparing it to the regrettable but trivial incident properly labeled the Díaz-Lanz leaflet flight. The thrust of my toast was not lost on my guests.

Castro Slams the Door

Castro's performance of October 26 on the "bombing" spelled the end of my hope for rational relations between Cuba and the United States. It also triggered the separation from the regime of those with any previous standing in the Cuban establishment. Felipe Pazos who had been so optimistic a few weeks earlier and so apparently close to Castro was appalled at the speech; he told President Dórticos how damaging it was in terms of Cuba's relations with the United States. Dórticos, an individual distinguished more for adaptability than for straightforwardness, seems to have encouraged Pazos to speak out and may have even given him the notion that he shared his views. He reported Pazos's statements to Castro in a manner that infuriated the latter and led him violently to denounce Pazos at a Cabinet meeting.[8]

By the end of November Pazos was replaced by Che Guevara at the National Bank. Manuel Ray, the able Minister of Public Works, an engineer both competent and of high repute, was also eliminated and replaced by Camilo Cienfuegos's Communist brother. The Minister of the Treasury, Rufo López-Fresquet, did not resign for several weeks but his participation in the government became minimal and his adversary position increasingly notorious. The appointment of Che Guevara to the National Bank—I recall the "Ché it isn't so" headline in the *Times of Havana*—was all the confirmation one could ask of the fact that the attempt to find a basis for constructive relationships between the Cuban Revolution and the United States government had foundered.

Guevara had long been noted for his anti-Americanism, a passion that antedated his Marxism and predisposed him, as it did Castro, to the acceptance of the doctrines of the major enemy of the United States. Guevara was devoted to wiping the American establishment and the American private-enterprise system out of Latin America. With him you knew where you stood. I had little direct contact with him. He had been traveling abroad during part of my first year in Havana. His anti-Americanism was so notorious that I had never called on him though I had made it a practice to call on leading officials of the Cuban government. Initially famed as an exponent and practitioner of guerrilla warfare, he was now entrusted with vital financial and economic responsibilities. His association with Castro was not an easy one for either man; they shared a sense of continental mission that made Cuba a crowded spot when both were there.

The United States government now was forced to recognize that normal or quiet diplomacy had proved worthless in dealing with the Cuban government. On October 27 the United States issued the first of what was to be a series of statements by both governments setting forth their respective policies and grievances.[9] The American statement was delivered by me to President Dórticos and Foreign Minister Roa on the day after Castro's outrageous harangue on the "bombing." The text had, however, been drafted some days earlier. It was released to the press and published in the principal Cuban papers still more or less free from official interference.

The Cuban people now had before them a statement of the American view on the relations between the two countries as an antidote to what seemed to us the gross distortions of the Cuban government. Most significantly, the statement stressed the firm American commitment to nonintervention in the domestic affairs of Cuba. This, I hoped, would convey the message that Cubans who disagreed with the direction in which Castro was moving should not rely on the government of the United States to share with them their responsibility for expressing views and taking measures oriented toward a change of course.

So far as Castro was concerned, it had now become clear and would become clearer that he denied to the United States and to American private interests in Cuba any rights whatever that he felt bound to respect. That minimum of reciprocal confidence and trust that makes productive relations between governments possible no longer existed. The American attempt to establish such relations had been decisively rebuffed.

Chapter 12

What Course for
the United States?

CASTRO's vicious fiction about the "bombing" of Havana and his appointment of Che Guevara to head the National Bank marked a watershed in Cuban American relations. Henceforth, as long as Castro ruled Cuba, productive diplomacy was out of the question. I so reported to the Department of State early in December. Ernesto Dihigo, the distinguished Cuban Ambassador in Washington, was evidently of the same opinion; he left his post for good on the seventh of December.

Nevertheless there was agreement on the American side that the channels and the forms of diplomacy should be maintained. The situation in Cuba was chaotic and fluid; Cuban toleration for the prevailing disorganization and for the mismanagement of the country's interests at home and abroad might be short-lived. Effective opposition from within the Cuban community still seemed a reasonable expectation in view of the Castro excesses and of the supposed character of that community. Castro's own chances of escaping death from assassination or accident appeared poor.

The maintenance of diplomatic relations was also justified by more immediate considerations. Although progress on major policy questions was precluded, there were many pending matters, particularly those in which individual American citizens were interested; these, in spite of Castro's attitude, could still be discussed with Cuban officials. There was an important volume of trade even though the Cuban government had begun the imposition of restrictions that were to escalate to an almost complete cessation of commerce within the year.

The continued presence of the Embassy was further justified because, as had been the case for generations, there were thousands of Americans with their wives and children residing on the island. American-owned properties were numerous and important. American visitors were still coming to Cuba in appreciable numbers though Castro had effectively discouraged the tourist traffic—a traffic often described as Cuba's second crop (after sugar). American newspapermen and others were constantly running afoul of touchy and arbitrary revolutionary officials and having to be looked after by the Embassy's devoted and hardworking consular officials. And the number of Cubans desiring to leave the utopia that Castro was promising his countrymen and to emigrate to the United States had risen rapidly and was making increasing demands on the consular staff.

The Guantanamo naval base, with its three thousand or so Cuban laborers residing in neighboring Cuban territory and with its water supply on Cuban soil, was a potential source of friction and of diplomatic exchanges. I must record, however, with gratitude and appreciation, that under the able and tactful administration of Admiral "Mike" Fenno the base in my time gave the Embassy little to worry about.

Castro was, in my judgment, disappointed at the American decision to maintain relations with his government in the face of his rejection of the American attempt at accommodation. He aimed at an eventual rupture even though for tactical reasons he permitted President Dórticos and Foreign Minister Roa to make statements that seemed to temper his intransigence about everything involving the United States.

As 1959 wore to a close, the destinies of Cuba so far as the internal regime was concerned were firmly in Cuban hands in spite of the increasingly oppressive power of Castro and his activists. There was relative freedom to express dissent, and some dissent was in fact expressed. The police and other forms of totalitarian pressure and terror designed to insure uniformity of public opinion had been projected by Castro and his inner circle but were not yet in place. Most of the mass media were not under governmental control though their influence, in spite of the courage and the good intentions of some of their owners and editors, was weakened by reputations achieved in the pre-Castro period. A leadership willing to fight Castro and his policies would have had scope for its activities. But there was none.

The magnitude of the Castro charisma was thus enhanced by the dearth of alternatives. The supporters of Batista, not all of whom were corrupt and bloodstained, were barred from effective political action because of the nature of the regime with which they had been identified. The leadership left over from the democratically elected governments that had preceded the Batista dictatorship was almost completely passive (when not publicly pro-Castro as in the case of former President Prío).

Castro was now stepping on the revolutionary accelerator. He erased the anti-Communist complexion of most of the labor unions in November through a vigorous exercise of the magic of his personality that persuaded his followers that anti-Communists were apt to be counterrevolutionaries and that there was an imperative need for revolutionary unity in the labor movement. He had made a beginning of intimidating the nonrevolutionary press. He had established complete control over the Federation of University Students and was eradicating anticommunism from the faculties. In all of this he often employed the gangster methods with which he had became familiar in his student days to supplement the popular enthusiasm he so easily stimulated.

Castro was conditioning his people to the idea that Cuba would eventually have to defend itself against a direct or an indirect attempt by the United States to overthrow the Revolution. This thesis was extremely valuable to him in terms of the consolidation of his personal power, the denial of civil rights, and the building up of the state security system. Castro harvested an added dividend in that many of his opponents were swayed by his oratory about the certainty of American intervention; they devoutly hoped he knew what he was talking about. They looked outwardly instead of working inwardly for deliverance and were thus unavailable as activists in the fight against Castro.

Many of Castro's opponents had a predisposition (often inherited) to look to the United States rather than to their own efforts to correct their situation. The wishful thinking thus engendered discouraged activities aimed at protecting the liberties, the future prospects, and the properties threatened by the radical revolution on which the Castro dictatorship was now so evidently bent. Why should the Cuban opposition take the risks and undergo the dangers and the sacrifices of counterrevolution in Cuba if the United States could be relied upon to take the leadership, the responsibility, and the onus of the ejection of Castro? Some brave men and women persisted in the struggle against Castro, while the exodus of Cubans from their homeland began to assume major proportions. Many of those who departed did so in the conviction that they would soon return to find their country and their way of life restored to them without the need to exert serious effort on their part.

The fact is, of course, that until March 1960 the policy followed by the United States toward Castro's Cuba was one of complete adherence to the treaty commitments that forbid the intervention of one American republic in the domestic affairs of another. Furthermore, the United States had indicated a willingness to modify aspects in the long-standing relationships between the two countries that might be deemed to restrict the options available to the Cuban government in the conduct of its own affairs.

Official American spokesmen did their best to dispel any pretext for a belief in the possibility of American intervention in Cuba. In the presentation I made to President Dórticos on October 27, the day after the Castro performance on the bombing, I emphasized the American commitment to nonintervention in the affairs of its neighbors, the American hope that its neighbors, especially Cuba, would follow the same policy, one to which they also were committed, and the American determination to redouble efforts to prevent illegal actions against the Cuban government originating on American territory.[1]

In a statement he made in October at the Inter-American Peace Committee (a group set up by the Organization of American States to look into critical situations between American republics), Assistant Secretary Rubottom strongly reiterated the American commitment to nonintervention.[2] He said that the United States "deplores activities or threats carried on from outside any American country designed to overthrow the government of that country by force or foment civil strife within it." He added that the United States "believes that responsibility for the political affairs of any state should remain with the *residents of that state* without outside interference, subversion or aggression of any kind" (italics added).

Mr. Rubottom had eloquently reaffirmed the pledge of the United States not to interfere in any way with the responsibility of the people of an American state for the affairs of that state. Outside interference in an American republic was contemplated by Mr. Rubottom only in the event of collective action through the Organization of American States on behalf of the principle of representative democracy. Such a collective endeavor was as inconceivable then as it is now—particularly if instigated by the United States.

In spite of American intentions and of efforts to make clear those intentions, Castro was assisted in his campaign to build up the beleaguered-citadel mentality among his uncritical supporters by the fact that there were illegal flights and movements of men and weapons from Florida to Cuba on anti-Castro missions. Castro distorted these into instances of connivance by American authorities in endeavors to overthrow the Cuban government. These incidents, though not in great numbers or in any way threatening the existence of the Cuban government, were a source of embarrassment to the United States government and especially to its representatives in Havana. Much was done to improve supervision and controls particularly of airports but 100 percent enforcement of American law was never achieved. (Nor have the Cuban authorities, with all the resources of an absolute despotism, thoroughly sealed off their island territory from persons desiring to abandon it clandestinely or to enter it for subversive purposes.)

This type of covert activity has a long history in the Caribbean. Filibustering expeditions from Florida to Cuba go back to the early days of the American possession of Florida, that is, a century and a half. They vary in frequency and intensity according to the state of public opinion in the United States about conditions in Cuba and the size and energies of the Cuban exile community. The record of law enforcement against them is a spotty one.

Thus, for example, in 1895 the final Cuban insurrection was almost destroyed at birth when American officials held up three vessels laden with men and munitions on which the leaders of the insurgency had counted to give their movement a decisively vigorous initial impact.[3] Only men with the drive and the faith of José Martí and Máximo Gómez would have persevered after a setback of this magnitude. But many other similar expeditions sailed from Florida unmolested to the indignation of the Spanish government. In the lively memoirs of Frederick Funston, then a young soldier of fortune and later a distinguished officer in the Army of the United States, there is an account of the venture in which he was a participant and which brought much-needed men and artillery to the insurgents.[4] Funston's group was helped to evade the law while on American soil by influential citizens, and it enjoyed cooperation from the employees and rolling stock of the Flagler railway company.

During the fifties filibustering from Florida in the interest of Batista's opponents was frequent. Again law enforcement was imperfect. Former

President Prío was led handcuffed through the streets of Miami because of alleged violations of the American neutrality statute. On the other hand a number of successful expeditions by sea and air brought men and supplies to the anti-Batista forces in Cuba including those under Castro in 1957 and 1958. Castro, however, took the position in 1959 and 1960 that any failure to enforce the law against his opponents was evidence, not of poor enforcement or of the difficulties encountered in all law enforcement, but of collusion by the American government in the effort to thwart and overthrow the Cuban Revolution. These incidents were in fact so welcome to Castro for his own purposes that, as I have earlier mentioned, he went to the length of having his agents in Florida arrange for one or more clandestine flights to Cuba which would be captured on Cuban soil and used to reinforce Cuban propaganda about the malevolence of the "imperialists."[5]

Castro and Communism at the End of 1959

In my view, evidence that either the Cuban or the Russian Communists were plotting with Castro behind the backs of the Cuban people to suppress the liberties of that people could have justified a departure from the American commitment to nonintervention. But as 1959 gave way to 1960 there was no such evidence. There was no Communist armed force identifiable as such, with the capacity to dominate the Cuban people—still anti-Communist in its great majority. There was every evidence that Castro continued to enjoy tremendous popular support both in spite of and because of his defiance of the United States. The situation was not comparable to that in Guatemala five years earlier when the United States was generally praised or blamed for having decisively helped to overthrow a government which the United States believed had proved itself receptive to the penetration of international communism.

The Cuban Communists had been worried at Castro moves which might produce internal or external conflict capable of destroying the Cuban Revolution and with it the positions being achieved within the Revolution by the Cuban party. The party's views as to the pace of the Revolution were more moderate than Castro's.[6]

Early in November the Central Intelligence Agency in Washington, after evaluating all the available information on Castro's relations to the Communists, had stated, through its Deputy Director General, General

C. P. Cabell, that the Cuban Communists did not consider Castro, a man of bourgeois origins, to be a member of the party or even pro-Communist. The General pointed to continued evidence of substantial opposition to the Communists in the ranks of Castro's own party, the 26th of July movement. He concluded that Castro was not in fact a member of the party and did not consider himself to be a Communist.[7]

I concurred in this CIA estimate of the state of affairs at that time. Castro's sympathies for the Cuban Communists were to increase steadily as he found them more useful than any other organized force in Cuba in carrying out his revolutionary concepts and manning his expanding security apparatus. At this particular juncture, however, Castro was making Castroites out of his Communist compatriots rather than being taken into the Communist camp himself. Two years later he was to imply that he had long been a devout Marxist-Leninist. Only Castro could have allowed himself such a statement; only a man with his magic could have gotten away with it.

Castro's passionate anti-Americanism, rather than a predilection for communism on his part, was drawing him to the attention of the Soviet Union. It is probable that for months there had been unpublicized contacts between Cuban revolutionaries and Soviet agents.[8] Castro wanted to find out if he could count on any help from the Soviet Union in the event of a conflict with the United States. The Russians welcomed opportunities to make trouble for the United States, but I am confident that they were then far from contemplating the sort of all-out help for Cuba which the rupture of Cuban American trade relations the following year made necessary if Castro and his Revolution were to survive.

In early November 1959 the Castroite daily, Revolución, probably at Castro's instigation, pointed out the presence in Mexico City of Soviet Vice Premier Mikoyan and advocated that Cuban representatives approach him.[9] The suggestion, perhaps originally intended as a trial balloon, led to the invitation which Mikoyan accepted to come to Cuba in February to inaugurate a Soviet trade exhibit. Revolución argued that the visit to Havana of such an able and influential Russian official would permit Castro to discuss with him the economic problems of the Revolution and the resumption of the diplomatic relations broken off nearly eight years earlier by Batista. (Mikoyan's visit to Cuba and the resulting Cuban-Soviet agreement are discussed in chapter 14.)

An American Note Sends Castro Into Orbit

Nonintervention and the avoidance of provocative actions or attitudes could not for long be the total American policy toward Cuba. The United States and its interests there were under constant destructive attack. I spent a couple of weeks in the Department of State in December participating in discussions of the situation Castro had created. Many possible courses of action were examined and rejected or put in cold storage. The upshot was a decision to continue for the present the American attitude of patience and restraint in the hope that developments in Cuba would sooner or later reward such an attitude. It was also decided to build up a record of the injuries the United States and its citizens had received at the hands of Castro.

Opinion in the United States had become irritated and frustrated at Castro's verbal excesses in the face of the conciliatory policy of the American government. American enterprises which had contributed to the economic and the social development of Cuba and could show a better record of conformity to Cuban law than many purely Cuban enterprises were now being treated as convicted criminals. There was a most respectable demand for a firmer policy toward Cuba. There were indeed those who thought that our government should respond to the Castro excesses with excesses of its own, that the situation warranted a test of strength which the United States could not fail to win. Many of the proposals made at this time were somewhat incoherent reflections of a logical exasperation that a situation so long taken for granted should have erupted in this fashion.

I still believed that Cuban society would find Castroism inherently unacceptable and would eventually reject it; I was convinced that this process would not be accelerated by American pressures—quite the contrary. As 1959 drew to a close, I was pleased that it was American policy to avoid actions that would penalize the Cuban people as a whole for the actions of Castro and his henchmen, that is, for the misguided behavior of those who, hopefully, would be running the government of the island only briefly. American policy was designed to make it clear that when Castro fell, his overthrow would be due to inside and not outside causes.

This policy did not, however, preclude placing on the record the numerous acts of arbitrary despoilment of which Americans in Cuba had been the victims at the hands of INRA. Since Castro had decreed the Land Reform

Law there had been at least fifty such cases. In many of them the productive capacity of the properties affected had been damaged well beyond the specific losses of land, cattle, and equipment misappropriated by the eager incompetents under Castro's personal supervision.

Normally the making of this type of an official record would have been justified only after the injured parties had exhausted the administrative and judicial remedies available to them in Cuba. But two conditions now warranted a more expeditious procedure. In the first place, the INRA's actions did not represent the application of the Land Reform Law or of any other Cuban law; they were purely arbitrary exercises of personal power. Secondly, Castro and the INRA were engaged in intimidating and dismantling the administrative and judicial machinery in Cuba that might have furnished remedies to those who believed themselves the victims of abuses of executive power and of denials of due process.

I returned to Havana on January 10, with the delivery of a note on the lines described above as my first order of business. At the airport I made a conventional statement of pleasure at being back in Cuba and pledged myself to work for the improvement of the relations between the two countries. The next day I presented to the Foreign Ministry a recital of the seizures and occupations of lands and buildings, the confiscations and removals of equipment, the taking of cattle, the cutting of timber, the plowing under of productive pastures, and the moving of fences and boundary markers of which American individuals and corporations had been the victims without any sanction in Cuban law, without written authority from their chief, and, of course, without court orders. A press release summarizing the note was made available in Washington.[10]

Castro and his propagandists pretended to be outraged and to regard the note as a negation of my expressed desire to improve relations—an improvement they implied could only be achieved through that slavish submission to all of Castro's whims fast becoming the test of the true revolutionary in Cuba. Castro's irritation peaked in a television interview ten days later.[11] He said that the note and the attendant publicity could have had no other purpose than to encourage counterrevolution—a task on which he falsely alleged the Embassy had long been engaged. He rehearsed his familiar and uncomplimentary views about the United States, its past, present, and future policies toward Cuba and the caliber of some of its public men, including Vice President Nixon. His statements were so offensive that Secretary of State Herter recalled me to Washington for a prolonged stay, though I had been back in Cuba only briefly. To emphasize the depth of Washington's displeasure with Castro I was instructed to bring Mrs. Bonsal with me—at government expense!

In the course of this same address Castro had made some offensive remarks about Spain and Spanish priests. The Spanish Ambassador, Juan Pablo de Lojendio, Marquis of Vellisca, was so stirred that he rose from the bed where he was recovering from a slight indisposition and rushed to the studio to confront the speaker. Mrs. Bonsal and I were at home viewing this characteristically late, late show when we saw the Ambassador walk into the studio and vigorously interpellate the Prime Minister who was well into the third hour of his discourse. Present was a large live audience including President Dórticos, members of the Cabinet, a number of the military, and the customary courtiers. Castro was visibly taken aback as could clearly be seen by the viewers throughout the nation—he had long lost the habit of dialogue.

Instants later Mrs. Bonsal and I and the hundreds of thousands of viewers saw the whole mass of the Castro-selected audience surge toward the angry and vocal Ambassador and hide him from our screen. We learned next day that only the cool-headedness of Juan Almeida, the commandant of the armed forces, saved the Ambassador from serious bodily harm. The courageous diplomat was at once declared *persona non grata* and given twenty-four hours to leave Cuba.

I called on the Ambassador the next morning and had the story from him. I was photographed as I arrived at the Spanish Embassy. My visit of farewell to an old friend and valued colleague was given publicity of a nature not hard to imagine. Next day Castro's paper, *Revolución*, in commenting on the matter took an attitude based on the cliché of Cuban folklore to the effect that Spaniards are the least intelligent of human beings and proceeded to allege that the action of confronting Castro on television was not one that would have occurred to a Spaniard. The writer asked himself where the Spanish Ambassador could have acquired such an idea and answered himself to the effect that the instigator must have been that snake in the grass, the American Ambassador. I admired Lojendio's spirit in challenging Castro literally in his den but regretted that the only practical consequence of his action was to remove from Cuba an energetic and intelligent diplomat. Lojendio's act of defiance was unmatched during this period, though there were plenty of Cubans with even more reason than the gallant Ambassador to take issue with Castro.

Chapter 13

The American Commitment to Nonintervention Reaffirmed

My unexpected return to Washington enabled me to discuss with Secretary Herter and with the President a draft of a statement summarizing the policy I believed the United States should follow now that Castro had rebuffed American moves toward a rational relationship. Castro's most recent pronouncements including those which had led to my temporary recall gave some urgency to a public expression of the President's attitude. My draft was carefully studied both in the White House and in the Department of State. On January 26, 1960, with very few changes, the President released it as a considered statement of American policy. Here is its text:

> Secretary Herter and I have been giving careful consideration to the problem of relations between the Governments of the United States and Cuba. Ambassador Bonsal, who is currently in Washington, shared in our discussions. We have been, for many months, deeply concerned and perplexed at the steady deterioration of those relations reflected especially by recent public statements by Prime Minister Castro of Cuba, as well as by statements in official publicity organs of the Cuban Government. These statements contain unwarranted attacks on our Government and on our leading officials. These attacks involve serious charges none of which, however, has been the subject of formal representations by the Government of Cuba to our Government. We believe these charges to be totally unfounded.

121

We have prepared a re-statement of our policy toward Cuba, a country with whose people the people of the United States have enjoyed and expect to continue to enjoy a firm and mutually beneficial friendship.

The United States Government adheres strictly to the policy of non-intervention in the domestic affairs of other countries including Cuba. This policy is incorporated in our treaty commitments as a member of the Organization of American States.

Second, the United States Government has consistently endeavored to prevent illegal acts in territory under its jurisdiction directed against other governments. United States law enforcement agencies have been increasingly successful in the prevention of such acts. The United States record in this respect compares very favorably with that of Cuba from whose territory a number of invasions directed against other countries have departed during the past year, in several cases attended with serious loss of life and property damage in the territory of those other countries. The United States authorities will continue to enforce United States laws, including those which reflect commitments under Inter-American treaties, and hopes that other governments will act similarly. Our Government has repeatedly indicated that it would welcome any information from the Cuban Government or from other governments regarding incidents occurring within their jurisdiction or notice, which would be of assistance to our law enforcement agencies in this respect.

Third, the United States Government views with increasing concern the tendency of spokesmen of the Cuban Government, including Prime Minister Castro, to create the illusion of aggressive acts and conspiratorial activities aimed at the Cuban Government and attributed to United States officials or agencies. The promotion of unfounded illusions of this kind can hardly facilitate the development, in the real interest of the two peoples, of relations of understanding and confidence between their governments. The United States Government regrets that its earnest efforts over the past year to establish a basis for such understanding and confidence have not been reciprocated.

Fourth, the United States Government, of course, recognizes the right of the Cuban Government and people in the exercise of their national sovereignty to undertake those social, economic and political reforms which, with due regard for their obligations under international law, they may think desirable. This position has frequently been stated and it reflects a real understanding of and sympathy with the ideals and aspirations of the Cuban people. Similarly, the United States Government and people will continue to assert and to defend, in the exercise of their own sovereignty, their legitimate interests.

Fifth, the United States Government believes that its citizens have made constructive contributions to the economies of other countries by means of their investments and their work in these countries and that such contributions, taking into account changing conditions, can continue on a mutually satisfactory basis. The United States Government will continue to bring to the attention of the Cuban Government any instances in which the rights of its citizens under Cuban law and under international law have been disregarded and in which redress under Cuban law is apparently unavailable or denied. In this connection it is the hope of the United States Government that differences of opinion between the two Governments in matters recognized under international law as subject to diplomatic negotiations will be solved through such negotiations. In the event that disagreements between the two Governments concerning this matter should persist, it would be the intention of the United States Government to seek solutions through other appropriate international procedures.

The above points seem to me to furnish reasonable bases for a workable and satisfactory relationship between our two sovereign countries. I should like only to add that the United States Government has confidence in the ability of the Cuban people to recognize and defeat the intrigues of International Communism which are aimed at destroying democratic institutions in Cuba and mutually beneficial friendship between the Cuban and American peoples.[1]

I have quoted this document in full because I believe that the policy it expressed, if consistently followed, would have helped create conditions in which the Cuban people might have found their own way out of the chaotic situation in which the magnetic, extremist, and unbalanced dictatorship of Fidel Castro was plunging them. In that event, the Cuban American relationship, with all its reciprocal advantages and with the modifications required by changing conditions, could have been preserved. This is admittedly hypothetical: it is only too clear that the measures which the government of the United States later adopted for the purpose of over-throwing Castro produced results directly contrary to those anticipated.

By its solemn renewal of its commitment to nonintervention in Cuba, the United States pledged itself to refrain from actions aimed directly or indirectly at changing the political situation there or at least that is my judgment of the intent of the document I have quoted. The President's statement was designed to convince the Cuban people that, so far as the United States was concerned, the question of Castro's or another's leader-ship was theirs to decide, whether they liked it or not. Some of them did not, and many more did not believe it.

There was, of course, nothing in the President's statement that implied a passive acceptance by the United States of the injuries inflicted by Castro on the trade of the United States with Cuba and on American investments in that country. In matters of trade, for example, the Cuban government had for months been taking measures designed to reduce imports from the United States on the plea of balance-of-payments problems but in fact in order to diminish the dependence of Cuba on the United States. (American exports to Cuba which had been valued at $547 million in 1958 sank to $435 million in 1959 and were to decline to $224 million in 1960, with much of the decrease reflecting Cuban governmental action.)

These Cuban measures had been taken in the face of a stated willing-ness on the part of the United States to renegotiate the tariff arrangements between the two countries so as to adjust situations which the Cubans had claimed hindered their industrialization and diversification aspirations. The rejection of the American offer and the Cuban measures in question pro-duced for the American side a freedom of action which allowed though it did not oblige the United States to adopt retaliatory measures proportion-ate to the injury sustained. A reduction in the sugar quota in an amount re-lated to the losses of American exporters to Cuba could have been considered though the extreme mutuality of the relationship at that time and the reciprocal entanglement of many of its elements made decisions difficult.

Nor did the President's statement leave American investors in Cuba entirely without remedy against the arbitrary and unfair actions of the Cu-ban government. As I understood it, there was implicit in the statement a renouncing of any use by the United States on behalf of its injured citizens of the leverage of American superior power in the economic field to obtain for those citizens treatment deemed equitable by the United States and thus to coerce the sovereignty of Cuba. But the statement reasserted the practice to be followed when the United States government reached the conclusion that in a particular instance its nationals had experienced a denial of justice. The President contemplated that the case should be the subject of a diplomatic claim and that, if the two governments were unable to reach agreement, "other appropriate international procedures" would be used to seek a solution. This clearly implied resort to arbitration.

Admittedly the President's position was unsatisfactory in terms of immediate relief for Americans injured by revolutionary measures. But the days when President Coolidge had asserted that the duty of our government was to protect the person and the property of an American citizen wherever he went just as though he were in the United States were long past. There had been a very considerable retreat from what Professor Bryce Wood has described as "the high water mark in the declamatory assertion of the right to protect American citizens abroad."[2] An American judgment to the effect that what Mr. Coolidge called "the fundamental laws of justice" in property matters had been violated was no longer a sufficient justification for forcible American action.

After recognizing the sovereign rights of the Cuban government, the President's statement went on to say, "The United States Government and people will continue to assert and defend, in the exercise of their own sovereignty, their legitimate interests." The availability of an adequate supply of sugar was such a legitimate interest, one closely involved in the general welfare of our country. For many years nearly a third of the sugar consumed in the United States had come from Cuba. If Cuba, either because production was materially diminished in consequence of the loss of efficiency resulting from drastic changes in the sugar industry or because of a Cuban governmental decision to find other destinations for sugar normally sent to the United States, seemed likely not to fill the American quota, the United States government would have been entitled to evaluate the prospects and to take steps well in advance of the anticipated shortfall in Cuban sugar for the American market. These steps, under the sugar system which has been in force in the United States for a generation, would have involved a reduction of the quota from Cuba and increases in quotas from other sources regarded as reliable suppliers.

The President's statement also contained a rejection of the charges against the United States government and its officials in which the Cubans had been indulging themselves. It stressed American determination to prevent the use of its territory for illegal acts directed against other governments. It pointed out how much better was the American record than the Cuban in this respect, though, considerately, it did not make the point that the illegal acts originated on Cuban territory had been performed under the sponsorship of the Prime Minister and with the resources of the Cuban government.

The President's statement was favorably received in Cuba, in the United States, and in Latin America.[3] Many editorials in the American press expressed the hope that Castro would respond in the conciliatory spirit of President Eisenhower. President Dórticos rushed out what in Cuban terms could be described as a temperate response. Castro himself was silent for a time. Public opinion in Cuba which had believed the United States and Cuba on the verge of a break was tranquilized. A relaxation of tensions and an opportunity for constructive thinking and acting in a calmer atmosphere had been achieved, if only briefly.

Castro's brief abstention from invective and calumny against the United States was helped along by my distinguished colleague, the Argentine Ambassador in Havana, Julio Amoedo. An able, lively, and engaging man, he had achieved an excellent personal relationship with Castro and with some of those around him. He approached Castro on the evening of the President's statement of January 26. He impressed on Castro the extremely adverse effect of the Prime Minister's raucous anti-Americanism on government and public opinion in the other American republics, and the alarm felt lest Castro provoke a definitive break between Cuba and the United States.[4] Amoedo was successful to the extent that Castro was, for him, relatively inoffensive for a few weeks.

Some confusion has since arisen with regard to the Amoedo attempt to change Castro's attitude toward the United States.[5] It has been asserted that it included an offer of aid for specific purposes, including the financing of land reform, made to Castro by Amoedo with the authorization of the government of the United States. There was no such authorization. Under the circumstances which unfortunately prevailed at the time, such an offer would have been regarded in the United States as craven appeasement and would have been scornfully rejected by Castro as attempted bribery. The notion that the Amoedo approach contained an American offer contingent on a rejection by Castro of whatever deal Mikoyan might propose when he reached Cuba the following week is equally devoid of foundation. There could be no doubt in anyone's mind, however, that, had the sort of reconciliation between the Cuban Revolution and the United States for which Amoedo so valiantly worked been effectuated and relations between the two governments placed on a rational basis, Cuba could and would have participated in the expanding concept of government-to-government assistance which was informing the evolution of American policy toward Latin America. Amoedo could well have made this point to Castro without any specific authorization.

Within a couple of weeks after the President's statement, the highly competent Chargé d'Affaires in Havana, Dan Braddock, had skillfully extracted from the Foreign Minister, Dr. Roa, an admission that the Cuban government had no specific charges to prefer against the American Ambassador. This admission contradicted the statement Castro had earlier made as well as the entire trend of comment in the Castro-oriented press. My return to Havana was not expedited, however, as it was considered that the longer my absence the greater the implied reprimand to a now, on the surface, more conciliatory Cuban government.

During February there was an exchange of views between the two governments about negotiations on pending matters. Although both governments were at this time convinced that there was no possibility of fruitful discussions, there was on both sides a desire to maintain a negotiating stance. The United States had been sincerely ready to seek accommodation but had reached the conclusion that, as the Cuban government was then constituted, there was no prospect of success in this direction; the gap in basic concepts between the two governments was too great. Castro and Guevara were equally convinced that the positions they had taken or intended to take were not susceptible of negotiation with the United States; the Cuban revolutionaries were the prisoners of their own statist concepts and of the "anti-imperialism" that is the breath of life to them.

Dr. Roa demanded that, before negotiations could begin, the United States should bind itself to take no steps against Cuba while they lasted.[6] This was interpreted in Havana and in Washington to mean that if the

United States wanted to negotiate with Cuba, it would have to pledge itself to make no alteration in Cuba's sugar quota while the negotiations were in progress. The United States rejected a condition that would have involved an executive commitment precluding the exercise of a congressional prerogative, the passing of sugar legislation. (The Congress had not yet made the grant of executive discretion in this matter which the administration had requested in January.) The Cubans were perfectly familiar with this aspect of the matter when they made their demand. Indeed, for the Cuban Foreign Minister to ask the American executive to tie the hands of the American Congress while the Cuban dictatorship was daily taking wholly arbitrary and hate-inspired actions against American interests in Cuba was as unrealistic as it was impertinent. If, however, negotiations had been initiated and if they seemed to be progressing in an atmosphere of good faith and a desire for results, there would have been no congressional inclination to rock the boat by taking action adverse to Cuban sugar. This Cuban demand, had other conditions been favorable, would not have prevented negotiations; it was advanced for propaganda purposes and to underline the unilateral nature of the American sugar legislation on which Cuban welfare was then dependent.

Chapter 14

The Castro-Mikoyan Deal, February 1960

Days after his coup in 1952 and even before the United States had recognized his regime, Batista broke off diplomatic relations with the Soviet Union. Thereafter, unwavering support of the United States in the cold war, then at its height, was the major element in Cuba's foreign policy. Nevertheless, the Russians made a number of highly welcome purchases of Cuban sugar during the years of the dictatorship. These were, of course, at the prices prevailing in the world market (generally 40 percent and more below what the United States was paying). Though the Russian purchases had amounted to less than half a million metric tons or below one-twelfth of the Cuban crop in any one year they had benefited the Cuban government both economically and politically.[1]

Now that the Cuban regime was taking an increasingly anti-American and anti–private enterprise attitude, it was logical for Havana and Moscow to seek a rapprochement. To the degree that Cuban American economic relations might suffer from the deterioration of the political relations between the two countries, the Maximum Leader was interested in seeking, and Khrushchev in providing, assistance that would help Castro to pursue his anti-American policies.

Yet when Mikoyan reached Havana in early February 1960, the opportunities for an expansion of Cuban-Soviet trade seemed limited in spite of the goodwill that could be assumed to exist on both sides. Russia might increase the relatively modest takings of Cuban sugar that had been the

129

major feature of that trade in the past few years. The Castro-Guevara objective of reducing Cuban dependence on trade with the United States could be furthered through the development of imports from the Soviet Union and from Eastern European countries to replace some of those being obtained from the United States or from United States influenced sources. Crude oil might be an item here. Soviet oil was already moving to Argentina, Brazil, and Uruguay—why not to Cuba also? Yet these possibilities did not then seem seriously to threaten the substance of the trading relationship between Cuba and the United States.

The accepted wisdom, as 1959 gave way to 1960, was that Cuban dependence on the American market for the disposition at premium prices of half its sugar and the dependence of the American people on Cuba for some 30 percent of the sugar consumption in the United States represented a relationship the disruption of which was in the interest of neither partner. Furthermore, the Soviet policy of autarchy in the matter of consumer goods in general and of foodstuffs in particular seemed to limit the degree of dependence on Cuban sugar that would be acceptable to the policymakers in the Kremlin. This seemed true even though the per capita consumption of sugar in Russia—about two-thirds of that in the United States—was inadequate for a country the leaders of which were trying to persuade their citizens that they were about to achieve a standard of living higher than that prevailing in the United States and in Western Europe. It seemed reasonable to believe that increased Russian sugar consumption would be achieved primarily through the expansion of beet-sugar production rather than through the establishment of a major source of supply from a far-distant country under the guns of the United States.

Castro extended the most lavish hospitality to Mikoyan and his party. There were receptions, there were tours of the countryside, there were speeches in profusion. Despite a natural reticence the business community gave Mikoyan a banquet—some said this reflected top-level persuasion. The Soviet Vice Premier placed a wreath on the Martí monument though many thought this action inappropriate to the point of being insulting on the part of the representative of a country with so deplorable a record in the matter of respect for the right of self-determination of small countries. Mikoyan told the Cubans he approved of their land reform but pointed out that in Russia they ordered these things better: there they had not even promised compensation to the dispossessed landowners!

Mikoyan drove a hard bargain with the Cubans in spite of all the anti-imperialistic pleasantry with which his visit was studded. He agreed that over the next five years Russia would buy a million tons of sugar per annum from Cuba. This meant about twice as much sugar as the Soviet Union had ever before bought from Cuba in a single year. It was a most helpful outlet for approximately one-sixth of the total crop and was equivalent to about one-third of what was normally shipped to the United States. Some commentators have said that it reflected Soviet shortages arising from drought conditions and from an intention to increase the per capita consumption of sugar in Russia. Under the prevailing conditions there was concern in some quarters as to whether the Russians would be able to absorb what they had agreed to buy from Cuba without dumping some of it on the world market and thereby adversely affecting the outlet for the one-third of the Cuban crop usually sold on that market.

It was generally understood that the initial Russian sugar purchase was at a price of 2.78 cents per pound. This was slightly below the then prevailing world-market price—the Russians received a quantity discount. The price was low compared with the level of 5.0 cents per pound which the American sugar system then guaranteed the Cuban producer of sugar under the Cuban quota in the United States. Furthermore, only 20 percent of the payment was to be made in dollars and the remainder in Soviet goods under a clearing arrangement. In addition, the Russians offered the Cubans a credit of $100 million at a low rate of interest for the purchase of Soviet goods, presumably for developmental and industrialization purposes.

This deal did not in itself jeopardize the American economic position in Cuba. The amounts involved did not threaten the Cuban capability for supplying the American market or even suggest that there was an alternative outlet for the sugar normally supplied that market. There was nothing in the deal to indicate that the Russians could greatly expand their purchases from Cuba. There was some puzzlement as to what goods Cuba might receive from the Soviet Union to make up the 80 percent of the value of the sugar sent the Soviet Union. Crude oil was a major Soviet export. Yet the three principal refineries in Cuba, operated in accordance with Cuban concessions and legislation, were refining crude oil from nearby Venezuela.

In any event there was really nothing the United States could do to prevent Cuba and the Soviet Union from trading with each other. The United States could not argue that this particular deal undermined Cuba's position as a supplier of sugar to the American market. Trade between the Soviet Union and most of the American republics had been going on for years. Relations between Moscow and Washington continued to be conducted in "the spirit of Camp David" (where President Eisenhower and Mr. Khrushchev had had a cordial meeting in September 1959) until the U-2 blowup in May, three months after Mikoyan's visit to Cuba.

When I endeavored to raise with departmental officials the larger issue of whether the United States was in a position to discuss with Moscow the deterioration of Cuban American relations and to ascertain whether it would not be possible to persuade the Russians—perhaps on a reciprocal sphere-of-influence basis—to avoid actions that would encourage the Cubans in their aggressive designs on legitimate American interests, I was told that representations even of an informal nature were not feasible. At a later date I was reliably informed that the American agenda for the summit conference that aborted after the U-2 incident did not include Cuba.

Chapter 15

Nonintervention Abandoned, March 1960

THE American policy of nonintervention, moderation, and restraint in dealing with Cuba was frustrating to Castro and Guevara. It had much support in the United States and in Latin America. Worse yet from Castro's point of view, it was sapping that sense of emergency in the face of imminent American aggression he had inculcated in his supporters. In an atmosphere of concentration on purely Cuban issues, opposition to his personal dictatorship could be expected to grow.

A French Munitions Ship and Castro Explode

Unhappily an event now occurred that was made to order for the man who had so convincingly demonstrated his talent for distortion and prevarication in the case of the "bombing" of Havana four months earlier. On March 4 the French cargo vessel La Coubre arrived at Havana laden with arms and munitions for the Cuban government; it promptly blew up with serious loss of life. With hardly a pause for breath, Castro conveyed to his people the notion that "functionaries of the North American Government" were responsible for the explosion.[1] The accusation would have been ludicrous if it had not demonstrated so much shamelessness and venom.[2] Some observers concluded that the disaster was due to the careless manner in which the Cubans set about unloading the vessel's dangerous cargo. There

133

could have been sabotage; the Cuban Revolution by this time had made many bitter enemies. But it was preposterous, without even a pretense of investigation, to accuse the United States government.

Even more preposterous was the rapidity with which Castro leapt to his conclusion. He compared the La Coubre disaster to the sinking of the Maine in Havana harbor in 1898. The revolutionary folklore in vogue in 1960 described the earlier sinking as a deliberate clandestine act by warmongering American officials—one designed to inflame American public opinion to support war with Spain and thus to cheat the Cuban patriots of their imminent victory and of the independence of their country. Castro did not recall that the investigation of the Maine explosion had been in progress for six weeks before any report was issued. For his purposes no investigation was necessary. Cubans and Americans wishing for reconciliation or at least a relaxation of tensions were rudely jarred out of the relative hopefulness that had prevailed since the end of January.

Castro's reaction to the La Coubre explosion was perhaps what tipped the scales in favor of Washington's abandonment of the policy of nonintervention in Cuba that had been reiterated as recently as the President's statement of January 26. The pleasantries exchanged by Mikoyan and Castro in February had been given the most alarming significance in some Washington quarters. The economic arrangements between Cuba and the Soviet Union seemed intolerable to people long accustomed to a dominant American position in Cuba. The Embassy had had no reply whatever from the Cuban government to its representations regarding the cases of Americans victimized by the continuing abuses of the National Institute of Agrarian Reform. The abuses themselves continued unabated.

In addition, the Washington atmosphere was beginning to be heated by the imminence of a presidential election; the administration wished to buttress the defenses of its foreign policies while the opposition was seeking weak points to attack. The American posture of moderation in the face of Castro's insulting and aggressive behavior was becoming a political liability, even though as late as April such disparate commentators as Jules Dubois, Joseph Alsop, and Herbert Matthews were counseling restraint and the avoidance of economic sanctions in dealing with Castro.[3] Threatening sounds began to emanate from various quarters along the Potomac.

The new American policy—not announced as such but implicit in the actions of the United States government—was one of overthrowing Castro by all the means available to the United States short of the open employment of American armed forces in Cuba. The political, military, and economic elements of the new program were only belatedly, and sometimes through unofficial chanels, made known to us in the Havana Embassy. In fairness to State Department officials charged with keeping the American Ambassador in Cuba informed of developments and asking his advice about contemplated measures, I must record my impression that the various highly placed people in different agencies who took decisions and set in motion activities related to Cuba did not keep the Department of State effectively abreast of what they were planning and doing. As my narrative will reveal, we in the Havana Embassy became aware only gradually and imperfectly, and without real opportunity for comment and discussion, of the new policy of our government.

I later learned that within a couple of weeks of the *La Coubre* incident and about the time I returned to Havana, the top-level decision (for nine months advocated by Vice President Nixon) was taken to allow the Central Intelligence Agency to begin recruiting and training anti-Castro Cuban exiles for military service.[4] The purpose was to create a force that would be able to assist in ridding Cuba of the extremism that was engulfing it. This seems at first to have been done on a contingency or standby basis with the actual use of the recruits undecided.

The operation soon became notorious in spite of the secrecy in which its sponsors attempted to shroud it. The nature of the activities and the number of people involved made concealment impossible. I assume that Castro's intelligence service knew of the project within weeks, perhaps within days, of its inception though, of course, the goal and the details of what later became the Bay of Pigs expedition had not yet been determined. It became common knowledge in Havana that summer that the CIA was helping the anti-Castro guerrilla fighters who appeared sporadically in a number of rural areas.

The economic measures in the American program for the overthrow of Castro included the advice given the oil-refining companies in June to refuse to process Soviet crude oil acquired by the Cuban government, the total suspension of Cuba's sugar quota in July, and the removal of key American and Cuban personnel from leading American companies in such a manner as to create serious difficulties for the Cuban economy. These measures are the subject of chapter 16.

A Curious Debate on Sugar

Mrs. Bonsal and I returned to Havana on March 20, 1960, after an absence of two months. The conditions in which the Embassy operated became increasingly dreary and sterile because of the atmosphere created by the mendacious, repetitious, and comprehensively fraudulent anti-Americanism of Castro, Guevara, and Dórticos. I did not share the opinion of some in our press and in the Congress to the effect that the dignity of our country was impaired by the return to his post of the American Ambassador.[5] I thought it important for the reasons earlier set forth that the forms and channels of diplomatic intercourse be maintained. It seemed to me that there was more than an even chance that some critical incident or accident might change the picture completely. Also I continued to be convinced that if the United States adhered to the policy set forth in the President's statement of January 26, it was not only logical but possible that, given time, an effective anti-Castro movement would develop in Cuba.

Soon after my return a remarkable argument about sugar took place. Earlier in the year the American executive had asked the Congress for a grant of discretion in the fixing of sugar quotas, a function that had been a legislative prerogative for a quarter of a century. (The purpose of the request was to give the executive flexibility in reacting to the Cuban situation; Congress did not act until July.)

The fact of the executive request had naturally aroused great interest in Cuba both among the friends and the enemies of the regime. The Foreign Minister, Dr. Roa, asserted that any reduction by the United States in the amount of sugar Cuba could ship to that country would be economic aggression in violation of American commitments as a member of the Organization of American States.[6] Roa had fully absorbed the key Castro doctrine that to the Revolution all is permitted but that those it designates as its enemies have no rights, not even the right of self-defense.

On the other hand, Guevara, in the course of a campaign to defend the deal he and Castro had made with Mikoyan, was arguing that Cuban sugar sales to the United States were undesirable. He proposed to undermine the long-held belief of most Cubans that the presence in Cuba of an efficient sugar industry with a market in the United States for a major share of the product at prices considerably higher than were normally obtainable elsewhere was a vital asset for Cuba—one not lightly to be jeopardized. This Cuban view with which Guevara was now taking issue was the complement of the traditional American concept—one which I fully shared—to the effect that the advantage for Cuba had as its counterpart for the United States the well-tested fact that Cuba was a sure, flexible, and strategically defensible source of most of the sugar the United States in peace or war could not or did not wish to produce on its own soil.

Guevara, in defending the deal made with the Russians in February from charges the Russians had—as indeed they had—driven a hard bargain, said that the critics "never stopped to analyze what amount of slavery the three million tons of our sugar we customarily sell at supposedly preferential prices to the 'Giant of the North' has meant and means for the Cuban people."[7] This statement played into the hands of those in the United States who were beginning to advocate drastic economic measures as a means of "bringing Castro to his senses"; perhaps it was designed to do so.

On April 20 I addressed the annual meeting of the American Chamber of Commerce in Cuba. On the subject of sugar I observed that I would not "participate in the remarkable argument as to whether a reduction in the United States quota for Cuban sugar would constitute economic aggression or whether on the contrary it would represent a decrease in the enslavement of the Cuban people the said quota has been said to signify." I emphasized the great advantage to both countries of the existing sugar arrangement. Though I could not comment on the aspect of the matter that was then before Congress (the grant of discretion to the executive to vary quotas), I expressed the hope that the mutual benefit which both countries had so long derived from the production and the consumption of sugar would be preserved.

The Miró Appointment Amid Brief Calm

In retrospect, these first few weeks following my return to Havana seem relatively relaxed in spite of the sugar controversy and the by now routine scurrilities of the revolutionary leadership. The artificially stimulated hysteria following the *La Coubre* explosion had died down. I was confirmed in my view that the less the United States did to furnish Castro with pretexts—

though he needed none—to play his "Cuba beleaguered by Yankee imperialism" tune the more the attention of the Cuban people might be diverted from the alleged menace from abroad to the eccentric anarchy with which their affairs were being conducted and their rights suppressed at home. Even in some advanced sectors there seemed to be developing an attitude of doubt as to the pace of the Revolution. The frenzied screams about imminent invasion and economic aggression from the United States were falling on increasingly skeptical ears. The Revolution badly needed evidences of active hostility from the United States. Had these been withheld instead of becoming public knowledge before the middle of July, the course of affairs in Cuba might have taken a more palatable direction from our point of view.

During these weeks I saw Roa on routine matters. Toward the end of April he spoke of the possibility of serious talks on the whole range of matters pending between the two governments. Though I expressed polite receptivity, the attitudes of Castro and Guevara made it impossible to take the Minister seriously; there was no follow-up though I reminded Roa of his initiative.

Another development at the end of April was as great a surprise to Roa as it was to me. A request was conveyed directly from Castro's office through the Cuban Embassy in Washington that the United States accept José Miró-Cardona to succeed Ernesto Dihigo (who had resigned) as Cuban Ambassador in Washington. Miró had been Prime Minister during the first six weeks of the Castro regime. He lost his next post, that of Ambassador to Spain, when, as earlier reported, his Spanish counterpart in Havana interrupted a Castro television performance, and the two governments in consequence reduced their reciprocal representation to the chargé level.

Miró's political and legal backgrounds were incompatible with the direction in which the Revolution was moving. His nomination and his willingness to serve seemed equally incongruous. Since his return from Spain in January he had not once been received by Castro nor was he after his appointment to Washington. He and Roa were enemies. (Roa's revolutionary proclivities derived in part from the fact that he had few admirers in the former Cuban establishment.)

My recommendation that Miró be accepted for the Washington post was acted on favorably. I briefed him thoroughly on the sad state of Cuban American relations. He was aghast at what I told him but pledged his best efforts to improve matters. I remember his confiding to me and to a group of my Latin American colleagues his belief that Castro was about to make a radical and favorable change in his policies toward the United States and Latin America and that we could anticipate one of those dramatic metamorphoses characteristic of the Maximum Leader. As the weeks passed Miró became increasingly discouraged. Early in July, after an attempt by President Dórticos to use Miró's prestige and influence in a maneuver designed to increase government control over the University of Havana, he gave up the struggle and sought political asylum in the Argentine Embassy.

The Miró appointment seems to have been part of an opportunistic Castro tactic to placate the Latin American diplomatic representatives in Havana. Those representatives were increasingly concerned at the course of the Revolution and particularly at the deterioration of Cuban American relations. Castro naturally wished to put as much of the onus for that deterioration as possible on American shoulders. I knew that the Argentine Ambassador had suggested the Miró appointment to Castro some weeks earlier; the adoption of the suggestion could be interpreted as evidence of a conciliatory disposition.

Toward mid-May my Latin American colleagues were involved under the spirited leadership of the Argentine Ambassador, Julio Amoedo, in an operation designed to find out whether Castro's Cuba intended to adhere to the principles that made Latin America a part of the democratic world and of Western civilization as contrasted with the totalitarianism of the Soviet Union and of Eastern Europe. The confrontation, if it could be called that, took place at a dinner at which Castro was the guest of honor and the Latin American ambassadors were the hosts. The affair ended on a note of bland frustration. Castro was, however, left in no doubt as to the concerns of the Latin Americans. He was displeased when one of the guests raised the question of "foreign," that is, Communist, influences in the Revolution.

My association with the Latin American diplomats was a most rewarding and pleasant part of my Cuban experience. In addition to the closest and most friendly relations between us individually, it was our custom to lunch together regularly and to exchange information and ideas on the situation in Cuba. My colleagues were unanimous in condemning the suppression of human rights to which the Cuban government was so seriously applying itself. They approved of the policy of moderation and restraint which the Eisenhower administration had heretofore followed. In general—there was lack of unanimity on this point—they were opposed to any exercise of American military or economic power to rectify a situation which many of them were confident would be taken care of by the people of Cuba if left to themselves.

Castro Destroys the Anti-Castro Press

Ironically enough, on the same evening of his appearance before the Latin American ambassadors with their concern for democracy and human freedoms, Castro ordered a major forward step in the assertion of his total authority. The *Diario de la Marina*, the oldest daily newspaper in Havana and one identified with conservative—its enemies said reactionary—interests in political and property questions, was shut down. Under the courageous direction of its editor and part owner, José I. Rivero, the *Diario* had been criticizing the trends and the actions of the revolutionary government. It had long been subjected, in common with all of the independent press, to harassment and interference with government backing from an extremist minority of its employees and workmen. All privately owned papers had been obliged to publish the hostile comments of this minority as a *coletilla* ("little tail") appended to such of their editorials or news dispatches as failed to please the revolutionary element.

The crisis in the case of the *Diario* came when the minority group tore up the forms of an editorial that was to appear the next day and, with the help of thugs supplied by the Prime Minister, closed the plant down after sabotaging it extensively. The gangster-type violence employed was characteristic of Castro's personal style. The other surviving independent daily, *Prensa Libre*, suffered much the same fate a few days later. *Información*, a paper which carried no editorial comment and merely printed news dispatches from the various agencies, was abolished before the year was out, leaving the newspaper field to government concocted and financed sheets.

The owners, editors, and top people of the papers in question behaved as bravely as one could ask. The reader reaction to this deprivation of unofficial news and comment was practically nil. So far as one could judge from the attitude of the public they had served, *Diario de la Marina* and *Prensa Libre* sank amid only the gentlest of ripples.

The absence of serious reaction to Castro's abrogation of the rights for which the Revolution had been fought was not the least surprising and disappointing of the developments of those weeks. Castro had demonstrably betrayed the Revolution and the people who had made it with him. But former President Prío, for example, who might have been regarded as a personification of the democratic aspirations thwarted first by Batista and now by Castro, had not broken publicly with the Maximum Leader. (By mid-summer, however, he concluded that Cuba was no longer a suitable residence for a man of his wealth and background and took his departure—to which Castro interposed no obstacles.)

Castro had indeed rejected constitutional democracy, human rights as understood in the Western world, and the constructive Cuban American relations to which he had earlier pledged himself. But this repudiation of his promises did not cost him any significant part of his support in Cuba, nor did it endanger a predominance unaffected by the contradictory attitudes he has taken over the years on subjects of major importance.

The Cuban Political Scene in May 1960

In May 1960 a Princeton group polled what it described as a representative sample of the Cuban population and reported that 43 percent were *strongly* in favor of Castro, 43 percent in favor, and only 14 percent opposed. Allowing for the fact that this type of operation in the Cuba of those days was bound to be weighted in favor of Castro, I now believe that we in the Embassy, as well as our largely anti-Castro informers, gave the state of affairs shown by this poll less weight in our own evaluations than we should have. We underestimated the degree to which pre-Castro Cuba in most of its manifestations had been rejected by the great majority of the people.

The political opposition to Castro at this time consisted of three elements: Batista's old supporters—largely neutralized because the record of that dictatorship was still fresh in people's minds; the members of the traditional parties, including, but not exclusively, those who had participated in the movement against Batista and had accepted Castro's leadership of that movement without surrendering their political identity; and, finally, those who had been enthusiastic members of Castro's 26th of July movement and had abjured their former political loyalties as had Castro but were now disillusioned at his abandonment of the cause for which they had fought at his side. Then there was a growing opposition consisting of large numbers of formerly influential people unidentified with pre-Castro politics but now seriously alarmed at the threat inherent in the Revolution to their property interests and to their way of life.

This opposition did not within itself generate a willingness to stand up to the Castro-dominated mobs with their subsidized gangster-type leadership and their backing from a flourishing security apparatus. The return to Havana of a prominent politician of earlier days, Aureliano Sánchez-Arango, furnished an instructive illustration of what had become the facts of political life.[8] This man had been a Communist but had later made for himself a respectable place in the politics of the Grau-Prío period (from 1944 to 1952). His old supporters turned out to give him a warm welcome at the airport. For their pains they were terrorized and beaten by government thugs. Señor Sánchez-Arango soon left the country convinced that any normal form of political activity was denied him by the Castro methods and by the absence of any effective mechanism for public debate on the issues of the times.

In my judgment the members of the opposition with the most promise were the men and women who had belonged to Castro's own party or movement in the struggle against Batista and who now found themselves thoroughly disillusioned with the direction of affairs under Castro and Guevara. Such men as Manuel Ray, Humberto Sorí-Marín, Raúl Chibás, and others seemed to have the possibility of eventually forming an opposition to Castro not based on a return to discredited methods and personalities but rather on the creation of a purified and progressive form of representative democracy in Cuba. Some of their conservative contemporaries described the men I have named as advocates of Fidelismo without Fidel; I can only say that under their direction the Cuban people would have been given a freedom of choice denied them under Castro.

During these months the most tangible symptom of opposition to Castro was the rush of Cubans to leave their homeland. This placed a heavy burden on the services of the American Consulate General. The officers and clerks involved deserve the greatest credit for the efficiency and the compassion with which they handled tens of thousands of applications for admission to the United States. The policy, in the American tradition, was one of making as easy as possible the entry into the United States of Cubans fleeing the conditions Castro was creating. The regulations were stretched as far as they would stretch. Castro, for his part, was not sorry to see these people go.

I have sometimes been asked whether this American policy was not a factor in the failure of a real opposition to develop as might have happened had these anti-Castro elements been obliged to remain in Cuba. I think not; the failure had other causes, including the absence of respected leadership and the conviction that somehow the United States would take care of the situation. That conviction had not been weakened when the United States was both preaching and practicing a policy of nonintervention though perseverance in such a policy would have eventually undermined it. As the adoption by the United States of a harsher attitude toward Castro became apparent, reliance on the United States was confirmed. Many of the Cubans who went to the United States in 1960 believed they would soon return to find the threat to their way of life had been radically extirpated by the Americans.

I would not wish to give the impression that there was no overt opposition to Castro during these months. A number of brave men from all ranks of society, including some who had been members of Castro's movement in earlier days, risked life and liberty, and some lost one or the other, fighting the dictatorship. But the overall position was as I have described it. Castro was fast consolidating his security and espionage apparatus and he was encountering little or no opposition.

The flavor of the situation is conveyed in the following exchange I had with a Cuban journalist. He approached me at a reception and said, obviously having reference to the alleged supineness with which the representative of the American government in Cuba was responding to the insults and calumnies being heaped upon his country by Castro and his people; "Mr. Ambassador, you are the most patient man I know." To which I rejoined; "Thank you, my friend, but I can think of many thousands of people within a radius of only a few miles from where you and I are standing who deserve your compliment, if it is one, more than I do."

Castro's demonstrated ability to disregard his earlier democratic promises with no appreciable weakening in his position had whittled away the misgivings of the Cuban Communist party known as the *Partido Socialista del Pueblo* (PSP). As of the spring of 1960 the PSP had achieved a close identification with Castro's Revolution, though its formal recognition of his leadership was delayed until August.[9] It had done missionary work in Moscow and in Peking to stress Castro's potential for the world Communist movement.

The Communists in Cuba, in Russia, and in China were attracted not only by Castro's successes at home. His anti-Americanism placed him in the frontline trenches of the "antiimperialism" so dear to the imperialists in Moscow and Peking. The Cuban Communists were becoming less fearful of the risks inherent in the headlong pace at which Castro was driving his Revolution, as they became aware of the degree to which he was in complete control of the masses. The imminence of an invasion from the north, which Castro at first unscrupulously promoted as an essential element in the maintenance and the extension of his personal authority but which developments starting in March and culminating with the suspension of the sugar quota in July made more plausible, was a further factor in drawing the PSP closer to Castro. Blas Roca, the Secretary General of the party, became a convert to Castro's imminent invasion thesis, though he had previously rejected it.

The evolution of his position led Blas Roca in the spring of 1960 to visit both Peking and Moscow.[10] His purpose was to explain to Mao and to Khrushchev the opportunity available on the doorstep of the United States to further a movement of "national liberation" and to advance the cause of Marxism-Leninism. At the very least much trouble would be made for the United States which could perhaps be forced to attack the movement in a manner calculated, among other things, to take the mind of world opinion off the brutal Soviet performance in Hungary in 1956.

The success of Roca's mission to Moscow was assured by the impact on Khrushchev of the U-2 incident which so drastically evaporated "the spirit of Camp David" and led to the adoption by the Russians of a bitterly aggressive attitude toward the United States—one that was not relaxed until after the missile crisis in the fall of 1962. The restoration of diplomatic relations between Cuba and the Soviet Union was announced in Moscow on May 7 while Roca was there. It was the day after the cancellation of the summit meeting for which Khrushchev and President Eisenhower were already in Paris.

Chapter 16

American Sanctions: Oil and Sugar

In June and July 1960 the United States confronted Castro with situations in the economic field designed to accelerate his downfall. The American measures included the pressing advice given companies having a virtual monopoly of oil refining in Cuba to refuse to handle the crude petroleum the Cuban government was acquiring from the Soviet Union and the refusal to allow the importation into the United States of the sugar unshipped from Cuba under the American quota in effect for 1960. Also during the spring and summer of 1960 there was a concerted removal of key Cuban and American personnel from American companies in Cuba; this was supposed to hamper the functioning of important units of the island economy. This operation was coordinated—to the extent that it was—from New York. These measures were to be complemented, as necessary, to achieve the fall of Castro by United States directed and subsidized covert operations by United States selected Cuban opponents of the regime.

The Refineries Refuse Soviet Crude Oil

In spite of extensive exploration over many decades, Cuba has no significant known petroleum resources. In 1960 and earlier, the importation and refining of crude oil and the distribution of the resultant products, notably gasoline, fuel, and diesel oil, were in the hands of three large companies with worldwide assets: the Standard Oil Company of New Jersey

(Esso), the Texas Company (Texaco)—both American concerns—and the Anglo-Dutch enterprise known as Shell. There was, besides, a much smaller Cuban-owned refinery. The three larger companies did an efficient job in serving the public, but the prices charged and the balance-of-payments impact were question marks in the minds of the revolutionaries now in the saddle.

Although since the days of the Spaniards there had been some refining of crude petroleum at the Belot refinery in Havana (owned by Esso), the great growth of the industry took place during the Batista dictatorship. A decree-law of November 1954 established especially favorable conditions, including tax incentives, with the result that between 1954 and 1957 refining capacity on the island increased sevenfold.[1] Shell built a new refinery in Havana and Texaco did the same in Santiago. Esso's operations in Havana were transformed and greatly expanded. The total investment of over one hundred million dollars was a significant contribution to the public and private development program in which the Batista administration took great pride—much of it justified.

From the revolutionary point of view the refineries were obvious targets for a number of reasons. They had been built during the time of the hated Batista. They were the property of gigantic international corporations. (Standard Oil of New Jersey had gross annual sales worldwide perhaps twenty times greater than the public revenues of Cuba.) They typified exploitation and monopoly in the revolutionary mind. The companies bought their crude oil from their own producing wells in Venezuela at prices which the revolutionaries believed were excessive in comparison with the prices at which other crude oils, including those from the USSR, were obtainable on world markets. The companies were the prisoners of their own rather rigid pricing policies and of the fact that the government of the producing country, in this case Venezuela, was understandably anxious to maintain the pricing system of the companies. Any decrease in prices would involve a reduction of Venezuelan government revenues from the oil industry.

In Cuba, although there were three companies and competition in theory existed, the general belief was that the companies had divided up the market on an agreed basis. The fact that petroleum products had to be bought from large enterprises with foreign identification seemed to many incompatible with the goals of the revolutionary nationalism dominant in Castro's Cuba.

Even before the radical transformation of the regime in November 1959, the government had taken steps indicative of its intention to play a role in the petroleum industry. Thus the small Cuban refinery had been seized or "recuperated" from its owners on the basis that the latter had misappropriated public property. It had been declared state property and constituted the initial unit of the Cuban Institute of Petroleum, a name ominously reminiscent of the National Institute of Agrarian Reform.

The government had also seized the records of the companies involved in exploration for petroleum and had decreed that henceforth if oil were found in Cuba the share of the government would be 60 percent instead of the 10 percent provided in earlier legislation. These two actions paralyzed private exploration work. The government had issued a decree relieving the owners of gasoline stations from the obligation many had assumed to distribute only the products of the companies which had financed the construction of the increasingly elaborate filling stations on the American model being built all over the island. This meant, in the government's view, that the stations would no longer be the victims of the foreign "monopolies" but would be able to distribute national products received from the Cuban Institute of Petroleum.

In the face of this hostile attitude, the companies had done what they could to ingratiate themselves with the new regime and to play down the ingratiating they had perforce done in earlier times. They were leaders in the advance payment of taxes to relieve the treasury's cash shortages in January 1959. Showing a similar consideration for the country's balance-of-payments problems they had allowed their local currency accounts to rise and, after the establishment of exchange controls, had not pressed their demands for dollars to pay for their imports of crude oil. They hoped that the existence of an indebtedness which the government found it hard to liquidate and which was evidence of an understanding attitude on the part of the companies might restrain further unwelcome governmental actions. This hope vanished when Che Guevara took over responsibility for Castro's economic policies in November 1959.

Guevara's hostility toward the oil companies was given scope by the agreement reached with the Soviet Union at the time of Mikoyan's visit in February 1960. Russia was to take a million tons of Cuban sugar per year for five years and was to pay 20 percent of it in dollars and the rest in Soviet goods. This meant that for the first year of the agreement Cuba would have to acquire somewhere in the neighborhood of fifty million dollars worth of Soviet goods if she were to be compensated for her sugar. (I have used the price of 2.78 cents per pound and have applied it to a million Spanish long tons and rounded out the result so as to get an approximate figure indicative of the magnitude of Guevara's problem.) Hitherto Cuba's imports from Russia had been insignificant. Crude oil was an obvious item. Russia had it at prices well below those being paid by the refining companies in Cuba for their own Venezuelan product. A first shipment of Russian oil for the small Cuban refinery was received by the middle of April.[2] But the capacity of that plant was insufficient to permit the absorption of substantial amounts of the Soviet product.

Guevara had already shown an uncooperative attitude to the moderate pleas of the companies that they be granted the dollars owed them for the crude oil they had been importing. By mid-May a balance due of over fifty million dollars had accumulated. Guevara then informed the companies that the only solution of their problem of being paid the dollars due them for the oil they had imported, refined, and sold in Cuba would be for them to accept an amount of crude from Russia during the latter half of the year equivalent to roughly half the amount they would normally have imported from their own sources. In round numbers this amounted to about one million metric tons or seven million barrels. On an annual basis the arrangement involved the importation of some thirty million dollars worth of Soviet crude. (I have arbitrarily taken a price of two dollars per barrel in making this estimate —a price well below that at which Venezuelan crude was being acquired.)

There were many objections to Guevara's proposal. The companies contended that the government could not legally interfere with their right to import crude from sources of their own choosing. They said that the law obliging the companies to refine crude offered them by the government was meant to apply only to the royalty oil of Cuban origin to which the government might become entitled from the exploration concessions it had granted. The companies were probably correct on this point. They also objected to the quality of the Soviet crude and intimated that it would seriously damage refineries built to handle Venezuelan crude unless expensive alterations and adaptations were made.

While the Guevara proposal was under consideration by the companies, the Embassy kept the State Department informed of developments and was

new Ambassador to Cuba
s a rebel officer at the Ha-
airport. (Wide World Pho-

bassador Bonsal presents his credentials to Cuban Foreign Minister Roberto Agramonte. (Wide
rld Photos)

First meeting with Fidel Castro, March 6, 1959. (Wide World Photos)

The American Ambassador with two of Cuba's top political figures—President Osvaldo Dórticos (left) and Foreign Minister Rául Roa (center). (Wide World Photos)

Rául Castro visits the kitchen of the American Embassy during a Fourth of July celebration.

Castro gestures during his lengthy television appearance following the Diaz-Lanz "bombing" of Havana. (Wide World Photos)

DR. FIDEL CASTRO

(Above) Ambassador Bonsal confers with Secretary of State Christian Herter in Washington, January 1960, following a series of anti-American outbursts in Havana. (Wide World Photos)

(Below) Ambassador and Mrs. Bonsal return to Havana, March 1960, after their temporary recall to Washington. (Wide World Photos)

in touch with company representatives. I did not believe that the matter was one in which the Embassy should offer any advice. I considered it to be one between the government of Cuba and companies operating within the jurisdiction of that government. I believed that if the companies considered the government's action to be illegal, they should, nevertheless, do as requested, seeking their remedy in an appeal to the Cuban courts and eventually, if the United States government reached the conclusion that a denial of justice had taken place, in the filing of a diplomatic claim against the Cuban government. It was my impression during May that this was the position the companies had decided to adopt.

However, on the afternoon of Saturday, June 4, I received a visit from the chief executive in Cuba of a major American oil company who had just returned from Washington. He said that he was calling on me at the request of the Assistant Secretary of State for Inter-American Affairs, Mr. Rubottom, in order to bring me up to date on recent developments with regard to the Guevara demand that the refineries in Cuba handle Soviet crude oil. After confirming my impression that until very recently the companies' position had been that of going ahead with the operation under protest and attempting to secure recognition of their rights through the Cuban courts, he added that this position had been predicated on the assumption that the United States government would not wish to take a stand on the matter. This assumption had now proved to be contrary to fact.

My visitor went on to tell me that on the previous day representatives of the two American companies with refineries in Cuba had been summoned to the office of the Secretary of the Treasury, Robert Anderson, and had been informed by the Secretary that a refusal to accede to the Cuban government's request would be in accord with the policy of the United States government toward Cuba and that the companies would not incur any penalties under American antitrust laws should they take a joint stand in this matter. They were further told that the situation was being discussed in London with the Shell company along the same lines. My informant added that there had been a representative of the Department of State present at the meeting conducted by the Secretary of the Treasury. He concluded that the companies had decided to conform their policies to that of their government and that they would refuse the Soviet crude; they understood that the Anglo-Dutch company would follow suit—as indeed it did.

The recommendation made by Mr. Anderson to the companies does not seem to have been discussed beforehand with officials of the Department of State having responsibilities for relations with Cuba. I was reliably informed that a Department official, summoned at the last minute to attend Mr. Anderson's meeting, went to it "completely cold."

To say that I was startled at the news of Mr. Anderson's decision and at the channel through which it was conveyed to me would be putting it mildly. I wrote Mr. Rubottom that while I understood Mr. Anderson's adverse reaction to Guevara's demand that Soviet crude oil be refined in Cuba, I very much hoped that our government knew what it was doing in assuming the responsibility for so serious a challenge to the Cuban Revolution—one which involved the very existence of that revolution. I said that if the Cuban government and its Soviet friends were able to meet the challenge—as in the event they were—the result would be to give the Cuban Revolution a shot in the arm comparable to that which Nasser received when it was demonstrated that the Suez Canal could be operated in spite of the withdrawl of Western pilots—a maneuver counted on to "bring the Egyptian Dictator to his senses." I stressed that what we were doing was to present a situation to the Cuban revolutionaries and their presumably then reluctant Russian friends which involved the fate of the Cuban government.

On June 7 the three companies courteously but firmly, in separate communications so as to give the impression of company decisions independently arrived at, informed the Cuban government that they would not refine the proffered Russian crude. During the following three weeks I assume Guevara was in close consultation with the Russians. The latter solved the problem of finding the tankers to carry Soviet crude from the Black Sea to Cuba in sufficient amounts so that there would be no exhaustion in Cuba's stocks of oil.

After all the necessary arrangements had been made, the Cuban government—beginning on June 29—intervened the three refineries, that is, took over their management "temporarily" and proceeded to refine the Soviet crude which arrived in adequate quantities to cover Cuba's entire requirements instead of the 50 percent which Guevara had originally projected. Russian technicians readily overcame the difficulties alleged to be inherent in running the Russian product through the refineries in Cuba. There was no interruption in the availability of refinery products to consumers in Cuba. The Cuban Revolution had won a great victory and had had a powerful ally thrust into its arms.

The Cuban Sugar Quota Suspended

On July 6, a week after the intervention of the refineries, President Eisenhower announced that the balance of Cuba's quota for the supply of sugar to the United States for the year 1960 was suspended. Some writers have regarded this action as in the nature of a reprisal for the intervention of the refineries. I do not believe this was the case. The suspension of the sugar quota was a major element in the program for the overthrow of Castro.

I was notified of the decision to suspend the quota only a few hours before it was made public. I was deeply disturbed. I had anticipated that, in using the discretionary powers obtained from the Congress, the administration might have given some indication of its displeasure at the injuries done to American interests by the Cuban government and have reduced the quota or at least have done away with Cuba's opportunity to share in the reallotment of the unfilled quotas of other producing areas. An excellent summary of the many injuries received by American interests at Castro's hands had been prepared under the direction of the Embassy's able Economic Counselor, Eugene Gilmore; it would have justified a stiff American retaliation.[3] But the complete suspension of the quota, following hard upon Congress's granting of the discretionary powers that made it possible, seemed to me most unwise. In agreement with my principal associates in the Embassy, I sent a telegram to Washington to the effect that the contemplated action would nullify the benefits reaped from our previous policies of restraint and nonintervention. But the wheels in Washington had already moved too far to be reversed. With this action I contend that the United States turned its back on thirty years of statesmanship in the Latin American field.

Ernest Hemingway, as quoted in A. E. Hotchner's memoir, had put the case against cutting the quota in concise terms earlier in the year when he remarked: "I just hope to Christ the United States doesn't cut the sugar quota. That would really tear it. It will make Cuba a gift to the Russians."[4] And now the gift had been made.

In an intemperate speech just before the President's suspension of the quota, Castro had announced that action against the quota by the American authorities would cost Americans in Cuba down to the nails in their shoes. He did his best to carry out this threat. He had issued a decree described as a Law of Nationalization authorizing expropriations of American properties at the discretion of the Cuban executive.[5] Compensation was to be paid on the basis of Cuban government valuations from a fund created by the proceeds of sales of sugar to the United States in excess of three and one half million Spanish long tons at a price of at least 5.75 cents per pound. The victims were to receive thirty-year bonds bearing 2 percent interest with service contingent on the aforementioned fund. Since the fund would have no resources at all until American purchases of Cuban sugar reached amounts not attained since World War II at prices well above those then prevailing under United States sugar policy, it was clear that the intent of the law was the confiscation without compensation of American properties if Castro was displeased at the quota action of the American government.

I had earlier urged that whatever action the executive planned to take under the discretionary powers it was seeking from the Congress should be discussed with the Cubans at the highest possible level, that is, with Castro, before adoption so that the Cubans could be made aware that the proposed action was in retaliation for specific anti-American measures of the Cuban government. I thought the Cubans should be given a final opportunity to consider the situation they had created and to ponder the possibility that a different course of action on their part would better serve their interests. Such an approach by the United States would have very much improved the posture of the United States with opinion in Cuba and in the Latin American countries. I deprecated the prevailing spirit in Washington which was that of "taking a good solid slap at Cuba."[6] But, of course, I then had no notion that a complete cutting off of Cuban sugar was in the cards.

In his proclamation President Eisenhower explained the suspension of the quota in terms of the necessity of insuring the American people's supply of sugar, which was endangered by threats resulting from conditions in Cuba under Castro.[7] There seems to me no doubt, however, that the discretionary powers under which the suspension was decreed were extracted from the Congress on the basis that they were a necessary weapon to overthrow Castro and defeat Communist penetration of the territory of America's former staunch friend and ally. (The committee sessions at which the matter was discussed were secret.)

The publicly stated reason for the suspension of the quota, that is, the danger to the American sugar supply presumably resulting from the decreased efficiency of the industry under Castro and INRA, lacked plausibility. It was not reasonable to suppose that Cuba would voluntarily give up the

American market or that Russia would wish to compete with the United States for Cuban sugar as long as the flow of sugar to the United States was uninterrupted. There might, of course, be moderate decreases in Cuban production because of revolutionary conditions. There might even be increases in Russian takings above the one million tons a year contracted in February. But as of July 1960 the availability of Cuban sugar to the American market in the quantities that had prevailed over the period since World War II did not seem in jeopardy from any decision which the Cubans or the Russians might be expected to take under the conditions that existed prior to the President's suspension of the quota.

The immediate loss to Cuba as a result of the President's action was the seven hundred thousand short tons remaining unshipped from Cuba's initial quota for 1960 (about one-quarter of the total quota) plus another two hundred thousand tons representing the probable reallocation to Cuba of deficits in the production of other areas having quotas in the American market. The value of this sugar was in excess of ninety million dollars; had the Russians not come to the rescue, its loss would have been a serious blow to Cuba.

But the blow to Cuban American relations was far more grievous. The keystone in the arch of those relations had been the interdependence resulting from the fact that for generations hundreds of thousands of Cubans had earned their living supplying sugar to the American market—at premium prices since 1934—and that tens of millions of Americans had consumed the product of Cuban plantations and mills. Now all this was destroyed by a stroke of the Presidential pen—a stroke which had done for Castro something it might have taken him years to do for himself, indeed something he might not have been able to encompass at all in the face of resistance from his own people to the destruction by their own government of the major source of their prosperity and of the welfare of their country. Furthermore, I do not believe the Russians would have taken sugar from Cuba which the United States was prepared to purchase. The opportunity we now presented them with was one I am convinced they would gladly at that time have done without.

Chapter 17

Revolutionary Progress and American Frustration

THE United States government measures described in chapter 16 went far beyond the retaliation warranted by the injuries American citizens and interests had up to that time suffered at Castro's hands. Such retaliation should have been roughly proportionate to those injuries rather than evidence of an intention to overthrow the regime through an exercise of superior force. Admittedly, even justified American retaliation would have led to Cuban counterretaliation and so on with the prospect that step by step the same end result would have been attained as was in fact achieved. But the process would have lasted far longer; measured American responses might have appeared well deserved to an increasing number of Cubans, thus strengthening Cuban opposition to the regime instead of, as was the case, greatly stimulating revolutionary fervor, leaving the Russians no choice but to give massive support to the Revolution and fortifying the enervating belief among anti-Castro Cubans that the United States was rapidly moving to liberate them.

The Soviet Union Driven Into Castro's Arms

Prior to the revelation of the American decisions on oil and sugar Russian scepticism as to how much of an asset Castro's erratic personality and leadership could represent for Soviet policy in the Western Hemisphere was fully justified. The Russians did not then think of the Cuban Revolution as Marxist-Leninist, though they applauded Castro's hostility toward "imperialism." The Soviet Union did not then, in my judgment, contemplate replacing the United States as Cuba's major trading partner and economic patron though Moscow was willing to help Castro harass the United States. I do not believe the Russians wished for a confrontation with the United States over Cuba. I suggest that until July 1960 the Moscow bureaucrats advised Castro to proceed with moderation in his dealings with Washington.

Now, however, the Russians were faced with the abandonment of the policy of restraint the United States had pursued toward Castro. The Soviet Union had the choice of furnishing the oil Cuba needed and buying the sugar Cuba had formerly sold to the United States or of letting the Cuban Revolution perish from economic strangulation. It was inevitable that a world power engaged in a global confrontation with America would decide to come to Castro's rescue.

The Soviet Union's assumption of responsibility for Cuba's economic welfare gave the Russians a politico-military stake in Cuba. Increased arms shipments from the Soviet Union and Czechoslovakia enabled Castro to strengthen his rapidly expanding armed forces. And the Russian attitude so resolved the remaining doubts of the Cuban Communist party that it formally recognized Castro's leadership in August of that year though it did not claim him as a party member.[1]

As for Castro himself, I believe that he was genuinely shocked at the finality of the President's action in suspending the Cuban sugar quota. He had shared the conventional wisdom about the irreplaceability of Cuban sugar in the American market and the improbability of Russia as a satisfactory substitute for the United States in the Cuban economy. Rather than a sweeping American initiative in terms of economic sanctions, he had anticipated an eventual American intervention by American armed forces in support of a puppet regime made up of his Cuban enemies—a regime against which he and his supporters would wage a long and eventually successful guerrilla struggle. He had used this threat of an American invasion to rally his supporters, to build up his defense and security apparatus, and to justify, in the name of a national emergency, the accelerated suppression of the liberties of his fellow Cubans.

Castro's goal was the elimination of the American presence in Cuba. The intensity of his feelings on the subject was pathological. The bulwarks of that hated presence were the American investments, the quota for Cuban sugar in the American market, and the trade relations between the two countries. Now suddenly the initiatives of the American government had created for him conditions vastly more favorable for the rapid completion of his program than the piecemeal attacks on American interests to which he would have remained reduced in the absence of those initiatives. I cannot avoid the conclusion that Castro and Guevara warmly welcomed the fact that the reluctant and cautious Russians had been forced into the Revolution's own warmly welcoming arms by the drastic actions of the Americans.

Increasing numbers of Castro's fellow citizens, including both his friends and his enemies, became convinced that the American economic measures would soon be supplemented in the politico-military field. The policy on which the American government had embarked required the complete overthrow of the Cuban Revolution at an early date, if that policy were to make sense in the eyes of these Cuban observers. Meanwhile Cuba had been dumped on Moscow's doorstep by the United States and Mother Russia, pending developments, had no choice but to feed the foundling.

Khrushchev's Rockets

President Eisenhower's total suspension of Cuba's sugar quota caught Castro and Khrushchev by surprise—to say nothing of the American Ambassador in Havana! They were unprepared for anything so drastic. Castro's immediate reaction was to extract a maximum of political advantage from what he plausibly defined as large-scale economic aggression designed to destroy him. He interpreted this American decision to mean that the military attack he expected from the United States would come sooner rather than later. He announced for the tenth of July a monster rally at which he would lead his people in protest.

Khrushchev was now confronted with far more than he had bargained for in February when he had allowed Mikoyan to make trouble for the Americans in Cuba. The Russian sugar economy would have to be profoundly readjusted so that the Soviet Union could replace the United States as an importer of Cuban sugar under conditions that would permit the Cuban Revolution to survive. This would require weeks of study, action, and negotiation. The Soviet Union would need to evaluate future American policy toward Cuba and the risks involved in supporting Castro before long-term commitments could be made.

But in the field of propaganda Khrushchev had a facile response to the American threat to Cuba's well-being. The Russians had often made points with their supporters by means of empty atomic threats. "Massive retaliation" was a game at which two could play. On July 9, three days after President Eisenhower's sugar proclamation and the day before Castro's protest meeting, Khrushchev announced: "The USSR is raising its voice and extending a helpful hand to the people of Cuba. . . . Speaking figuratively, in case of necessity, Soviet artillerymen can support the Cuban people with rocket fire." From the point of view of the United States this ambiguous statement was a welcome diversion from the hitherto dominant issue of economic aggression by the United States against Cuba. The Russian rocket threat against the leading power of the Western world stole the headlines from the American sugar offensive against Cuba.

Castro was furious at Khrushchev's rocket-rattling.[2] It was a cruel downgrading of his struggle for the political and economic independence of his country. The Soviet leader had made it clear that he thought the fate of Cuba now depended upon the will and ability of the Soviet Union to "rocket" the United States and not upon the will, the courage, and the fanaticism of the Cuban people united around their Maximum Leader. The American attack Castro had anticipated might now be prevented by Khrushchev's threat and not defeated by Castro's valor and leadership. This was the first of the bitter pills his Russian friends have forced him to swallow.

Khrushchev's threat cut the ground from under Castro's monster rally scheduled for the following day, the tenth of July. Castro, either actually or diplomatically ill, did not attend. When the assembled crowd found that the major attraction was to be President Dórticos, it drifted away in large numbers. The gathering was lacking in the glamor and the fervor Castro alone could produce.

Castro followed the proceedings on television. He realized that his Revolution was in trouble. This was its first clear loss of drive. Castro was, I believe, highly irritated at his Russian friends, but he moved quickly to repair the damage they had done and to do so without offending them since his fate was now in their hands.

On the evening of the mass meeting he had not attended, Castro made a fifty-minute television appearance, speaking from his alleged sickbed. Khrushchev had already helped him to bring public attention back to the theme of economic aggression by sending him that same day an offer to buy the sugar which the United States had rejected for 1960 (though at the world-market price which was considerably below the American price and with payment largely in Russian goods). In dealing with the rocket matter, Castro emphasized the absolutely spontaneous nature of the Khrushchev statement, thus divorcing himself from any responsibility for bringing Russia into the Cuban picture at the politico-military level—a prospect that was still repugnant to many of his supporters. Then, however, he forced the pace of Russian involvement by treating the Khrushchev statement not as a figurative or symbolical one directed against the United States but as a specific commitment made by Russia to the Cuban Revolution in the event of an armed attack or threat of an attack from the United States. (Two years later he was to escalate this alleged commitment in a manner that led his overconfident Russian allies to a serious defeat and gave Castro a galling demonstration of his own place in the world of big-power confrontations.)

Castro's Wholesale Nationalizations

In spite of his superheated oratory Castro did not at once invoke his so-called Law of Nationalization to confiscate American properties in Cuba in retaliation for the suspension of the sugar quota. I hoped he was holding his hand in part because of a meeting of the Foreign Ministers of the American republics scheduled for the following month in San José, Costa Rica. Castro might, I thought, wish the Cuban position at that meeting to be as nearly as possible that of an innocent victim seeking redress from gross economic aggression by the United States.

I believed that the American position at the forthcoming meeting could stand some strengthening. Moscow's rocket-rattling and the injection of the Soviet Union into the political problems of the Western Hemisphere had served to divert attention from the spectacle of a confrontation between Cuba and the United States. But the reactions to Castro's anti-American actions and provocations was quite different in public opinion and even in some official opinion in the other American republics than it was on the banks of the Potomac. I believed that the American position at the forthcoming meeting would be helped by a conciliatory gesture.

Also—entirely aside from the tactics of inter-American politics—I favored a last effort to salvage or at least to preserve for a few weeks or months longer what was left of the American presence in Cuba. To gain time in which favorable developments might occur seemed well worth a serious effort.

I, therefore, made an informal recommendation that Washington indicate a willingness to propose a negotiating position even though negotiation with Castro seemed beyond the realm of the possible. The basis of such a position might be the expression of a willingness on the part of the United States, in spite of the wiping out of the balance of the 1960 quota, to contemplate taking some sugar from Cuba in 1961. No announcement had yet been made of American policy for that year; the President retained discretionary authority to fix the Cuban quota at any level he saw fit below the maximum provided in current sugar legislation.

My proposal reflected my conviction that the economic pressures available to the United States were not apt to bring Castro to his knees, since the Soviets were capable of meeting Cuban requirements in such matters as oil and sugar. I believed that the Cuban government was doomed by its own disorganization and incompetence and by the growing disaffection of an increasing proportion of the Cuban people. (In the absence of peremptory American pressures with consequent acceleration of revolutionary action and fanaticism, this belief might have proved sound.) I referred, although with skepticism, to the rumors of a bitter power struggle in the Castro entourage; this involved a Guevara drive to exclude others, including Raúl Castro, from Castro's inner circle. I concluded that it was vitally important that the fall of the regime appear due mainly to its own shortcomings and not to the application of economic sanctions by the United States.

I recommended that prior to any announcement of the action to be taken by the United States with regard to Cuban sugar in 1961, I be authorized to approach the Cuban government in an attempt to restore some semblance of reason and mutual benefit to the relations between the two countries. After rehearsing the course of these relations and the manifold injuries inflicted by the Cuban regime on legitimate American interests, I would propose the establishment of a joint claims commission to which the Cuban government would make available annually a negotiable sum of money for the payment of adjudicated claims. My plan included a method for settling differences, possibly through arbitration. In return, the United

States would commit itself to the establishment of a negotiable sugar quota from which, in part at least, the Cuban government would find the resources needed to finance the settlement of American claims.

In conclusion I pointed out that, although the Cuban government would probably reject such a proposal, the fact it had been made would help the United States with both Cuban and hemispheric opinion. I stressed the importance of a serious effort by the United States to arrest the disastrous destruction of American economic interests in Cuba and of the American trading position. It was demonstrably futile to suppose that these economic assets abandoned or destroyed by the United States were not readily susceptible of being restored by the Russians so far as the requirements of the Revolution were concerned.

In the Washington mood of those days I recognized that my proposal had only the faintest of chances of being considered at all.[3] Even those faint chances were destroyed when, on the night of August fifth, at a youth meeting in a local stadium and in an atmosphere of hysterical enthusiasm, Castro announced the nationalization of all thirty-six American sugar mills, the two oil refineries already intervened, and the two utilities—the telephone company, intervened for over a year, and the electric light and power company. This was a clean sweep of the key American properties. Others would follow in short order. In the language of the Revolution, a major step in the emancipation of Cuba from American domination had been taken.

These initial nationalizations were followed by others covering all American properties on the island.[4] Then it was the turn of the Cuban capitalists. By mid-October properties used for productive purposes had largely been socialized if they were of any significance in the economic picture. The series of events stimulated by the American adoption of a hard-nosed economic policy toward Cuba produced the elimination of significant private property on the island in little more than three months.

The actions of the Cuban government against American interests were vigorously protested in notes eloquent and erudite which it was my duty to present and which were answered in notes strident and intemperate. But the writers of the notes on both sides realized that they were not contributing to the settlement of matters which both governments had entrusted to the kind of tests with which the international lawyers and the diplomatic drafting officers had little to do.

The nationalizations strengthened the Revolution materially and in

"Don't just stand around—go out and confiscate something!"
(Drawing by Alan Dunn; © 1960 The New Yorker Magazine, Inc.)

other ways. They eliminated from important jobs a large number of Cubans and Americans identified with private enterprise and with democratic concepts and turned these jobs over to ardent revolutionaries to whom power and prestige now belonged. The successful looting of the economy both from the point of view of material assets and from that of positions of influence gave the Revolution a significant forward thrust.

These drastic Cuban actions against American property and American trade might have taken place even in the absence of the actions on the American side I have described. I do not believe that a continuation of the policies of nonintervention, nonaggression, and restraint which I had advocated would have changed the policies on which Castro and Guevara were bent. But it would have made the implementation of those policies very much more difficult in that the Cuban government would have had to be on the offensive against American and Cuban private interests instead of appearing to react defensively to American actions designed to overthrow the Revolution. The whole process which was completed between the end of June and the beginning of October 1960 might have taken several times as long. It might have taken place in an atmosphere of declining rather than, as was the case, of rising revolutionary fervor. Cuban and American assets of value to the anti-Castro cause would have been preserved much longer. An effective resistance to Castro could conceivably have had time to grow up. For a longer period of time, conditions would have been more favorable for one of those accidents or incidents that would have changed the whole face of affairs. A continued American policy of moderation would have stimulated friction and frustration in the revolutionary ranks.

The Foreign Ministers of the Americas Deal with Castro

The Foreign Ministers of the American republics met at San José on August 25, nearly three weeks after Castro's sweeping nationalizations of the major American private properties in Cuba. The United States delegation was led by the Secretary of State, Christian Herter. There were two questions on the agenda: first, how to cope with Trujillo, the Dominican "Benefactor," who had engineered and financed an attempt to murder President Rómulo Betancourt of Venezuela, and second, the degree to which the Cuban situation represented an unacceptable Communist penetration in the hemisphere. The United States cooperated with Venezuela and others in the condemnation of Trujillo. But the meeting was able to find no significant area of agreement between the United States and the other delegations as to Castro's Cuba and what to do about it.

The American delegation presented a resolution condemning the Cuban government both for having denied representative democracy to the people of Cuba, thus violating the resolution which the Foreign Ministers of the American republics, including Castro's Dr. Roa, had so cheerfully signed at Santiago only a year earlier, and for having admitted and encouraged the penetration of Cuba by international communism thus going counter to the resolution Secretary Dulles had persuaded the Caracas meeting to adopt in 1954. Although the United States reaffirmed its commitment to nonintervention and its determination not to use its troops to attack Cuba, it soon became clear that the American resolution lacked adequate support.

Many of the other delegations were more concerned at the political strength in their own countries of widespread sympathy for what were then regarded as the renovationary aspects of Castroism with its vindication of what had generally been considered to be a peculiarly fragile and incomplete sovereignty than they were at the perils of international communism so clear to the American delegation. Also since the United States had already presented the Cuban Revolution with situations, notably in the matter of oil imports and sugar exports, from which it was only rescued by the Russians, the American position on the cherished doctrine of nonintervention—including nonaggression in the economic sense—was weaker with some of the other delegations than it would have been in the absence of these actions.

Eventually the American delegation had to settle for a resolution that did not even mention Cuba. It was passed by a vote of nineteen to nothing, with Mexico abstaining, after Dr. Roa, having poured forth a stream of denunciation and vituperation more harmful than not to his cause, flounced himself and his delegation out of the meeting. The resolution strongly condemned "intervention or the threat of intervention by an extra-continental power" as well as all attempts by the "Sino-Soviet powers to exploit the political, economic or social situations of American states for their own ends" and pronounced any form of totalitarianism to be irreconcilable with the inter-American system. The resolution also viewed with disapproval some practices in violation of cherished inter-American dogma of which the United States—though not mentioned—was considered guilty by some of those present.[5]

The achievement of even this result had cost the United States and other like-minded delegations a tremendous effort. The fact that the United States was then rapidly moving toward the Alliance for Progress concept so far as economic assistance to the other American republics was concerned undoubtedly helped. (At Bogotá the following month the United States pledged half a billion dollars in such assistance.)

In terms of American hopes the outcome at San José was a serious disappointment. The Mexican delegate who had abstained announced that the resolution was not aimed at Cuba. The Foreign Ministers of Venezuela and Peru, although they had been instructed by their governments to sign the resolution for which their delegations had voted, refused to do so and had to be replaced by junior members of those delegations at the final ceremony.

Castro chose to regard this mild and ineffective resolution, this embodiment of the frustrations of the United States in dealing with him and with the other American republics, as an intolerable and unacceptable insult at the hands of the "imperialists" and their puppets in the Organization of American States. Early in September he issued his "Declaration of Havana" as a reply to the "Declaration of San José."[6] This lengthy document, a compilation of the more virulent themes dear to antiimperialism over many generations, was "passed by acclamation" at a mammoth mass meeting in Havana early in September. It accused any Latin American government that was not hostile to the United States of betraying its own people.

Castro unblushingly asserted that the approval of this declaration by his followers represented the purest sort of democratic process—one reminiscent of that pursued in the assemblies of the citizens of the ancient Greek cities. Along with members of my staff I watched the affair over television. Any hardy soul in the vast crowd who had ventured even so much as to ask a question about some detail of the poorly drafted, mendacious, and prolix document, much less object to it, would have been torn limb from limb. Few greater farces have been perpetrated, even by Castro, in the name of popular participation in the governing process.

It is worth recalling that during the fall of 1960 the leaders of the Cuban Revolution (except Guevara) continued bitterly to resent suggestions that their movement was Communist dominated.[7] Castro's confession that he was a Marxist-Leninist, with its implication that he had always been one, was over a year in the future. The fact that Cuba's "liberation" from the American presence would involve an oppressive dependence on the Soviet Union and an onerous involvement in the Soviet bloc was only dimly, if at all, perceived by Castro and his inner circle. I speculate that the Maximum Leader was counting on a sweeping victory for his movement in the rest of the continent. He perhaps visualized a status for himself in Latin America similar to that achieved by Nasser in the Arab world, a status that would guarantee Soviet help without Soviet domination.

No doubt Castro was fully and currently informed of the CIA-directed recruiting, financing, arming, and training of his Cuban enemies for action against his Revolution. That summer and fall he had little difficulty in destroying a few desperately brave guerrilla fighters on Cuban soil in spite of the assistance they had received in the form of arms drops generally attributed to the CIA. He can hardly have imagined that these limited activities would prove to be the major hostile action contemplated by the United States in the military field. He was still preparing for the all-out invasion by, and the long guerrilla struggle against, the Marines and their "mercenaries." His confidence in his eventual victory reflected his faith in his own talents as a guerrilla fighter and his absorption of the theories of antiimperialism.

At home, however, and partly because his opponents believed that the United States would move effectively to their rescue, Castro's problems were minimal. His confiscation in October of 186 major Cuban business enterprises, thus completing the virtual elimination of socially significant private property in Cuba, produced discontent but not a sign of effective resistance. The passivity of the former possessing classes was startling. The traditional structure of law and property that had seemed so firm only two years earlier had crumbled before the words of Castro much as the walls of Jericho are said to have done before the trumpets of Joshua. The Revolution was vastly encouraged by the demonstrated impotence of the old order. The dispossessed and their friends believed that the United States would soon set things in order again. The rush to leave Cuba grew apace.

Chapter 18

The End of My Mission and Electoral Politics at Home, October 1960

The Trade Embargo

ON the nineteenth of October the United States prohibited exports to Cuba except for nonsubsidized foodstuffs, medicines, and medical supplies.[1] These exceptions, as well as imports from Cuba, were to be banned within a few months. The stated purpose of the measure was to defend the economic interests of the United States against the discriminatory, aggressive, and injurious economic policies of the Castro regime. This is the origin of the "blockade" from which Castro has extracted so much propaganda mileage.

The embargo was a recognition of the fact that the basis for the conduct of trade between the two countries had been destroyed by the action of their governments. The embargo was not an action in a vacuum by the United States, the cancellation of which would restore a *status quo* acceptable to both parties. It was rather a final step in a series of actions taken by each government. The embargo caused the Cuban revolutionaries and their new friends some inconvenience, especially in the early months of its enforcement. But it did not prevent Cuba from obtaining through third parties, especially Canada, a part of the imports formerly bought in the United States. Nor have American attempts to secure the cooperation of its friends and allies in Western Europe and elsewhere in supporting the embargo been successful. Castro's ability to buy goods of the kind and quality needed in Cuba has been curtailed more by his inability to stimulate Cuban export earnings and by low prices for world-market sugar in some years than by the American embargo.

The measure has been a godsend to Castro. For the past ten years he has blamed on what he calls the American blockade of Cuba the shortages, the rationings, the breakdowns, the incompetencies, the inefficiencies, and even some of the unfavorable weather conditions that have afflicted the Cuban people. As the threat of invasion from the United States has receded and has seemed less plausible even to Cuban audiences, the embargo has been used to keep alive the legend of the American menace and thus to stimulate the beleaguered-citadel mentality on which Castro still relies so heavily for the maintenance of his own authority.

My Final Weeks in Havana

I was permanently recalled to Washington in late October. Seldom has a diplomatic mission functioned in the circumstances that prevailed during my final weeks in Cuba. The government of the country I represented was constantly being held up by their rulers to the people of the country to which I was accredited as the incarnation of all evil—past, present, and future. Property of citizens of the United States valued at hundreds of millions of dollars had been stolen by the Cuban regime under circumstances that recognized to the despoiled no shadow of legal right or recourse. The government I represented had done its best to impair the economy and trade of the country to which I was accredited. It was an open secret that the government I represented was hastening the training and the arming of exiled Cuban citizens in order to contribute to the forcible overthrow of the government with which I was maintaining a semblance of diplomatic relations.

To top this off, members of my staff certified to the Cuban government as entitled to diplomatic immunity were detected by the Cuban authorities in activities such immunity is not supposed to cloak.[2] Though the activities in question were of a relatively trivial nature—one of them had to do with bugging the offices of the Communist Chinese News Agency—much was made of them by the now wholly official mass media in Cuba. The resultant excitement added to the sense of hostility and tension Castro was so eager to intensify.

Obviously diplomatic relations under such conditions could not last indefinitely. Yet I believed it desirable on our side to prolong them. Castro's own position seemed to me shaky in spite of the fanaticism of many of his supporters. There was talk of growing resistance to him. The frequent extravagances in his behavior, the disorganization that surrounded him, the neglect of the simplest sort of precautions—all these made him seem a very poor risk indeed. (But the law of probability, like most other laws in Cuba, was suspended!)

There were still practical reasons for maintaining relations with the Cuban government. Although since July American citizens had been advised by their government to leave Cuba, there remained hundreds of them on the island. Their welfare was a concern of the Embassy which could at least serve as a means of communication with Washington if the vicious anti-American propaganda in which the regime was indulging should place the lives of these people in jeopardy. The fear of mob outrages against our fellow citizens was constantly in the minds of all of us at the Embassy. (On the other hand, it seems reasonable to suppose that Castro and his people, in spite of their verbal excesses, were still reluctant to offer as a motive for the expected American invasion the protection of the lives of Americans because the Cuban authorities were unable or unwilling to guarantee their safety.)

In addition to the residents there were still numbers of American transients—businessmen and journalists principally. These people often got into trouble with the authorities either through their own imprudence or more often because of the arbitrariness and the hostility of the Cuban police and plainclothesmen. The Consul in charge of attending to these protection cases was Denny Kessler, one of the ablest, most energetic, and resourceful Foreign Service officers I have known. His death at an early age deprived the service of a promising and devoted officer.

The maintenance of American consular services in Cuba was also justified by the needs of the thousands of Cubans desiring to leave the paradise Castro was promising them and to seek refuge in the United States. A long line of applicants formed every morning and extended for blocks in the neighborhood of the Embassy office building. It was often photographed by American correspondents to the annoyance of the Cuban authorities who, however, photographed it for police purposes.

My principal official function during those final weeks was to present notes protesting the various Cuban depredations of American properties. I do not remember having seen Roa during this period; he was either at the United Nations or traveling about. His understudy was one Carlos Olivares who had risen rapidly in the bureaucracy because of his sympathy with pre-vailing trends.[3] He had been private secretary to President Urrutia and was reported to have fabricated some of the evidence with which Castro destroyed his own choice for the post of President of Cuba. My calls on Señor Olivares were unpleasant experiences because there was completely lacking between us that minimum of mutual confidence essential to fruitful diplomacy.

An opportunity for the exercise of revolutionary bureaucratic ingenuity —presumably by Olivares—was afforded when Castro went to the United States in late September to attend the General Assembly of the United Nations. This was the occasion when the exhibitionism and the extravagances of Castro and his troupe helped create the atmosphere in which Khrushchev took off his shoe and with it thumped his desk at the General Assembly. Castro's security in the United States was a delicate and difficult problem. There had been shooting affrays in New York between his partisans and his enemies in the course of which a stray bullet from the gun of a Castroite thug took the life of a little girl from Venezuela.[4] For the sake of his own safety, Castro was asked to confine his movements to a specified area in Manhattan. He chose to consider the restriction highly insulting, though it in no way interfered with his attendance at the United Nations which was the sole known purpose of his trip to a country which he made a practice of vilifying and slandering.

Soon after the restriction on Castro's movements in New York had been announced, I received official word that my own movements in Havana would be limited so as to permit me to travel from my house to my office and very little besides. This seemed silly and petty since nothing had happened in Havana to change the nature of my activities or the risks to which I was exposed—though if anything had happened to Castro in New York, my chances of escaping attack in Havana would have been poor.

During this difficult period my relations with my Latin American and with my Western European colleagues as well as with the Canadian Ambassador were especially close and helpful. I have already indicated the importance to me of the regular exchanges with the Latin Americans. I shall always remember with gratitude the many proofs of friendship which I received from these distinguished and able members of the profession to which I was proud to belong.

But neither the antics of the burgeoning Castroite bureaucracy nor the warmth of my relations with most of my colleagues could distract my attention from the sad events of those weeks. The acceleration of the revolutionary pace was causing the departure of many Cubans and Americans who had contributed and could under democratic circumstances have continued to contribute to the economic and social progress of the community of which they had so long been a part. It was distressing to see homes broken up and careers, both useful and successful, terminated. The resulting gaps in the country's human resources will take a generation to fill. We Americans have profited from the integration into our society of thousands of able and constructive people. Cuba has been drained of thousands of its most valuable citizens.

A heartbreaking experience stands out in my memory of those final weeks in Havana. Three young American adventurers were captured only hours after landing on Cuban soil with a guerrilla band. They were armed and there could be no doubt of their intention to make war on the Castro regime. A peremptory drumhead proceeding condemned them to death; the sentence was to be carried out in hours. I could do nothing for these Americans through formal channels. An intercession by the American Ambassador in favor of men whom Cuban officials believed, not implausibly, to have engaged in activities of a type notoriously sponsored and financed by the CIA would have done the prisoners more harm than good.

I consulted with the Papal Nuncio, Monsignor Luis Centoz, an admirable and venerable figure with considerable diplomatic skills. I found him disposed to intercede with the authorities on humanitarian grounds. These young men had only been trying to do against Castro, and for comparable reasons, what Castro had done against Batista and for which he had been formally tried, imprisoned, and later amnestied. The Nuncio agreed that he would endeavor to secure a proper trial that would give the prisoners an opportunity to make a defense and perhaps permit passions to cool. We hoped that the outcome of such a trial might be imprisonment rather than execution. The Nuncio's efforts, in spite of his zeal, his sincerity, and his prestige, proved fruitless. As a last resort I wrote President Dórticos a confidential letter disclaiming any intention of passing on the merits of the cases but appealing to the President's humanitarian sentiments and imploring him to delay the carrying out of the death sentences long enough to give the young men an opportunity to prepare and present their defenses. My letter went un-answered. The three were shot.

In spite of the conditions I have described, Mrs. Bonsal and I learned with real regret on October 18 that the Secretary of State had decided to re-call me to the United States "on extended consultation" meaning in effect that I would not be returning to my post. I have given the reasons for which I thought we could have put up with the situation for a few weeks or months longer. We hated to leave the staff and friends with whom we had endured so much. The American officers and clerks deserved the commendations that were heaped upon them. In addition to being faced with the discom-forts inherent in the state of Cuban American relations, they had been con-fronted months earlier with the Department's decision that the dependents of American official personnel should depart from Cuba. As of late Septem-ber, Mrs. Bonsal and one other officer's wife, who was working as a secretary in the Embassy, were the only family members left in Cuba. I must also pay tribute to the Cuban personnel that worked so hard and so faithfully during those difficult days and weeks especially. Their loyal goodwill was beyond praise.

The Secretary's message expressed the hope that I would serve tempo-rarily as the United States representative on the Council of the Organization of American States, a position that had become vacant on the resignation of Ambassador John C. Dreier who had filled it with distinction and devotion for many years.

Mrs. Bonsal and I sailed from Havana for West Palm Beach on October 28 accompanied by our good friend, my faithful and highly efficient secre-tary, Viola Keskinen. The only jarring note was some good-natured, rather sheepish shouting of the regime's slogan "¡Cuba si! Yanquis no!" by the workers on a neighboring dock. We were seen off by the representatives of friendly countries, by the American press contingent in Havana, by the mem-bers of our splendid official family, and by a number of old friends.

Cuba in the 1960 American Election

Mrs. Bonsal and I had left Cuba ten days before the American presiden-tial elections in which Senator John Kennedy nosed out Vice President Richard Nixon. The timing of my recall in part reflected the administra-tion's desire to improve the Vice President's position in his debate with the

Senator over Cuba. The manner in which the contenders handled the Cuban issue seems to me worth recalling.

The Democrats did not fault the administration for the economic warfare it had waged against Castro in such matters as the suspension of the sugar quota in July. The notion that the Cuban people were almost to a man anxious to throw off the rule that Castro had violently and mysteriously imposed seemed to be accepted by both candidates. The Vice President was intent on persuading the electorate that the administration had taken appropriate steps and would continue, if reelected, to pursue a policy that would help the Cuban people eventually to get rid of Castro. Senator Kennedy ridiculed the Nixon statements on this point and endeavored to give the impression of advocating a more vigorous and a more effective policy with the same object in view.

Until the final weeks of the campaign Cuba was not a prominent issue. Senator Kennedy had abandoned his earlier favorable view of Castro as the inheritor of the Bolívar tradition in Latin America.[5] There had been substantial agreement in American public opinion with the policies of moderation and restraint followed during 1959 and the early months of 1960. Developments in the spring and summer of 1960 had stimulated interest in Cuba and hostility to Castro because of his anti-Americanism in word and deed. The President's suspension of the sugar quota had not been seriously questioned in the United States.

As the campaign drew to a close, the issue of Cuba became increasingly divisive. The administration's alleged responsibilities for letting things in Cuba come to the pass that they had reached was a tempting target.[6] During the final weeks of the campaign Senator Kennedy unkindly remarked, "I wasn't the Vice President who presided over the Communization of Cuba."[7] Earlier, in a speech in Cincinnati on October 6 almost entirely devoted to Cuba, the Senator stressed the warnings that former Ambassadors Arthur Gardner and Earl E. T. Smith had just divulged they had vainly given to the Department of State as to the Communist proclivities of Castro and his entourage.[8] At the same time he was scathing in his denunciation of the warm relations with the Batista regime personified by these two Ambassadors. He recalled that Vice President Nixon when he visited Cuba in 1955 had said publicly that he was "very much impressed with the competence and stability" of the government of Batista. The Senator harped on the gold telephone presented Batista in appreciation of the "burdensome rate increase" granted the telephone company. His attack on the Republican administration's policies toward Batista in some ways paralleled the views of Castro on the same subject.

Senator Kennedy was particularly critical of the administration's belated recognition of the importance of broad economic assistance programs for Latin America in general and for Cuba in particular. (He quite naturally failed to state that the Republican policies in that direction had now evolved so that they were appreciably more forthcoming than had been those of the Democrats when they left office in 1953.)

The positive element in the Senator's position was expressed in the following paragraphs:

> What can a new administration do to reverse these trends? For the present, Cuba is gone. Our policies of neglect and indifference have let it slip behind the Iron Curtain—and for the present no magic formula will bring it back. I have no basic disagreement with the President's policies of recent months—for the time to save Cuba was some years ago.
>
> Hopefully, events may once again bring us an opportunity to bring our influence strongly to bear on behalf of the cause of freedom in Cuba. But in the meantime we can constantly express our friendship for the Cuban people—our sympathy with their economic problems—our determination that they will again be free. At the same time we must firmly resist further Communist encroachment in this hemisphere—working through a strengthened Organization of the American States —and encouraging those liberty loving Cubans who are leading the resistance to Castro. And we must make it clear to Castro once and for all that we will defend our naval base at Guantanamo under all circumstances—and continue to seek reparation for his seizures of American property.

On the issue of assisting Cubans to overthrow Castro, the Senator was explicit when he said (on September 23), "The forces fighting for freedom in exile and in the mountains of Cuba should be sustained and assisted, and communism in other countries of Latin America must be confined and not permitted to expand."[9] Later he stressed that "we must . . . let the Cuban people know our determination that they will some day again be free."[10] And at another point he urged that the United States authorities be called upon "to end the harassment which this Government has carried on of liberty-loving anti-Castro forces in Cuba and in other lands."[11] He went on to say, "While we cannot violate international law, we must recognize that these exiles and rebels represent the real voice of Cuba and should not be constantly handicapped by our Immigration and Justice authorities." Later he was critical of the fact that "these fighters for freedom have had virtually no support from our Government."[12]

Mr. Nixon was in the unhappy position of defending the administration's record of what had been against the vigorous and imaginative attack of his political enemies with their partisan view of what might have been. He deplored Senator Kennedy's defeatist view and urged that Cuba was not lost to the Communists. He said, "There . . . isn't any question but that the free people of Cuba are going to be supported and that they will attain their freedom."[13] But by this he apparently did not mean the same thing as Senator Kennedy. Thus on October 20 he remarked in a tone of virtuous reproof:

> I think that Senator Kennedy's policies for the handling of the Castro regime are probably the most dangerously irresponsible recommendations that he's made during the course of the campaign. In effect, what Senator Kennedy recommends is that the United States Government should give help to the exiles and to those within Cuba who oppose the Castro regime, provided they are anti-Batista. Now let's see just what this means. We have five treaties with Latin America, including the one setting up the Organization of American States in Bogota in 1948, in which we've agreed not to intervene in the internal affairs of any American country and they as well have agreed to do likewise.[14]

And then the Vice President, after denying any intention on the part of the administration to violate its international commitments, proceeded to give his prescription for getting rid of Castro:

> Now what can we do? We can do what we did with Guatemala. There was a Communist dictator that we inherited from the previous administration. We quarantined Mr. Arbenz. The result was that the Guatemalan people themselves eventually rose up and they threw him out. We are quarantining Mr. Castro today. We are quarantining him diplomatically by bringing back our Ambassador, economically by cutting

off trade—and Senator Kennedy's suggestion that the trade that we cut
off is not significant is just 100 per cent wrong. We are cutting off the
significant items that the Cuban regime needs in order to survive. By
cutting off trade, by cutting off diplomatic relations as we have, we will
quarantine this regime so that the people of Cuba themselves will take
care of Mr. Castro. But for us to do what Senator Kennedy has suggested would bring results which I know he would not want and certainly which the American people would not want.[15]

Mr. Nixon was lavish in his praise of the "wise policy of restraint and
forebearance" which he said the administration had been following. He did
not mention the crude oil situation nor did he, except in passing, dwell on
the suspension of the sugar quota. He wanted to get rid of communism in
Cuba, but he wanted to do it in concert with the other American republics
and "without the use of force toward Cuba or any other sister Republic."

To the end of the campaign Senator Kennedy charged that the Nixon
policy recommendations were too little and too late and that the trade embargo to which the Vice President pointed with such pride was of no real
significance. But he was sufficiently sensitive to some of the Nixon counter-
charges to send Mr. Nixon a telegram denying that he had ever advocated
intervention in Cuba in violation of American treaty commitments or of
international law.[16] At the same time he remained critical of the alleged fact
that the anti-Castro Cuban "fighters for freedom have had virtually no support from our Government."[17]

The use of American government resources to assist Cubans fighting or
wishing to fight Castro became a serious issue between the candidates. Mr.
Nixon later accused Senator Kennedy of having been disingenuous, to say
the least, since the Senator knew from his secret official briefings that the
administration was doing what he was publicly accusing it of not doing,
namely the training and the arming of anti-Castro Cubans.[18] Mr. Nixon,
though in a sense the father of the operation, could not publicly admit its
existence. This whole argument seemed unrealistic to thousands in Cuba and
in the United States—including the writer—who, though not having the
benefit of secret briefings, were fully aware of the fact, if not of the details,
of CIA preparations against Castro involving the recruitment and the training of anti-Castro Cubans.

Chapter 19

President Kennedy, the Bay of Pigs, and the Missile Crisis

The Break in Cuban American Relations

CASTRO took the initiative that led to the formal break in relations between Havana and Washington. In a speech on the night of January 2, 1961, he, for the nth time, described the American Embassy as a center of counterrevolution, subversion, and espionage; then he demanded that it reduce its personnel to the level maintained at the Cuban Embassy in Washington. The latter establishment had no significant responsibilities, had been inactive for over a year, and had a total of eleven employees. In contrast, the American Embassy was maintaining contact with the Cuban government, was performing legitimate functions of interest to the American government and was serving tens of thousands of Cubans anxious to escape from their country. Its staff was several times as large as that of the Cuban Embassy in Washington.

I suspect that Castro's demand was a notion that came to him while he was orating; once the words were out of his mouth he could not retreat. Nor did the United States, once it was determined that Castro meant what he said, have any choice other than to close the Embassy in Havana.

Immediately after the break in relations Castro ordered a full-scale mobilization of his armed forces to repel an invasion from the United States which he asserted was imminent. He demanded of his people an all-out revolutionary defense posture and thus distracted attention from his own impulsive expulsion of the American Embassy. With the intelligence available to him, he could not have supposed that the lame-duck administration in Washington would take the momentous decision to invade Cuba, though Castro was convinced the invasion would come in time and would include not only the Cubans notoriously training in Guatemala under CIA auspices but also American Marines in the "imperialist" tradition.

A New Administration in Washington

With the inauguration of President Kennedy, Castro briefly dropped the invasion-scare motif from his repertory and conveyed to his people a hope that with the change of administrations in Washington an improvement in Cuban-American relations was possible. He did this in part to relieve the strain and the expense of his full military mobilization. He may also have been influenced by the Latin American cliché that described the Republicans as the party of big business, the "big stick," and protectionism, while the Democrats were identified with the Good Neighbor Policy, nonintervention, liberal trade policies, and nostalgic memories of Franklin D. Roosevelt. (As of 1970, the Bay of Pigs, the Dominican intervention, and the war in Vietnam have blurred this conventional distinction.)

But Castro knew that the Senator Kennedy who had been relatively sympathetic to him had long given way, because of Castro's own extravagant anti-Americanism, to the presidential candidate who had bitterly castigated the Republicans for losing Cuba and had promised that he would follow a more effective anti-Castro policy. President Kennedy's inauguration in fact brought with it no change in the Cuban policy of the United State government. The overthrow of Castro was the objective of that policy—an overthrow to be encompassed by all means short of an involvement on Cuban soil of American armed forces. The program included the economic measures already described plus an American-created military force made up of anti-Castro Cubans to be used in an operation or operations that would lead to the downfall of the regime. The economic measures had already been adopted by the Eisenhower administration; the question of perfecting and executing the covert military part of the program was left to the incoming administration.

The situation the new President faced in Cuba warrants a brief summing up. Diplomatic relations had been severed. Trade relations were grinding to a complete halt. The Soviet Union had assumed responsibility for the survival of the Cuban economy. The Cuban Revolution had moved forward with increased speed and fervor after the American economic measures of June and July 1960. All American and Cuban private property significant in the production of Cuba's goods and services had been confiscated. The anti-American extremism personified by Castro with his hold on his people had stimulated a true fanaticism which Washington did not fully understand. The administration's imperfectly secret preparations for an invasion of Cuba by a force of exiles and refugees and the possibility that American armed forces might also participate in such an invasion were responsible for the increasing quantities of arms and military equipment sent by Russia to Castro after the middle of 1960.

President Kennedy entrusted the formulation of policy in the Latin American area to a task force headed by Dr. Adolf A. Berle, Jr. Dr. Berle had performed high-level assignments in the Roosevelt and the Truman administrations. He had served briefly as Ambassador to Brazil. He had been in touch with Latin American affairs both during his government service and during his business and legal careers. He was well and favorably known to the leaders of the "democratic left" in Latin America and in Puerto Rico. He had achieved a well-deserved fame as an analyst of the American economy and of the organization of American society for the production of goods and services.

As the old administration gave way to the new, the United States government was increasingly committed to assisting the economic development and the social progress of the American republics in ways that would have been inconceivable a decade earlier. The process had been expedited by Mr. Nixon's misadventures in Latin America in the spring of 1958 and by the abrupt rise of Castro and Castroism. But it also had deep roots in the thinking of American and Latin American statesmen and economists over many years.

Dr. Berle at first hoped that he would be able to arouse the governments of the other American republics to share his alarm at the Castro take-over in Cuba and at the peril inherent therein for the rest of Latin America. The new American policy of practical sensitivity to the needs of the region for large-scale assistance would, he hoped, be an asset in moving toward a consensus on the Castro issue. It soon, however, became clear that support from the principal members of the Organization of American States for an effective anti-Castro program was no more in the cards in early 1961 than it had been in the summer of 1960 at the San José meeting. Such a program, especially one championed by the United States, was a negation of cherished inter-American doctrine and politically unacceptable in many of the American republics.

Not until Castro granted facilities to the Russians for the installation of missiles that threatened the security of the United States and possibly of other countries of the area and was proved guilty of positive subversive acts—as distinct from mere oratory—against other American republics did the latter agree to political and economic nonintercourse with Cuba. Even then Mexico remained outside the agreement.

The effort under Dr. Berle's direction to persuade the other republics to accept the American view about the Castro menace and what to do about it was, in my opinion, pursued with more perseverance and energy than a realistic appraisal of the situation would have warranted. The attitudes of key countries such as Argentina, Brazil, Chile, and Mexico demonstrated the futility of attempting to obtain from the OAS with their approval support for an intervention designed to overthrow Castro. (A favorable vote not including all or at least three of these four countries would have been futile.) The governments of these major countries and of several others were not yet convinced of the Communist orientation of the Cuban government or of the reality and intensity of the Castro drive for continental leadership. They had significant pro-Castro sentiment at home to consider. Though they were anxious to participate in the Alliance for Progress and believed in it as a weapon against the spread of Castroism, they rightly concluded that the United States would not use the Alliance as a lever to persuade them to accept American concepts for dealing with Castro.

Setting the Stage for the Bay of Pigs

During the early weeks of the new administration I was absorbed by my duties as interim American representative on the Council of the Organization of American States. Yet I kept in touch with Cuban developments and was fortunate in that my Havana colleagues, the Brazilian and the Argentine Ambassadors, visited the United States and gave me much useful information and comment on Cuban conditions and on the views of their governments as to the options available to the inter-American community in dealing with Castro. I was called on by Dr. Berle to serve as his contact with the numerous Cuban leaders in exile anxious to see him.

I was not briefed on what was being covertly prepared against Castro though the existence of such preparations was becoming increasingly public knowledge. Those fully informed about the operation were kept to a minimum; most of the principal officers of the Department of State were excluded as was the head of the intelligence side of the CIA.[1] I speculate that my noninclusion reflected a normal desire on the part of those directly concerned to maximize positive thinking about their project. My views or prejudices regarding much of the CIA's concept of foreign relations were well known within the bureaucracy. I was, however, one of those under serious consideration at the White House for the post of Assistant Secretary for Inter-American Affairs shortly to be vacated by Mr. Thomas Mann, who was to be named Ambassador to Mexico.

My lack of information about the operation that was to be unveiled at the Bay of Pigs taken in conjunction with my assignment to serve as Dr. Berle's contact with the Cuban exiles placed me in an anomalous position. I often received from my Cuban friends bitter complaints about the manner in which the CIA was directing the secret operations—operations on which they could not believe I had no more information than any reader of the daily press. All I could reply to my friends was that I had listened to what they said!

During these weeks prior to the unleashing against Castro of whatever was to be unleashed, American officials recommended to their Cuban contacts that the base of the Cuban exile opposition, then known as the *Frente* ("Front"), be broadened to include all of the anti-Castro elements except those so irredeemably identified with Batista as to be liabilities in Cuba in 1961.[2] My assignment from Doctor Berle gave me a role in this matter. I saw Dr. José Miró-Cardona, a man of integrity and goodwill, on several occasions. I also had interviews with Antonio Varona, a former Prime Minister with courage and convictions, with that old fighter Aureliano Sánchez-Arango, and with others.

The goal of a broader coalition of anti-Castro elements ran counter to the interests of some of the old-line political groups aspiring to retain control of the Frente. They viewed with particular suspicion and distrust people who had been ardent supporters of Castro and had defected from him. To the argument that these people represented an effective political force with possible influence over the Cuban masses and, therefore, should be mobilized in the fight against Castro, the conservatives opposed the argument of ideological unacceptability. There was perhaps an unspoken consideration in the minds of some. From the moment they became convinced the United States government was forging a weapon for the violent overthrow of Castro, they were imbued with a flattering though in the event a misplaced confidence in the success of the venture. Their political instinct led them to the tacit conclusion that it would be desirable to restrict rather than to expand the number of sharers in the spoils of a victory guaranteed by American support.

Nevertheless the efforts to broaden the Frente through the introduction of more progressive members and thus to invest the anti-Castro forces with a political coloration that would justify support by the New Frontier met with some success. A Revolutionary Council formed in March included, among other new figures, Manuel Ray; he had been Castro's Minister of Public Works until the upheaval of November 1959 when Che Guevara replaced Felipe Pazos at the National Bank.[3] Ray was a reputable engineer who headed what was then known as the *Movimiento Revolucionario del Pueblo* (MRP) and was believed to have a significant following among Cubans hostile to communism and disenchanted with the betrayal by Castro of the democratic revolution he had promised.

The Ray movement was, however, viewed with jealousy and suspicion by the more conservative of the anti-Castro leaders. Those of us in the American government who had worked on the Frente to get Ray and his party brought into the Revolutionary Council were denounced for our pains. Writers in the refugee press in Miami spoke gloomily of leftist influences in the Department of State and of Fidelismo without Fidel.[4]

Meanwhile the military side of the operation that was to culminate at the Bay of Pigs was wholly controlled by the CIA. Many of the Cuban leaders considered that that control was exercised insensitively, arrogantly, and ignorantly. Exile politics were the haphazard concern of the Department of State, the CIA, and the White House. We in the State Department who were not briefed on the military aspect got into the act in part because the Cubans wanted someone to whom they could appeal from the dictates of CIA and in part because they believed that their friends at State had some familiarity with Cuban conditions and personalities.

Thus the exile anti-Castro movement in both its military and its political aspects was manipulated, if not coordinated, by different agencies of the United States government. The two aspects were generally kept apart. The Cuban politicians saw relatively little of the Cuban freedom fighters. Their contacts were carefully regulated by the CIA. The Cubans on both the military and the political fronts were on the payroll of the United States government and had little recourse against distasteful decisions by the holders of the purse strings. Regardless of the merits in particular cases, it was difficult not to feel compassion for the humiliating situations in which these Cubans sometimes found themselves.

President Kennedy and the Bay of Pigs

President Kennedy had inherited from the Eisenhower-Nixon administration the operation that became, with his approval and guidance, the Bay of Pigs expedition. I share the conviction of millions of Americans that John F. Kennedy was a very great man and their lasting sorrow that his term of office was cut short so tragically. The unconditional loyalty he inspired in his followers has, however, tended to cloud the historical truth about some of the matters in which he was concerned. President Kennedy, in a most forthright and high-minded manner, accepted full responsibility for the Bay of Pigs fiasco. He deprecated recrimination and public attempts to find scapegoats. Yet two of his principal memorialists have endeavored to diminish the President's own involvement.

Both Theodore Sorensen and Arthur Schlesinger describe the President as the victim of a process set in train before his inauguration and which he, in the first few weeks of the new administration, was unable to arrest in spite of his misgivings. Mr. Sorensen writes of errors in the decision-making process "which permitted bureaucratic momentum to govern instead of policy leadership."[5] Mr. Schlesinger uses language which seems to amount to the same thing when he remarks that "Kennedy saw the Cuban project, in the patois of the bureaucracy, as a 'contingency plan'. He did not yet realize how contingency planning could generate its own momentum and create its own reality."[6]

The fact, of course, is that President Kennedy had made a promise during the campaign to pursue a more successful policy toward Cuba. He had castigated the Republicans for permitting the communization of the island. He was committed to help the Cuban opposition eliminate Castro.

Although it may be, as reported by Arthur Schlesinger, that some of the candidate's most forthright expressions about arming the Cuban patriots were made on his behalf by one of his aides and that the candidate was not in agreement with what was said in his name, he did not retract these statements.[7]

Overriding these points of detail was the fact that President Kennedy was pledged to a new and vigorous policy on all fronts; he could hardly remain passive and indifferent toward Castro's Cuba. He was impressed by the arguments concerning the commitments already made to the Cuban exiles, the preparations in progress, the fear that the Castro armament would soon be greatly increased from Moscow, and the fact that the members of the Cuban Brigade in the semiclandestine camp in Guatemala were at a peak of morale and must be used or they would "spoil," with prejudicial consequences for the United States. The plans submitted to him by Allen Dulles and Richard Bissell with Pentagon approval were in accord with his own thinking and with the policy of his administration for dealing with the Cuban situation. His assumption of full responsibility was more than a gesture of generosity and nobility: it was a highly creditable recognition of the truth of the matter.

President Kennedy's misgivings about the proposed operation did not arise from principle but from possible errors in the calculations of the experts whom he entrusted with its execution. The only articulate opponent of the whole concept among the President's top advisers was Senator William Fulbright. Arthur Schlesinger's words in describing the Senator's presentation in opposition to the CIA project deserve to be repeated and remembered, "He [Senator Fulbright] gave a brave, old-fashioned American speech, honorable, sensible and strong; and he left every one in the room, except me and perhaps the President, wholly unmoved."[8]

During these weeks of preparations, both military and political, I assumed that the semisecret operation being organized in the backwoods of Guatemala would involve a repetition against Castro of the Castro pattern against Batista though with greater forces and better equipment. I speculated that there would be more than one landing—perhaps as many as half a dozen—leading to the establishment of guerrilla strongholds in the mountainous areas in various parts of the country. The existence of these areas of guerrilla operations and the possibility of supplying them from outside Cuba by means of airdrops would encourage the anti-Castro movement throughout the island. Thus, if all went well, Castro might in time be confronted with the same sort of repudiation and civic resistance that had brought down Batista.

The notion that the plan, on which, it was later revealed, the Joint Chiefs of Staff and the CIA had agreed, involved a one-shot confrontation of Castro's already formidable armed forces with a vest-pocket-sized force of Cuban exiles trained in regular combat rather than in guerrilla operations and political subversion never occurred to me. That plan amounted to asking the fifteen hundred patriots we landed at the Bay of Pigs to seize control over their seven million fellow citizens from over a hundred thousand well-trained, well-armed Castroite soldiers and militia!

President Kennedy had decided, when he became responsible for the operation, that American participation would be limited to recruiting, financing, equipping, training, and counseling the Cuban opponents of Castro.[9] He had specifically ruled out the use of American armed forces or even of American officers or experts in combat against the forces of Castro. He had insisted on the need to preserve the appearance of a purely Cuban venture. He had made clear that the expedition would be entirely on its own as soon as it entered Cuban territorial waters. The American government supplied the Cubans with obsolete aircraft and decrepit shipping chosen with the idea of nonidentification with the equipment of the American armed forces.[10]

The President's ground rules seem to have been imperfectly transmitted to the Cubans involved in the enterprise. Most of them believed firmly that the United States would do whatever might be needed to insure the success of an operation in which so much American prestige was being invested.[11] They (and many Americans, too) were convinced that the American position would, regardless of earlier disclaimers, adapt itself to the circumstances that might be encountered as the operation developed. They anticipated that American scruples would evaporate in the face of any serious emergency.

The President, however, resisted all requests, even prayers, to allow a degree of American intervention that might have saved the situation as it developed on the beach at Girón. The one exception which he did authorize would probably not have played a significant part in the battle, though it might have facilitated the evacuation of some of the brave Cubans who were captured by the Castro forces in the final debacle; the air cover in question failed because of a mix-up in scheduling.[12]

I am convinced that the President showed a surer instinct for the realities of the relations of the American government with the Cuban people than did those of his advisers who urged upon him a modification of his position in order to save the expedition. For if the enterprise had succeeded due to the presence of American armed forces and not owing to the military prowess of Castro's Cuban opponents and to the civilian uprisings the military successes of the Brigade were supposed eventually to produce, the post-Castro Cuban government would have been totally unviable; it would have required to be constantly shored up with American help. It would not have commanded the respect of the Cuban people. The heroes of that people would have been those who resisted the Americans by force of arms even if unsuccessfully. The scenario on which I believe Castro had counted from the start would have been created, and the United States would have become bogged down in a prolonged guerrilla war in Cuba. I believe the President sensed this and that much credit is due him for resisting the pressures of those who wished him to throw in American forces on those tragic April days. His decision was a most painful one for him: it conflicted with his sense of responsibility for the fate of the Cubans who had, on the basis of American assurances, enlisted in an American-sponsored, almost an American-guaranteed, effort to free their country from Castro.

With the wisdom of hindsight I believe that two factors escaped those in Washington responsible for Cuban policy in early 1961. In the first place, they underestimated the fanaticism and the combative spirit of those who supported Castro unconditionally. His support was not effectively diminished by the gyrations, the betrayals, and the absurdities that his enemies believed would damage his position. The notion that this support would melt away and that tens of thousands of Cubans trained in the use of modern weapons would defect or refuse to fight if the few hundreds of Castro's opponents, whom the United States had armed and trained, obtained an initial success was simply wishful thinking.

Second, the concept that an anti-Castro force could be put together capable of holding its own with Castro over a period of time even with the advantage of an initial success or two gained through surprise was probably erroneous. This involves no disparagement of the bravery and of the fighting qualities of the members of the Brigade that landed at the Bay of Pigs or of similar volunteers who could have been made available. The fact was that the number of those ready to risk their lives fighting Castro was less than those willing to defend him and his regime. As long as the assumption of the anti-Castro Cubans was that the United States was solidly behind the effort to overthrow Castro by force and would not let the effort fail, this disparity tended to increase. The expectation of a United States sponsored and managed thrust against Castro, in which the United States would, in the interest of its own prestige, do all that was necessary to insure success up to and including an injection of American armed forces, seriously weakened the Cuban opposition to Castro.

In this matter I share the opinion of my old friend and colleague Ambassador Ellis O. Briggs, who has written, "The Bay of Pigs operation (1961) was a tragic experience for the Cubans who took part, but its failure was a fortunate (if mortifying) thing for the United States, which otherwise might have been saddled with indefinite occupation of the island."[13] It is my view that even if the most optimistic expectations had been realized and the Castro forces had been driven from the principal cities (an almost inconceivable development on the basis of what we know now), "our Cubans" would have had to meet a prolonged opposition from well-armed and highly motivated irregular forces in town and country. This situation would, eventually if not immediately, have involved intervention with American forces plus, of course, a danger of confrontation with the Russians, though it seems to me reasonable to suppose that the Russians would have traveled much less of the road toward nuclear warfare in defense of a hypothetical Castro in the hills in 1961 than they did in defense of their real missiles in 1962. Thus, although the disaster of the Bay of Pigs was of a nature almost inconceivable at the time and one deeply humiliating to all Americans and particularly to those who held that the good name of our country had been diminished in the conception and conduct of the operation, I now believe the outcome was the most favorable realistically to be desired granting the undertaking and the policy that motivated it.

A successful Bay of Pigs could conceivably have brought the United States one advantage. The strain on American political and military assets resulting from the need to keep the lid on in Cuba might have led the President of the United States to resist, rather than enthusiastically to embrace, the advice he received in 1964 and 1965 to make a massive commitment of American air power, ground forces, and prestige in Vietnam. Our country might have been saved an adventure that has had such deplorable consequences for the American position in the world and for the coherence of our society at home.

The fiasco at the Bay of Pigs had only one useful result. It caused serious questioning of the CIA's role in covert activities in the conduct of the foreign affairs of our society—one that we like to think of as an open one. It drew the attention of the President and of the Secretary of State to the necessity of discharging more stringently and more effectively their responsibilities in these matters.

The Bay of Pigs, in spite of the minor stage on which the tragedy was played out, was a serious setback for the United States. It consolidated Castro's regime and was a determining factor in giving it the long life it has enjoyed. Though the threat of the early arrival of Russian weapons and planes for Castro's forces had been a factor in the timing of the expedition, the Russians themselves played no part in the affair. The Russian profit was in terms of American defeat rather than of direct Russian triumph; the nuclear mumblings of Mr. Khrushchev had no impact on the conduct of the United States.[14]

The only people on the free-world side of the episode to come out of it with credit were the members of the Cuban Brigade. They fought bravely until fighting was no longer possible in the face of overwhelming strength and of a situation for which they were unprepared. Their conduct while they were in captivity was one of exemplary fortitude.

After the Bay of Pigs it became clear to all concerned in Washington, in Havana, and in Moscow that for the time being the Castro regime could be overthrown only through an overt application of American power. The Kennedy administration seems at no time to have planned such an application in the absence of military developments in Cuba that would make the island a security threat to the United States as distinct from an adverse element in relation to American interests and objectives in the other American republics. It was a misunderstanding on this point that led Castro to request and the Russians to install the missiles that brought the United States and Russia to the point of nuclear war in October 1962.

The Missile Crisis

The Missile Crisis of the fall of 1962 does not really belong to the story of Cuban American relations, though if the crisis had not been resolved when the Russians "blinked," it is probable that a by-product of the confrontation between the United States and the Soviet Union would have been the elimination of Fidel Castro. But the exercise had little to do with him. The conflict began when the United States discovered that there were Russian missiles under Russian control on the island, and it ended when the Russians took their missiles away.

The experience was a humiliating and a painful one for Castro, but it did not in the long run materially affect his position in Cuba. Nor did it modify American policy toward the Cuban Revolution. No one in Washington seems seriously to have believed that the Russians would have ever given Cuba physical control of these missiles or even have instructed Castro's men in their use. The issue was entirely one between the United States and the Soviet Union.

The Russians realized that the downgrading of Castro on this occasion might present some dangers for a regime in the maintenance of which their prestige was engaged. They assisted Castro in his attempts to save as much face as possible. Mikoyan spent what must have been extremely tedious weeks cajoling and soothing his government's slighted and ruffled client and supporting him in his rather pathetic efforts to prove to his people that he was not a complete cipher in this whole affair.

I have seen no wholly satisfactory explanation of why the Russians took the risk of installing these missiles. The story that President Kennedy unintentionally gave Khrushchev's son-in-law (who presumably misunderstood the President) the idea that an American invasion of Cuba was in contemplation and that when Castro heard this he persuaded the Russians to put in the missiles is unconvincing.[15] More plausibly, the Russians gambled that President Kennedy, still a relatively new and untried man, having absorbed one humiliation in Cuba would swallow another. The manner in which the President met the challenge was magnificent and warrants the continued pride and gratitude of his fellow citizens.

American policy toward Cuba was not changed by the Missile Crisis.

The removal of the missiles and the certainty that they could not be replaced without detection satisfied the security needs of the United States to the point that it was not deemed necessary to insist on the third-party inspection Castro had so hysterically rejected. The use of American armed forces in Cuba solely to eject Castro was never seriously contemplated at responsible levels of either the Eisenhower or the Kennedy administrations. The pledge given Khrushchev on this point was a face-saver for the Russians and not a concession by President Kennedy. After the Bay of Pigs and the ransoming of the survivors of that episode, the Kennedy and, later, the Johnson administrations engaged in no further plans to finance, arm, or train Cubans for expeditions to liberate the island from Castro's rule. In fact both administrations enforced American law that prevents filibustering activities on American soil.

Chapter 20

Cuba and the United States, 1970 and Beyond

THE problem of Cuba has dwindled steadily in importance for the United States during the sixties. Castro's influence in Latin America has faded because of his repeated failures to export his Revolution and because of an increasing awareness of the gaps between his promise and his performance at home. The Guevara fiasco in Bolivia—a fiasco for which Castro is not held blameless—has dimmed the Castro image and the promise of Castro-style guerrilla insurgency. Even in those Latin American republics threatened with social upheaval, the impulse from Cuba is much less than it was at the beginning of the decade. Although in the United States Castro-communism still enthuses the lunatic left and gives the irrelevant, if affluent, far right goose pimples, it has shrunk to the dimensions of a purely Cuban, rather than a potentially continental, phenomenon.

Fidel Castro is in his twelfth year as Maximum (and only) Leader of Cuba. During the past nine years he has described himself as a Marxist-Leninist. Earlier he claimed to be an upholder of constitutional democracy and then an advocate of a special brand of humanism. The term Castroism, or Fidelismo, best identifies the eccentric, sweepingly revolutionary, wholly arbitrary exercise of absolute personal power made possible by Castro's phenomenal charisma and by his talents as a leader. Castroism has destroyed the social, the political, and the economic conventions and structures of the Cuban community into which Castro erupted. That community now in some ways resembles the societies of the Soviet world. The elimination of the rights of the individual as understood in the West and the abolition of private property in any socially significant sense have been achieved. The cult of the Castro personality is the backbone of the regime in a manner reminiscent of Sukarno's Indonesia and Nkrumah's Ghana.

As many as two million Cubans, a quarter of the total number, have found the conditions created by Castro and his Revolution unacceptable. They are not a political opposition in the usual sense since they participate in no political dialogue and are denied in their homeland any expression of their views or any legal way of working for a modification of the regime. Over seven hundred thousand people have emigrated from Cuba since Castro came to power. Thousands have clandestinely escaped at considerable personal risk. Several hundred thousand still in Cuba have registered as desiring to depart in spite of the severe hardships—immediate loss of job, forced labor, and confiscation of home and personal possessions—involved in that decision. Hundreds of thousands more would like to leave but are reluctant to register. Politically motivated executions are still a feature of the regime's defenses. Tens of thousands of Cubans are held in Castro's jails, concentration camps, and "rehabilitation" or forced labor establishments. After over a decade of the new order, profound dissatisfaction persists and is probably on the increase.

On the other hand, Castro and Castroism enjoy the fanatical support of millions of Cubans. The hundreds of thousands of men and women in the administration, the security apparatus, and the armed forces include a high proportion of these true believers. The two and a half million Cubans Castro claims are enrolled in the revolutionary vigilance committees found throughout the nation down to the block and hamlet levels number a substantial hard core of deeply committed followers of Fidel. Although Castro's prestige has declined, he still commands the effective allegiance of Cuban elements far stronger than those that oppose him. As long as Castro keeps his health and his charisma, a successful internal movement against him, though certainly possible, seems unlikely. Castro's immunity from assassination or from fatal accident has, however, already extended far beyond what the fates might be expected to grant a man with his record of ruthless dealing with so many of his fellow Cubans and with his disorganized way of life.

Since Castro allowed or engineered the departure of Guevara from the Cuban scene, there has been no one on that stage capable of filling Castro's shoes or of operating his form of personal, hypnotic rule. The men with whom Castro has surrounded himself have no potential of their own to mesmerize the Cuban people as Castro has done. Raúl Castro, his brother's designated successor, though a man of energy and aggressiveness, suffers from a notorious lack of magnetism as a public figure. President Dórticos, an adaptable, devious political manipulator, has little standing other than as Castro's choice for the position he has held at Castro's pleasure since the summer of 1959. The names of some of the others such as Carlos Rafael Rodríguez and Raúl Roa need only to be mentioned as possible replacements to be instantly discarded. When Castro goes the officials who serve him today will be punctured balloons.

Indeed the one feature of the regime on which all observers agree is its one-man character. After Castro his government will have lost its strength and vitality. The communization of the island society, the indoctrination of the young, and the institutionalization of the Revolution—to the extent that they exist—will not take the place of Castro in the scheme of things or prevent the change inevitable when he disappears.

Once the overwhelming Castro personality is removed, his nominal successors will be unable to prevent increased participation in the governing process by the various elements in Cuban society now serving uncritically under the Castro banner. Once the idol has fallen, the democratic, as well as the anarchic, instincts of the Cuban people will find outlets. But the political structure that existed at the time of Batista's coup in 1952 and the economic and social structures that prevailed when Batista was expelled six years later have little or no relevance to the Cuba of the future. Those vanished institutions resemble trees with abundant foliage and sound-looking bark which when blown down by a sudden gale reveal the shallowest of roots and pervasive internal rot. Their day has gone in Cuba regardless of the strength and vitality with which similar institutions flourish elsewhere.

Castro's regime, in contrast to those of Russia's European dependencies, was not created by Russian bayonets nor does it rely on them for survival. The presence in Cuban hands of Russian weapons was not a major factor in the origin of the regime. That regime, whatever one thinks of it, rests upon a Cuban base of coercion and acceptance.

The Russian presence in Cuba is largely the consequence of the American reaction to Castro's provocations. Russia took no critical initiative in bringing about the situation in the summer of 1960 that presented Moscow with the choice of either replacing the United States as Cuba's major trad-

ing partner or allowing an anti-American, anticapitalist revolutionary movement to die because of economic strangulation. Russia came to Castro's
rescue only after the United States had taken steps designed to overthrow
him. The Bay of Pigs consolidated Castro's power and set the stage for
Russia's long-term involvement in the Cuban economy.

Castro's Cuba is today far more dependent economically on Russia than
was pre-Castro Cuba on the United States. Castro is uncomfortably conscious that he could well be an expendable poker chip on the Soviet side of
the table in the game of world politics. Yet there are obvious limitations in
terms of prestige and strategy on Moscow's freedom of action in dealing
with its unsolicited and often, in secondary matters, nonconforming and
obstreperous Marxist-Leninist client.

When Castro goes, however, and the country begins to move away
from his one-man Marxism-Leninism, the Soviet Union will have to decide
how far its economic support of Cuba can be maintained in the face of
the deviationism and the revisionism that are bound to arise. The Brezhnev
doctrine of armed suppression of unorthodox client states will not be applicable in the Western Hemisphere without a confrontation with the
United States and with the Organization of American States. Moscow can
be expected to avoid such a confrontation. Nor will the Soviet Union's
economic leverage, strong as it is, be sufficient to keep Cuba in line, especially if alternate sources of economic support appear available.

Castro's Hatred of the United States

Castro's one-man rule and his dependence on the economic support of
the Soviet Union are major characteristics of the Cuban scene. A third is
the Maximum Leader's unremitting and relentless hostility toward the
United States. Castro constantly endeavors to instill in his people con-
tempt and disgust for American institutions, public and private, and a conviction that those institutions are doomed. According to him the future
rulers of our country are the Stokely Carmichaels, the student extremists,
and the other fringe elements of American society he so warmly clasps to his
bosom. His help to elements of this kind goes beyond hospitality and probably includes material assistance to them in their activities in our country.
(There is, however, no reason to believe that what Castro can do for them
has any decisive impact on their potential or that it represents a significant

fraction of the resources available to them from their home constituencies.)

Castro unfailingly presents the United States to his people as the source of all their troubles, past and present, including those which are Castro's own responsibility. Castro himself admits systematic distortion in the view of the United States he allows his people. A recent interviewer, Lee Lockwood, in discussing the Castro struggle for survival, asked the following question: "Is it also in the name of that 'struggle' that the Cuban press writes so one-sidedly about the United States?" Castro, according to Mr. Lockwood, replied as follows:

> *I am not going to tell you that we don't do that. It's true everything we say about the United States refers essentially to the worst aspects, and it is very rare that things in any way favorable to the United States will be published here. We simply have a similar attitude to the attitude of your country. I mean that we always try to create the worst opinion of everything there is in the United States as a response to what they have always done with us. The only difference is that we do not write falsehoods about the United States. I told you that we emphasize the worst things, that we omit things that could be viewed as positive, but we do not invent any lies.*[1]

The fact of the repeated publication in the United States of the extensive Lockwood interview with its panegyric of Castro's Cuba by Castro himself and the publication of much similar material disprove Castro's reasoning. In spite of the lack of relations and of communications, Americans interested in Cuba can choose from a wide range of contradictory reports and views on what is going on there. But as long as Castro controls the Cuban mass media, nothing positive about the United States will be published in Cuba. Even if we accept Castro's contention that nothing negative will be invented (my experience in Cuba and my familiarity with Castro's news media lead me to reject it), the Cuban people are getting a view of our country incomparably more one-sided than that of Americans about Cuba. Is it possible for the United States to contemplate constructive relations with a Cuban government whose major premise is that Cubans must be shielded from a rounded view of the infinitely varied human society of over two hundred million people that begins only ninety miles north of Havana?

Castro's major propaganda themes about the United States are: first, that the Cuban Revolution achieved the crushing defeat of an American imperialism, painted in the blackest of colors as a constantly exploitative and oppressive force dominant until Castro came along; second, that constant vigilance, including the maintenance of powerful and alert armed forces and an all-pervasive security apparatus as well as the most unquestioning unity around the figure of the Maximum Leader, are necessary if further assaults from the vanquished but unrepentant imperialists are to be beaten back; third, that the United States pledged itself not to invade Cuba as part of the bargain with the Russians at the time of the removal of the missiles in 1962; fourth, that the economic blockade of Cuba by the United States affords proof of the unremitting hostility of the United States and of its determination to destroy the Cuban Revolution; and fifth, that the Cuban Revolution is the wave of the future for Latin America, an area that must be freed from the same imperialist exploitation and oppression from which Fidel Castro freed Cuba.

These themes, in spite of their irrelevance as reflections of current American attitudes and of the fact that they coexist uncomfortably, are given some plausibility by the actions of the United States in 1960 and 1961—actions that have been earlier described. The United States did endeavor to overthrow Castro through a combination of economic and military measures. But the military side of the effort, consisting mainly in the preparation of the fifteen hundred brave men of the Cuban Brigade, was insignificant in comparison with what the United States would have done in this department had the United States been the aggressive, imperialistic power depicted in the Castro mythology. (The handful of Cubans who landed at the Bay of Pigs is regularly described by Castro and his men as "the mercenary hordes of American imperialism.")

The fact that there has been no threat of invasion in the past eight years and that the American authorities have been reasonably successful in controlling acts of terrorism or filibustering expeditions by Cuban refugees are neglected in the Cuban mass media. Indeed, Cuban propaganda has handled the American intervention in the Dominican Republic and the American commitment of troops in Vietnam in such a manner as to add plausibility to the Castro theme of an unrepentant United States awaiting the proper moment once more to attack Cuba.

Castro's magic enables him, at the same time that he is assuring his people of the imminence of an American invasion, to make much of the fact that President Kennedy, when the Russian missiles were removed, wrote Chairman Khrushchev that there would be no American invasion of Cuba. This helped the Chairman save some face but did not represent a change in American policy.[2] With the removal of the missiles that policy reverted to what it had earlier been—one of unwillingness to invade Cuba with American forces. This was the policy President Eisenhower, as well as President Kennedy, considered fundamental, except in October 1962 when what the Russians were doing in Cuba jeopardized American security. Reactions in the United States and in Latin America to the Dominican intervention of 1965 have, I believe, diminished rather than increased the almost nonexistent possibility of an American invasion of Cuba—always provided the Russians do not repeat their missile aberration of 1962.

As for what Castro and his friends describe as the economic blockade of Cuba by the United States, the reader will recall the series of events begun by Castro in 1959 which led by October 1960 to an almost complete cessation of trade between the two countries. The United States, in my opinion, unnecessarily and unwisely accelerated the process and played into the hands of Castro and Guevara by forcing the Russians into their welcoming arms. But the establishment of a normal trading relationship between Cuba and the United States calls for far more than a unilateral cancellation by the United States government of its embargo on exports to Cuba. There would have to be found a formula of compensation to the victims of Castro's depredations of American properties, and it would be essential, I believe, to make arrangements for the movement of Cuban products, notably sugar, to the United States. These problems are briefly examined in the next chapter.

The trade embargo itself, however useful it may be in Castro's propaganda at home and in this country, is currently of little importance to the Cuban economy. That economy has developed alternative sources of supply for what it would normally buy from the United States; its low export earnings under Castro are far more damaging to the people of the island than is the blockade on which Castro tries to persuade them to blame all or most of their troubles.

The United States and Cuba Today

The United States government is not the prisoner of a dogma of hate toward Cuba. Friendship for the Cuban people, the recollection of long years of close association, the conviction that a resumption of cordial relations would be mutually beneficial—all these are now components in the thinking of responsible people in the United States. A decade ago Castro contemptuously rejected the American attempt to reach an understanding with him and his revolution. American public opinion experienced a sense of injury, irritation, and alarm. The United States government tried unsuccessfully to overthrow Castro. Time and a plethora of other things to worry about have combined with the shrinking of the menace of Castro-communism to draw much of the heat from the American attitude.

For a measure of this cooling of American emotions toward Castro's Cuba, Mr. Nixon's points of view since 1959 furnish an instructive thermometer. The then Vice President was one of the earliest sponsors of the operation that culminated at the Bay of the Pigs in April 1961.[3] In the November 1964 issue of Reader's Digest, Mr. Nixon wrote, "The . . . view, which I share, is that Castro is a dangerous threat to our peace and security—and that we cannot tolerate the presence of a communist regime 90 miles from our shores." In the same article he reported that after the Bay of Pigs he advised President Kennedy to find "a proper legal cover" to invade Cuba. And he concluded the article as follows, "It is time to stand firm—and then move forward—in Cuba, in Vietnam, and in any other area where freedom is denied or threatened by the forces of world communism." He regarded "Cuba, along with Vietnam, . . . as the major foreign policy issue of the 1964 Presidential campaign, as it was in 1960."[4]

In the 1968 campaign Cuba played only a minor role. Neither major candidate said anything memorable about it. The voters were not seriously urged to support or to reject any change in the passive policy then being followed. But a number of Cuban exiles who had acquired American citizenship managed to persuade themselves, on the basis of Mr. Nixon's past stand and of utterances made by him or on his behalf during the campaign, that a vote for Mr. Nixon would help to bring about some affirmative action that would hasten the day of liberation for Cuba.[5] A year later President Nixon sent to Congress his "first annual foreign affairs message" described by him to the press as "in my view, the most comprehensive statement on foreign and defense policy ever made in this country."[6] That document consisted of forty thousand words—Cuba was not one of them.

The United States government has made only two conditions for the establishment of relations on the official plane.[7] The first is an end to the military alliance with Russia that makes Cuba a Soviet military satellite in an area of prime importance to the security of the United States and its allies. This would presuppose the removal of the estimated three thousand Soviet military men now in Cuba. The second condition is the cessation of Cuba's open advocacy and clandestine support of activities designed to overthrow the governments of the other American republics and indeed of the United States also. (I would myself add that a termination of the Castro practice of publishing only the most unfavorable possible information about the United States seasoned with fabricated calumny is important to the establishment of a self-respecting relationship on both sides of the Florida Straits.)

It seems to me highly unlikely that Castro will move in the matters mentioned above in such ways as to improve the situation between two countries that occupy such an important part of the geography of the Caribbean. There is no sign of change at the Cuban end. I am convinced that as long as Castro remains in power there will be no change: Castro needs the United States as a whipping boy and relentless enemy, the essential bulwark of his own personal government. We must accept that as long as Castro remains at the head of his regime in Cuba there can be no significant change in relations between Havana and Washington. The elimination of Castro is not, however, a development for which the United States should assume any responsibility or take any steps, overt or covert. The next great alteration in the politics of Cuba must both be, and be believed to be, the result of purely Cuban decisions. I propose, therefore, to evoke only to discard options sometimes advocated for dealing with Castro.

We must begin by holding fast to the fact that the current state of affairs in Cuba is a Cuban product, though supported by and dependent on the Soviet Union in the economic field. The people of the island—the enthusiastic Castroites and their opponents—are not living under a rule imposed on them from abroad or maintained by foreign soldiers. The existence of the regime, therefore, does not call into play either the Monroe Doctrine or the multilateralization of that doctrine implicit in the inter-American treaties designed to combat extracontinental aggression.

Much as we may dislike the current Cuban regime, we should have learned enough about the limitations on the uses of military power to discard the employment of armed force against Castro in the absence of any one of three rather unlikely contingencies. These are: interference by Castro with the aerial surveillance designed to make sure that missiles dangerous to

American security are not reinstalled on the soil of Cuba, Russia's military ally; the reinstallation, either actual or contemplated, of such missiles; and finally, the use of Soviet or other non-Cuban troops to suppress internal opposition to the Cuban government. (I do not, of course, advocate the suspension of the intelligence and the counterintelligence activities designed to frustrate Castro's own hostile actions against the United States and against Latin America. Beyond hoping that these American covert activities will be conducted with maturity, no realistic observer of the conditions with which Castro has confronted our country can object to their continuance.)

Castro and his Russian patrons are aware that the repetition in Cuba of the installation of Russian missiles deemed threatening to the security of the United States would be met by President Kennedy's successors in the same way as in 1962. The Russians are not anxious to provoke a challenge of this kind when they are deeply worried about the Chinese, when their dependents nearer home are giving them so much trouble and when they are, perhaps with some sincerity, endeavoring to find a basis for relations with the United States that will diminish the rate of increase in the burden of nuclear armaments borne by the long-suffering Russian people. The Soviet misunderstanding in 1962 of the American position is not apt to be repeated. The United States today continues to inspect Cuba from the air; Castro tolerates this though he occasionally makes noises as to its illegality. He would not have Russian backing for the provocation of a crisis on this issue.

In my judgment there is only one possibility—and I conceive it to be a remote one—that might trigger an intervention of American forces on Cuban soil. If internal opposition developed to the point that Castro or his successor could no longer rely on Cuban forces for the support of the government and consequently felt obliged to call in Russian troops to put down the Cuban enemies of the regime and if the Russians acceded to such a request, the United States would have no choice other than to send its armed forces to Cuba to counter the Russians. A Soviet intervention of the kind Castro so loyally justified in the case of Czechoslovakia would be totally unacceptable to the United States in the case of Cuba. United States counterintervention, in such a case, would have the support and probably the participation of other American republics. It would enjoy the backing of the Organization of American States. But I repeat that this seems to me a very remote contingency.

Nor does a renewal of significant American assistance to groups of

Cubans desiring to liberate Cuba appear within the scope of plausible policy. The Bay of Pigs fiasco has been so thoroughly analyzed and dissected and its shortcomings so clearly pinpointed that I would assume, if there were a next time, the United States would do better. But such an enterprise currently has no appeal to our policymakers or to majority public opinion. The talk as to what the Cuban exile activists in Florida could achieve if they were "unleashed" from the attentions of local and federal law-enforcement officers also seems to me highly unrealistic. I can see for these brave people in the future a significant, though auxiliary, role only when real resistance to the regime develops within Cuba—probably after the eclipse of Castro; the tragic state of the economy and its repeated failure to realize the Maximum Leader's goals may, however, accelerate matters.

The eventual key to a normalization of Cuban American relations consists in the forging of economic ties between two countries now totally lacking in such ties. The problems that will face Cuban and American negotiators when the time comes are briefly discussed in the following chapter. Both countries will have to be willing to reconsider and to unravel at least in part some of the measures they took against each other in 1959, 1960, and later. As long as Castro remains the ruler of Cuba the atmosphere will continue to be unsuitable for such negotiations or even for the establishment of the direct diplomatic contacts that would make them possible. American initiatives under present circumstances would merely furnish pretexts for further oratorical extravagances by the Maximum Leader.

What Can We Do Now?

There seems to me no prospect of any fundamental change in Cuban American relations as long as Castro remains in power in Havana. Yet the more relaxed American attitude about Cuba could produce progress in minor matters. Though diplomatic relations have remained severed since January 1961, the two governments have used several channels for the exchange of views and even for negotiations. The Swiss government has designated a succession of able diplomats of ambassadorial rank to handle American interests in Cuba while the Czech Embassy in Washington has represented Cuba in the United States. Through these channels, particularly through the Swiss officials in Havana, arrangements for the departure from Cuba of hundreds of American citizens and tens of thousands of Cubans have been worked out.

The details of the recovery of hijacked planes and the return of their passengers, though not (with one welcome exception) of the criminals involved, have been handled in this manner. The Swiss have also successfully disposed of numbers of welfare cases involving American citizens. The channel is available for the initial discussion of any matter which either government might wish to raise with the other.

Nor is communication between the two governments confined to third-party channels. When President Kennedy decided to ransom the survivors of the Bay of Pigs and Castro agreed to sell his prisoners, Castro negotiated with the Special Representative whom the President designated for the purpose (the late James E. Donovan). A recently published "inside" memoir has stated that there were approaches of an informal but serious nature involving highly placed officials in 1963.[8] Both countries have delegations at the United Nations in New York where contacts could be made if desired.

Furthermore, both governments have been generous in unilateral expressions of view about each other. Castro has been accessible to a number of American journalists. While official American statements about Cuba have, in the nature of things, been neither as frequent nor as prolix as Cuban utterances about the United States, the American position has been made clear to the Cuban authorities. Communication exists even though diplomatic relations do not. Existing channels are ample to permit either government to indicate to the other a desire to amplify those channels or even to resume normal diplomatic or consular ties. Not lack of channels but rather lack of will on both sides keeps matters in their present state of stagnation.

The relationship maintained by the Swiss has to some extent achieved an independent life of its own in spite of the eccentricities and the extravagances in which the Cubans have occasionally felt compelled to indulge.[9] The soothing effects of the passage of time and the skill of the Swiss diplomats have reduced asperities at some practical levels. There are, I believe, some steps of a minor character that might be contemplated in order to accelerate the coming of the day when two such close neighbors will establish the reciprocally profitable ties to which their geographical proximity, their still complementary economies, and their long tradition of friendship entitle them.

To begin with I favor a relaxation in travel restrictions between the two countries. An increased number of Americans visiting Cuba, including serious students and newsmen, would be desirable. The American public is currently too dependent on the reports of Castro's tame interviewers and unconditional admirers and on those of his bitter enemies. But obviously increased travel of Americans to Cuba would involve also a disposition on the part of Castro to relax his own restrictions on the admission of foreigners.

It would have to be pointed out to prospective American travelers that while in Cuba they would not enjoy the security provided in most countries in such matters as freedom from arbitrary arrest and the right of access of the citizen to the consular authorities of his country. But plenty of Americans would be willing to take their chances. And the presence of the Swiss officials in Cuba would make the status of the American traveler there less precarious than if he were going to Communist China or North Korea.

A relaxation by the United States so far as Americans traveling to Cuba are concerned need not require Cuban reciprocity in lifting the restrictions on the travel of its citizens out of that police state. Given the Castro position on the United States, it seems improbable that he will be inclined to increase exposure of his subjects to the real United States instead of the one he has fabricated for them in his speeches and his press. But if such a relaxation should occur the United States already has, thanks to the freedom flights for Cubans escaping permanently from Castro's domain, a thorough system for the screening of Cubans coming to this country.

Gift packages are currently available through charitable organizations in this and other countries for exiled Cubans to send to their friends and relatives in Cuba. Castro naturally views these packages with a jaundiced eye. They call attention to the hardships in the daily lives of the people over whom he rules, and they bring relief more often than not to those whom he considers the less deserving. But the traffic exists. It might be expanded and simplified. And why should not Cubans in Cuba be permitted to send gift packages to their own friends and relatives in the United States? Surely cigars, guava products, and so forth are not in such short supply that some minor exports on a nonreimbursable basis could not be contemplated even in the present deplorable state of the Cuban balance of payments.

Unfortunately, in the conditions in which we live in the latter third of the twentieth century, these mostly innocent exchanges of personal remembrances have to be hedged about with security precautions. Castro has alleged that some of the gift packages sent from the United States have contained explosives that have injured Cuban postal employees. The possibility of sending such packages from Cuba might inspire some senders to commit similar abuses. To avoid such possibilities the entire exchange should be confided to some organization acceptable to both sides.

If some relaxations on the movement of persons and on that of relief and gift packages can be brought to pass, the next step might be the establishment of direct air transportation for passengers and light cargo. Such a direct link has for years been nonexistent except for the "freedom flights" to which access is strictly limited and which carry little or no traffic from the United States to Cuba. It would be simple, if the will existed on both sides of the Florida Straits, to establish a service between Miami and Havana perhaps initially on a once-a-week basis with frequencies later dependent on the amount of traffic carried. The operation of the service might be entrusted to the Swiss who are responsible for American interests in Cuba, who have a fine airline, and who might be acceptable to Castro, depending on his mood of the moment.

Admittedly such matters as increased travel between Cuba and the United States, more relief and gift packages, and the establishment of a direct air link do not go to the heart of the present situation. I do not believe that as long as Castro remains the ruler of Cuba there is any possibility of substantial forward movement. The obstacle in the path of a normal relationship between the two neighboring peoples, other than the view of the United States which Castro has purposely made into a touchstone of revolutionary orthodoxy, is the paralysis of the formerly flourishing economic relations between them. The establishment of relations in this field on a basis of equity is a complex problem. The following chapter examines two major aspects of that problem.

Chapter 21

Future Economic Relations Between Cuba and the United States

I PROPOSE in this chapter to examine two problems for which solutions will have to be found before economic relations between Cuba and the United States can be established. These are, first, the development of a realistic method for settling the claims of Americans despoiled of their property by Castro and, second, the devising of arrangements that will permit the movement of Cuban sugar to the United States. It is, I believe, impractical to contemplate a return to the pre-Castro relationship between the two countries. The former ties rested on a level of trade and investment which are no more capable of being restored than is the generally American-oriented Cuban establishment Castro swept aside a decade ago.

Those ties were, however, of a magnitude that is worth recalling in the face of the nonexistence of any ties at all at the present time. During each of the years from 1951 through 1958 Cuban exports to the United States were valued at not less than $370 million or more than $490 million. Over 80 percent consisted of sugar and sugar-derived products. In these same years American exports to Cuba were never less than $370 million and in one year they rose to $580 million. The United States in the fifties absorbed roughly two-thirds of Cuba's exports and accounted for four-fifths of its imports.[1] A series of decisions for which both governments share responsibility, though the initiative was Castro's, drastically curtailed this mutually advantageous trade in the first two years of the new regime in Cuba; it was soon after completely eliminated.

During the fifties American investments in Cuba had a book value in excess of two billion dollars and played an important part in the Cuban economy and in Cuba's trade with the United States. Substantial new investments were being made by Americans in fields that promoted agricultural diversification and industrialization. Today there is little socially significant private property on the island. Most of what existed—both American and Cuban—has been confiscated. In addition tens of thousands of former residents of Cuba, including hundreds of Americans, have lost their homes and their personal possessions.

Compensation in Principle

The establishment of trade between Cuba and the United States presupposes a bilateral understanding covering principles and procedures for dealing with the claims of the American corporations and citizens despoiled of their properties without compensation in 1959 and 1960. Such claims, with a value of more than three billion dollars, have been filed in Washington by 1,144 corporations and 6,623 individuals. The claimants' valuation of their losses (currently being adjudicated by the Foreign Claims Settlement Commission in Washington) somewhat exceeds the annual estimated gross national product of Cuba at the present time; in comparison, the total national debt of the United States amounts to less than half of our gross national product for 1970. The properties in question may be divided into two categories: those which contributed to the production of goods and services and those which were the personal assets of the former owners, such as their homes, furniture, automobiles, and so forth.

If the political, economic, and social system in the context of which these properties were acquired still existed, the matter of valuation would be relatively simple in each case. But the old order has vanished. The nationalizations and confiscations reflect a revolutionary conquest at the expense of a now exiled or refugee element of Cuban society and of the American investors who were a part of that old order. Both the Cuban laws establishing the property rights in question and popular acceptance of those laws have disappeared.

American power over Cuban destinies has gone too; this was a factor that admittedly both stimulated American investment and gave it a sense of security adding to its value. Thus an American sugar mill derived a part of its value from the assurance that it enjoyed a legal share of the vitally important American quota for Cuban sugar and that the quota depended in part on American opinion of the treatment accorded by the Cuban government to the American investor. The American utilities benefited from a well-founded belief that the government in Washington would be constructively reluctant to see them treated in a manner that business-oriented opinion in the United States would consider unfair and would use powerful leverage to prevent such treatment.

Cuban investors also relied on the Cuban American relationship as an element of stability—this, however, did not prevent a great many of them from placing anchors to windward in the shape of significant investments in the United States. The chances of American investors to recover a part of their Cuban investments will run parallel with those of the former Cuban capitalists. Both will depend on the nature of the Cuban society that is established when the people of Cuba emerge from the Castro spell. I do not believe it possible at this stage to forecast what the Cuban people will eventually choose to replace both "imperialist-dominated" and "Marxist-Leninist" Cuba.

It seems to me unlikely, however, that post-Castro Cuba will wish to have its major utilities and its oil refineries once more owned and operated by foreign corporations or its sugar industry owned by private investors, a large fraction of whom would again be foreign. Conditions in Cuba after Castro are not apt to be such as to permit the payment to former owners of anything that would meet the definition of adequate and effective compensation based on earlier values. The fact of confiscation is a political fact, whatever one may think of its morality or of its equity. Cuban society will not be in a position to pay for the properties nor is it apt to decide that they should be returned to their former owners. Those responsible for the country's welfare after Castro disappears will be unable as a practical matter to saddle the country with a heavy debt that will not effectively increase the country's physical assets.

Nevertheless, a real obligation to the despoiled exists, even though the American tax system has permitted many of them to recoup a part of their losses at the expense of the United States Treasury. When it become feasible to open negotiations for a renewed Cuban participation in the American sugar market, the United States should insist that Cuba make available for the benefit of the American claimants an annual payment to be negotiated.

Distributions would be the function of a joint claims commission with agreed rules of procedure. The Cuban payment could be financed from taxes on the trade between the two countries and from other sources. Its amount would be determined in the light of conditions at that time. The American government's attitude should be a potent factor in bringing the sum set aside as close as possible to the Cuban government's real capacity to pay.

The determination of the principles on the basis of which the sums so accumulated would be distributed would be the responsibility of the proposed joint claims commission. In the event the commission disagreed on the principles of valuation and the adjudication of claims, provision should be made for appeals to international judiciary machinery or to arbitration.

Precedents involving compensation for this type of political confiscation do not encourage the hope that the sums eventually received will be more than a fraction of the values claimed by the former owners. The argument will be made on behalf of some of the claimants that the United States should adopt a harsh attitude toward the Cuban government in order to discourage other governments from similar attitudes toward American properties in their jurisdictions. I do not believe this position is valid. What took place in Cuba was the destruction of the entire private-property system, domestic and foreign. In the countries of Latin America, so long as the system of private property remains more or less secure, wholesale confiscations of American properties such as those that took place in Cuba are unlikely, though specific situations may and probably will continue to give rise to actions unpalatable to American investors and particularly to those with positions established generations ago and not sufficiently modified to take changing conditions into account. If the domestic private-property system is rejected by the communities concerned, the fate of American investments will be sealed, independent of what happened or happens in Cuba. If private investment and private property continue to be accepted by these communities, American investment, provided the policies of the American business community and of the American government are mature and realistic, should be reasonably secure.

Post-1960 American, Russian, and Cuban Sugar Policies

The establishment of a new trading relationship between Cuba and the United States will be an essential element in the creation of a situation in which Americans despoiled in Cuba may expect some compensation for their losses. In such a relationship a market for some Cuban sugar in the United States will be an indispensable factor. A review of the background of the present situation will help define the problem and indicate the conditions and the limitations of a possible solution.

In 1960 the Eisenhower administration announced, and in 1961 the Kennedy administration confirmed, the American decision to stop buying sugar from Cuba. In consequence the United States had to find new sources of supply for some 3 million short tons of sugar (about 2.7 million metric tons), equivalent to nearly one-third of the annual consumption requirements of the American people. The Soviet Union, Cuba's new patron, had to make it possible for Cuba profitably to dispose of that same amount of sugar annually; it represented about half a normal Cuban crop and nearly one-third of the amount then annually being consumed by the Russian people. The relative ease with which the United States and Russia made the required adjustments was not the least striking of the developments of those years.

The United States increased the marketing quotas of its domestic producers by some 800,000 short tons. Most of the new production came from beet areas though cane producers (some of them refugee Cubans in Florida) also benefited. The trend in the United States toward domestic self-sufficiency was thus accelerated. The balance of American requirements was obtained from other American republics and from Australia and South Africa. The principal beneficiaries were Mexico, Peru, the Dominican Republic, and Brazil; these countries experienced significant increases in their export earnings.

In 1960 Russia consumed about as much sugar as the United States but only two-thirds as much per capita. Retail prices were—and still are—several times higher than in the United States. Imports were sporadic at levels seldom reaching 10 percent of total consumption. At the prevailing low rate of consumption Russia seemed close to self-sufficiency in sugar. Then came the suspension by the United States of Cuba's quota in the American market. The Soviet Union was suddenly faced with a problem on whose solution the fate of the anti-American, anticapitalist revolution in Cuba depended.

Fortunately, from the Russian point of view and from that of Castro as well, Soviet management of the Russian economy was becoming oriented toward the needs of the long neglected and deprived Russian consumer. The

Russian leaders welcomed the opportunity to increase sugar consumption in Russia through the acquisition of Cuban sugar at prices which, while theoretically in the premium category (six cents per pound), involved 80 percent payment in Soviet goods and only 20 percent in free exchange. (Increased purchases of Cuban sugar by East European countries and by Communist China helped in the solution of Cuba's problem.)

For the Russians there was a period of adjustment. Russian storage facilities for Cuban raw sugar appear to have been strained to the point that some sugar spoiled. Some domestic beet production was diverted from human consumption to cattle feed to make room for Cuban imports. But through increased consumption per capita, through the development of markets for refined sugar among Russia's clients in the third world countries, and with assistance from other Communist countries Russia not only solved the problem of absorbing the portion of the Cuban crop formerly taken by the United States but did so in the context both of a resumption after 1964 of the upward movement of its home production and of a contractual willingness to buy far more Cuban sugar than Castro has so far produced for the Russian market.

Today Russia is less dependent on Cuba for sugar than the United States appeared to be in 1960 even though Russia has contracted to buy 5 million metric tons annually in the three years beginning with 1968 as compared to the 2.7 million tons of the Cuban quota in the United States in the late fifties. Castro has so far failed to produce for export to Russia even half of what the Russians pledged in 1964 they would buy in 1968. A brief review of the Cuban sugar record since Castro took over the industry will clarify the present position.

In 1960 Castro was sympathetic to the views of Guevara and others who held that the wicked capitalists had inflated sugar production in Cuba so that the people of the island were the slaves of a colonial, plantation economy. He decided to take some sugar land and devote it to agricultural diversification on a large scale. The paradoxical result was the production in 1961 of a bumper crop totaling 6.7 million metric tons of sugar, the largest ever (as of 1969) with the one exception of 1952.[2] (To make possible new land uses, more cane than normal was cut and less was sown. The industrial and the agricultural plants were still in the fairly good shape in which their former owners had left them. The organization of labor remained fairly efficient.)

In 1962 the crop was 30 percent below that for the previous year, and in

1963 it sank to a twenty-year low of under 4 million tons. This came at a time of booming world prices resulting both from short Cuban crops and from the fact that the United States was now buying significant quantities of sugar from countries which had heretofore relied on the world market for the bulk of their exports. In fact, the Soviet Union was obliged during these years to relieve Cuba of a part of its Soviet commitment in order that Cuba might increase its sales at the abnormal prices (sometimes above ten cents a pound) obtainable on the world market.

In 1963 Castro was faced with multiple failures in his agricultural diversification efforts and in his programs of industrialization. Guevara admitted that serious errors had been committed.[3] Sugar production in Cuba had declined drastically both because of Castro's policy and because of drought conditions at a time of sharply rising world prices.

Castro reversed his sugar strategy. In November 1963 he announced that the welfare of Cuba was tied to Cuba's ability to produce as much sugar as it possibly could.[4] He proclaimed that Cuba would never again sign with capitalist countries any restrictive agreements of the kind that had limited its production in the past; on the contrary, Cuba would increase its production as rapidly as possible in view of Cuba's unrivaled natural advantages for the growing of sugarcane. He threatened producers in other lands telling them that "they will soon find out that they cannot compete with us where sugar is concerned; we have in our hands an atomic bomb of sugar. What does this mean? It means that by the year 1970 we will be able to produce more than ten million tons of sugar, that we will be able to export ten million tons of sugar."[5]

Castro's sugar experts dutifully provided a series of gradually rising forecasts of Cuban sugar production culminating in the 10 million Spanish long tons the Maximum Leader had decreed for 1970. As a matter of fact, however, production in 1969 appears to have been about 5.5 million tons. Indeed, since Castro announced his "emphasis on sugar" policy in 1963, annual production has never (until 1970) been much over 6 million tons and has not equaled the 6.7 million tons achieved in 1961 when Castro was downgrading sugar. The efforts demanded of the Cuban people to produce 10 million tons in 1970 have apparently resulted in a record crop of 8.5 million tons.[6] But an absolute dictator's opportunities for statistical legerdemain are such that we may never know how much was really produced in the 1970 crop season.

In January 1964, on his return from Moscow, Castro reiterated the 10-

million-ton goal for 1970. He reported the agreement he had made with Russia according to which the latter pledged itself to take from Cuba 2.1 million tons of sugar in 1965, 3 million in 1966, 4 million in 1967, and 5 million each in 1968, 1969, and 1970 at a price of six cents a pound with 80 percent of the value payable in Russian goods. Actual deliveries to the Soviet Union were slightly in excess of the agreed 1965 figure. Thereafter Cuba has made available less than one-half the amounts Russia had contracted to take in each year.[7]

During the early sixties Russian policy appears to have been to cut back planned increases of domestic sugar production in order to make room for the large quantities expected from Cuba.[8] When Cuban production dwindled after 1961 and, by 1963, had fallen off by over 40 percent, the Russian authorities, committed to steadily increasing availabilities of sugar on the home market, found it necessary to resume the expansion of their domestic production.[9]

Relative scarcities on the world market, where quotas had been suspended largely because of the Cuban refusal to accept any restrictions, soon disappeared, and prices dropped to levels unknown since the depression years of the midthirties. In 1965 the average price sank to 2.1 cents per pound as compared with 8.4 cents in 1963 and 5.8 cents in 1964. In 1966, 1967, and 1968 it remained below 2.0 cents.[10]

By mid-1968 sugar was selling at little more than 1.25 cents on the world market.[11] The situation had become so critical that Castro, in part at the urging of his Russian patrons and underwriters and yielding also to the persuasiveness of Raúl Prebisch representing the interest of the developing nations in a more orderly sugar market, allowed his officials at Geneva to sign an agreement that limited Cuba's sales to the world market. He thus accepted the sort of arrangement he had so scornfully rejected four years earlier. The Cuban world-market quota in the new agreement (2.15 million metric tons) is of the same order of magnitude as that which Cuba had accepted in previous post–World War II agreements.[12]

There is no limit in the agreement to the amount of sugar Cuba can send the Soviet Union or other Communist countries. The Soviet Union, however, in signing the agreement has agreed to a limitation in 1969, 1970, and 1971 of its sugar exports to slightly over 1 million metric tons, which is equivalent to actual shipments in recent years. In the case of Cuban exports to Czechoslovakia, Hungary, and Poland (normally exporters of sugar), the agreement to which these countries are parties provides that if Cuban exports to them exceed 300,000 tons in any one year during the life of the agreement, the excess will be charged against Cuba's export quota to the world market.

There are also provisions regarding East Germany and Communist China which are not parties to the agreement. If these two countries increase their exports to the world market beyond a certain figure and if Cuba has exported to them in the preceding year more than 910,000 tons, the excess in their exports over 300,000 tons will be deducted from the Cuban quota in the world market. (Exports of these two Communist nonsignatory countries have, in general, substantially exceeded the limitation set forth in the agreement, but their imports from Cuba have been below the agreement figure. Therefore, these two countries could, in theory, increase their exports to the world market by several hundred thousand tons without causing a diminution in Cuba's export quota. But neither of these two countries is believed currently to have a physical capacity for seriously disrupting the world sugar market.)

Though other factors may be involved, the new agreement has contributed to an improvement in prices. The average in 1969 was 3.4 cents per pound. For most of 1970 it has remained well over 3.5 cents and at the year's end was over 4.0 cents. It is more than double the level to which it sank when quotas were in abeyance, reflecting Castro's refusal to sign an agreement.

Castro can point out to his people that the agreements he has signed with the world market and with the Soviet Union have not restricted Cuban production as did the previous world-market agreement taken in conjunction with the arrangement for the movement of Cuban sugar to the United States, then Cuba's major market. But he must derive little satisfaction from the fact that in the five years ending with 1969 the Cuban industry was not able materially to increase its production in spite of his repeated exhortations and of his contract with the Soviet Union. Cuba, as of 1969, had commitments—including the 5 million tons to Russia—for between 2 and 3 million tons annually in excess of what it is producing. (An illustrative Cuban crop distribution in a good year during the late sixties would be 2 million tons to the world market, 2.5 million tons to Russia, 1 million tons to other Communist countries, and 0.5 million tons for domestic consumption [rationed]. This total of 6 million tons is above the estimated crop for 1969 and above the average Cuban production since 1961.)

The Kremlin planners enjoy an enviable flexibility in sugar policy. Russian domestic production has been greatly expanded from barely 6 million metric tons in 1963 to over 10 million tons in 1969 and in 1970 is probably running at an annual rate of nearly 11 million tons. Consumption in the Soviet Union rose from under 7 million tons in 1963 to over 11 million tons in 1970. The outlook for further increases, as population and per capita consumption continue to rise, appears bright, though the rate of increase can be expected to decline as per capita consumption tends to stabilize.

As long as it is in Russia's political interest to do so, Russia can adjust its own sugar production and its people's consumption so as to absorb Cuban sugar over a very wide range—up or down. The Soviet authorities could probably handle the 5 million tons they committed themselves to take in 1968, 1969, and 1970, though Castro has not confronted them with any such amounts.

The economics of Russia's Cuban-sugar operations work out in favor of the Soviet Union. Russian purchases of Cuban sugar are at six cents per pound with 80 percent payable in Russian goods, whose values are fixed according to predominantly Russian views. (The American sugar system currently pays over seven cents per pound, in dollars, to its suppliers outside the United States tariff wall.) This Cuban sugar is then refined, distributed, and retailed to the Russian people at prices several times as high as it would bring in Western countries and, particularly, in the United States. Granting that part of this spread reflects differing systems of internal taxation, it is so great as to lead to the conclusion that a very handsome profit is earned by the Russian state on its sales of Cuban sugar to the Russian consumer. (Interestingly enough, the refined sugar that Russia is able to export because of its Cuban imports is sold to third world countries at prices which represent a very small fraction of what Russian consumers pay for the same article. These prices are also well below what Russia pays Cuba for raw sugar plus the cost of refining that sugar in Russia. I estimate the profit to the Russian state on Cuban sugar sold to the Russian consumer at at least twenty-five cents per pound.)

Cuban Sugar on American Tables Again?

Let us now turn to the problems that will be involved in arranging for the resumption of the movement of Cuban sugar to the United States when this becomes politically possible. Assuming that Russia renegotiates its contract with Cuba after 1970 at about current levels and that Cuban production becomes stabilized at more than 6 million but less than 7 million tons annually, Cuban sugar for the United States would have to be found at the expense of Cuba's other commitments. I can see no indication that Castro would be interested. Nor is it conceivable that the United States could agree to even minor purchases of Cuban sugar independently of some acceptance of the principle of compensation for the victims of Castro's nationalizations. Such acceptance by Castro is most unlikely. It may, nevertheless, be helpful to speculate on what may be possible once Castro disappears from the scene.

Under current American sugar legislation a resumption of diplomatic relations between Cuba and the United States would restore to Cuba a sugar quota in the United States of 1.3 million short tons (equivalent to 1,170,000 metric tons) or about 40 percent of Cuba's quota in 1960. This provision, however, is hardly likely to be invoked. I should expect it to disappear from the statute books. It was devised in terms of a temporary absence of Cuba from its normal commercial partnership with the United States. Its application today or tomorrow would be at the expense of friendly countries, largely in the Western Hemisphere, which have achieved over the past decade a respectable vested interest in their sales of sugar to the United States. These sales are a valuable item in the foreign-exchange earnings and, consequently, in the ability of these countries to satisfy their people's aspirations for economic development and social progress. It is inconceivable to me that the United States would reach an arrangement with Cuba that would abruptly deprive these American republics of a substantial portion of the sugar quotas they have enjoyed since 1961. To break the sugar pattern resulting from the Cuban Revolution would not be warranted by the advantages that would accrue from a partial resumption of the Cuban American sugar trade even from the narrow point of view of the United States.

If there were a change in Cuba's political orientation following the departure of Castro, the Russians might be tempted to eliminate, or at least curtail, their purchases of sugar from Cuba. Russia's own sugar economy is, as we have seen, readily adjustable. The participants in the International Sugar Agreement would presumably be willing to help Cuba by increasing Cuba's quota in the world market to the extent that the Soviet Union's own capabilities in that market were diminished by the decrease in Russia's imports of Cuban sugar. In the Russia of the seventies, the Soviet authorities would probably prefer to reduce Russia's exports rather than risk reversing the upward trend in domestic sugar consumption.

As I have suggested above, however, the mere availability of a Cuban-export surplus in the context of a restoration of Cuban American relations would not *ipso facto* make it possible for the United States to import such sugars. Nothing less than a reorganization in the marketing of sugar in international trade would be required to produce that result.

I do not propose to go into details about possible solutions. I will limit myself to indicating an approach that might be explored in order to develop a workable policy when the time comes. Roughly speaking, world sugar production and consumption are in uneasy balance at the level of 72 million metric tons; of this, about 20 million tons enter into international trade. The trend is for the major sugar-importing nations, including the United States, to increase their domestic producers' share of their total consumption. At the beginning of the current decade major industrialized sugar-importing countries produced 57 percent of their consumption requirements. By 1967 this had risen to 64 percent and the trend continues upward.[13] Thus the European Economic Community contemplates the production of significant export surpluses from an area where imports have been normal.[14]

Of the 20,000,000 tons of sugar that enter into international trade, less than half are dealt with in what is known as the *world*, or *free, market*. Almost all of the remainder is handled in accordance with three special sugar systems for which the United States, the United Kingdom, and the Soviet Union are respectively responsible. These three countries, partly for reasons of political economics, undertake to absorb specified amounts of sugar at premium prices from designated suppliers.

The American system was born in 1934; it reflected the New Deal agricultural adjustment philosophy and the Roosevelt administration's desire to rescue depression-distraught Cuba by guaranteeing to Cuba a share of the American market which, while little more than half what Cuba had enjoyed before 1930, was double that to which Cuba had been reduced in the trough of the world crisis. Following Cuba's elimination from the system in 1960, that system favors the other sugar-exporting nations of the Western Hemisphere, plus Australia, the Philippines, Taiwan, and others with quotas in the American market. (The Philippines had a quota in 1934 as one of the offshore domestic producers, like Hawaii and Puerto Rico; now that the Philippines is an independent nation its quota—about a million short tons—is a part of its treaty relationship with the United States.)

The Soviet system was initiated in 1960 when the Soviet Union fell heir to the former American responsibility for the Cuban economy. It covers Cuban exports to Russia and is, no doubt, coordinated with Cuban exports to other Communist countries, except perhaps Communist China.

The British system in its present form dates from the early thirties. It is largely designed to meet the requirements of the Commonwealth countries, including the former British West Indies, Australia, Mauritius, the Fiji Islands, and others. The United Kingdom buys specified amounts at negotiated premium prices from the Commonwealth (or colonial) producers and, in some cases, further specified amounts at the generally lower prices prevailing in the world market. The United Kingdom, in addition to buying raw sugars for domestic consumption, is also in the market for raw sugars to be refined in the United Kingdom and then reexported competitively in the world market.

All three of the countries maintaining these systems are net importers of sugar. All three have tended to stimulate the role of their domestic production, though the increase in their total consumption has counteracted the loss that otherwise would have taken place in the quotas of the tropical cane producers.

Ideally, the three special systems and the world market should merge to create a true *world* sugar market worthy of the name. Such a market, internationally operated and controlled, could allocate production and consumption quotas so as to lead to equitable prices for producers and consumers much as the American system has served the interests of both the producers for that market and the consumers within it. It would avoid the waste in the present system where sugar movements often depend on political or ideological factors rather than on economic advantage. But such a system is, realistically speaking, too far in the future to be considered in planning a way for Cuba once again to sell some sugar to the United States, its natural market.

The anomalies in the present arrangements are glaring. The United States buys no sugar produced in the Cuban cane fields on its doorstep. Each year over a million tons of Cuban sugar go to Japan and to Communist China—all the way across the Pacific. The United States buys a somewhat greater amount from the Philippines and Australia and brings it back across the Pacific. Japan buys sugar from Cuba and from wherever else it can get it at the cheapest possible prices.

I believe that Japan holds the key to the reorganization of sugar movements that would rationalize the sugar trade in the western Pacific area and, at the same time, permit a resumption of sugar exports from Cuba to the United States. Japan, with its phenomenal growth in economic power, should be ready to assume greater responsibility for the welfare of the sugar-producing countries in its natural sphere of economic influence by assuming the sort of burdens in regard to them that the United States, the United Kingdom—and more recently, the Soviet Union—have assumed in their own special contexts.

In 1969 Japan had a home production of over 600,000 tons of sugar while its imports were in excess of 2 million tons. Of the latter amount over 800,000 tons came from Cuba, nearly 600,000 from Australia, and over 350,000 from South Africa. The Philippines, an Asiatic nation currently bent on stressing its "Asianness," was sending all of its exportable sugar—about 1 million tons—to the United States.

Japan has, heretofore, used the bargaining power of its comparatively large imports from the world market (over 25 percent of the gross imports in that market) to get the sugar it needs under the most favorable possible conditions and has been a powerful influence for lower prices. It has been able to accentuate the price-depressant effect of the oversupply conditions that usually prevail in the world market.

As Japan consolidates its brilliant prosperity, it may reasonably be expected to take the lead in rationalizing the sugar trade in the area it increasingly dominates economically. It should undertake to meet its requirements of sugar from the countries in the western Pacific area and to do so at prices remunerative to the producers and, hence, comparable to those paid for sugar by the United States, the United Kingdom, and the Soviet Union. This could be achieved either through long-term contracts at fair prices or through the establishment by Japan of a sugar system comparable to those of the three countries mentioned. Surely Japan can logically be expected to shoulder the responsibility for the Philippine sugar industry heretofore borne by the United States and thus to contribute to the Asianization of the international relations of that country so ardently favored by so many of its leading politicians. In the case of Australia, Japan might also be expected to absorb a stated portion of the crop at a fair price instead of bargaining for the very lowest price in a normally oversupplied market.

Let us assume a willingness on the part of Japan to acquire all of the sugar it needs from the western Pacific area, that is, from the Philippines, Australia, and Taiwan, at prices comparable to what the United States is now paying for the sugar it imports from those countries. The United States would then be able to give Cuba a quota in the American market of some 1.5 million tons without displacing from that market any of the other Latin American countries that now share in it. Cuba would, of course, lose the sales it currently makes to Japan at world-market prices but would be more than compensated by the recovery of a part of its former American quota at premium prices.

Renewed purchases of Cuban sugar by the United States in the post-Castro era would trigger diminishing Russian enthusiasm for the current unnatural economic relationship between Havana and Moscow. Russian sugar purchases would shrink. Crude oil from Black Sea ports would logically give way to a renewal of the movement of Venezuelan oil to the island refineries. Yet it is probable that a commercial interchange far more substantial than that of pre-Castro days would subsist between Cuba and the Soviet Union.

On the basis of the assumptions we have been making, a rough guess at the allocation of a Cuban sugar crop of 5.5 million metric tons would be as follows: United States, 1.5 million tons; Soviet Union and other Communist countries, including China, 2 million tons; world market (minus Japan), 1.5 million tons; and local consumption, 0.5 million tons. These levels may logically be expected to rise so that Cuban crops in excess of 6 million tons—above the average for the sixties—would be marketable. That level of production probably makes sense in Cuban terms, also.

Countries other than Japan may have a role to play in the reordering of world trade in sugar. Canada is one of them. There are many unknowns in the picture. What is the possibility that Indonesia will regain the potential for sugar production that made Java so important a factor in the days before World War II? Will Communist China be able to produce what it consumes or will it become an increasingly important importer? No one today can claim to have the answers to these and many other questions that will suggest themselves as the problem is examined.

The general outlook for sugar is unstable—as it always has been. While increased consumption may be expected due to population growth and other factors, the trend toward self-sufficiency is a black cloud on the horizon of countries that depend on sugar exports. Cuba remains preeminently one of these in spite of all that has been done to develop other exports both pre-Castro and by the present regime. That country still depends on sugar for over 80 percent of its export earnings. And then, of course, there is the remoter nightmare of damaging technological developments in this age of rapid progress in so many fields.

Chapter 22

Conclusion

AN orthodox moralist might describe Castro as a cruel and unusual punishment for the shortcomings of Cuban society and of the Cuban American relationship. A radical moralist would thank the fates for having provided so phenomenal a personality to right the foreign and domestic wrongs of the Cuban people. But I am not concerned so much with whether Cuba deserved Castro as with the implications of the complete, speedy, and relatively nonviolent collapse of pre-Castro Cuba.

Castro has alienated Cuba from the region where the international aspects of its political and economic life should evolve. He has subordinated Cuba—here he had some unintentional help from the United States—to the Soviet Union, a power with no geopolitical interest in Cuba, now that it has been demonstrated that Castro's Cuba has no serious role to play in Latin America and that a Soviet power base in Cuba is unacceptable to the United States. He has dislocated and impoverished the island society because he has caused the departure of tens of thousands of trained and educated Cubans. He has restructured that society along lines that are, especially in such matters as political freedom, repugnant to the concepts of Western civilization as they have evolved over the centuries.

Judgments such as the above do not furnish a base for American policy toward Cuba. Those judgments, as takeoff points for positive action, must be made by the Cuban people. The United States government should do no more than to insure that the Cuban people, in making their own judgments about their own society, will not be coerced by the Soviet Union. Yet the Cuban experience furnishes more than a negative enlightenment to those endeavoring to think through American policy toward Cuba and toward the whole of Latin America.

To a greater or lesser extent—though not to the extent that prevailed in Cuba before 1959—there is an American presence in each of the other American republics. Though some progress has been made, many of these countries are also still tied to chaotic and irrational markets for some of the exported raw materials on which their welfare depends. Do current American policies strengthen these societies in their efforts to find evolutionary and self-reliant, rather than revolutionary, destructive, and bitterly anti-American, roads to economic development and social progress?

The answer to the question involves the nature of relations among twenty-one nations, of which only one has achieved or is apt to achieve, great power status and which in political strength, economic wealth, and material dynamism towers over the rest. The lines of attraction will run from the weaker to the stronger, while the lines of force will flow in the opposite direction, from the stronger to the weaker. The power of the United States manifests itself in relation to the other countries of the hemisphere either as influence or as intervention. Before pointing out how, under the conditions of today, intervention tends to destroy influence, an attempt at definition is in order.

Influence is a force that emanates from the United States because of the existence of the American community with its record of achievement. This influence, thus, reflects a recognition of the progress of the United States in many fields in which the other American republics desire to emulate American successes and to copy the principles and procedures to which those successes are (sometimes wrongly!) attributed. American influence derives from a competent performance in many fields, including the operation of self-government, the production of goods and services, advances in social fields, and technological and scientific progress. It flows from a consciousness of what the American people live for and of what they have proved willing to die for. It radiates from our popular arts including music, the mass media, theater, sports, and so forth. Although, in some cases, it may produce a misguided or ill-adapted emulation, it exists because the

American experience is considered relevant to the effort at progress in which the other American republics are engaged.

When, however, the United States does things or fails to do things at home or abroad that do not live up to the high opinion on which its influence has been based, the latter suffers. A belief that we have been indifferent or fumbling in our approach to racial, educational, or other social problems, evidences of a disposition on the part of sectors of our population to resort to lawlessness in preference to the mechanisms of our political and juridical order, and the alleged growth of selfish materialism in the more affluent sectors have done the image of our country much harm. Adventures such as those in Vietnam or the Dominican Republic diminish rather than increase our influence in Latin America.

The influence of the United States in the other American republics has been a powerful ally of American foreign policy in its dealings with those Republics. The recognition of the positive aspects of the American record in many of the arts of civilization has assisted our diplomats and our businessmen in the advancement of legitimate American interests in Latin America. In periods like the present when many aspects of our national life, including our policies toward other countries, are under severe scrutiny and violent criticism, American influence is diminished. But as our country rises to meet the crises of its national existence, as it has so often successfully done, that influence will be reasserted and strengthened.

American influence in Latin America was never so strong as it was during the first two terms of Franklin Roosevelt in the White House. Our country had formally abjured the right to intervene in the affairs of its neighbors—a right that had been asserted and exercised over the previous three decades. The United States government was struggling to revive an economy and to reform a society that had been buffeted by the Great Depression of the early thirties. At that time there was no Alliance for Progress, no American aid programs—only the spectacle of the most powerful nation in the Western Hemisphere inspiringly at grips with fundamental problems some of which were common to other nations of the continent.

Intervention, on the other hand, is the actual or threatened use of American power to secure a result that the country concerned does not wish to achieve. Some writers have confined intervention to those cases where the United States sends its armed forces to the territory of another American republic. I would define intervention more broadly—as any use of force or the threat of force, whether military, political, or economic, by the United States government (or even by a private American interest) designed to secure a positive or negative result or decision which the intervened country, if left to its own devices, would not have willed.

I would not define as intervention the assistance rendered by the United States to enable the country assisted to achieve goals it has truly set for itself. Nor would I so define fluctuations in the amounts of such assistance, particularly downward ones reflecting American fiscal policy. But the conduct of assistance programs can be a fertile field of intervention when the granting or withholding of assistance is made contingent on the recipient country's performance in a field or fields not directly related to the efficient utilization of the particular assistance being rendered.

The Bay of Pigs episode in April 1961, even though American forces were not involved on the field of battle in Cuba, was an unsuccessful American intervention in the domestic affairs of that country. The invasion of the Dominican Republic by American forces in 1965 was a successful example of this form of intervention. It achieved the immediate objective of its proponents, though there remains controversy as to whether the threat of "another Cuba" was real at the time. The forces deployed—over twenty thousand men—were so considerable, compared with the requirements of the gunboat diplomacy of earlier days, that it calls into question the feasibility of employing this type of intervention in the case of larger countries actually faced with the type of internal problem our policymakers believed existed in the Dominican Republic in 1965.

The success of the Dominican intervention, even with its coloring of hemispheric solidarity, has not increased support either in this country or in Latin America for retaining this weapon in the continental arsenal. The Bay of Pigs setback and the Dominican victory alike weakened American influence in the other American republics and, therefore, adversely affected the conduct of American diplomacy in those countries and the promotion there of American interests.

The principle that intervention destroys influence is clearly demonstrated in the relationship between Cuba and the United States and especially in the Castro experience. A Cuban society, preconditioned to passivity because of its dependence on an anarchic market for its major product, sugar, found its vital energies further sapped by the overpowering American presence. American intervention in Cuban affairs and, above all, a real, if unjustified, belief in the extent to which that intervention might go helped destroy the vitality of the Cuban political mechanism which might have served to place democratic control of the country's destinies in the hands of the electorate and of its chosen leaders. The rise of Castro and the failure of the American intervention designed to overthrow him proved that the effectiveness of American intervention was much less than had been believed both by its proponents and by its enemies. Even an initially successful intervention in Cuba, however, would have led to an American involvement in Cuba with unacceptable consequences because a viable Cuban government was not a conceivable end product of such an intervention. I cannot avoid the conclusion that intervention, as I have defined and described it in these pages, is as dead as colonialism as an effective political method in today's world.

Intervention, with the objective of overthrowing regimes of which the United States disapproves and bolstering those of which it approves, is, I believe, increasingly rejected by American public opinion. I would not expect to see a repetition of either the Bay of Pigs or the Dominican adventures in the development of American policy toward Latin America. The result of such abstention should be a restoration and a growth of the influence of the United States in the area.

But it must be recognized that American influence in these countries is also sapped by attempts to protect American private interests there through such devices as the Hickenlooper Amendment. The effect is to relate American aid or other "favors" (sugar legislation, for example) to the conduct of the government concerned toward American private interests within their jurisdiction. These interests are thereby given a status not possessed by other private interests operating in accordance with national legislation and subject wholly to the sovereign authority of the national government.

There are few more politically controversial and sensitive areas than the relations between government and private capital; in our country these have evolved since 1931 to an extent that many of us find hard to realize. The difficulty of legislation by a foreign power along the lines of the Hickenlooper Amendment is that it attempts to limit the freedom of action of the local governments and their responsibility for steps they may feel it desirable to take in the national interest. Their actions will sometimes be poorly conceived and may even be absolutely unjust; the point is that the consequences thereof should not include specific retaliatory action by another government.

The potential of private capital for assisting the economic development of the countries of the hemisphere is very great. A government which consistently maltreats foreign capital will not escape the consequences of its actions and peacefully enjoy the fruits of its depredations. Such a government will discourage further investment from abroad. It will destroy its foreign and indeed its domestic credit. Its ability to contract loans internationally, including those it could normally expect from the United States government as well as from the multilateral agencies, will be diminished. It will involve itself in international litigation. These evident consequences will have a far greater deterrent effect against unfair treatment of American investors than the formula that has appealed to our legislators. Indeed the Hickenlooper formula tends to invest disregard of American property rights with a certain patriotic or nationalistic aura and thus to work against a regard for fair dealing and for the need to encourage foreign investment with its capacity to contribute to desperately needed development.

In this matter of foreign investment, as in most things connected with Latin America, generalizations are misleading. There are many types of American investment. They have differing values from the point of view of the local community. An American investment that opens up a natural resource that the people of the country on their own would not have been able to develop deserves the welcome it has so often received in the Latin American past. During the first few years, if the enterprise is successful, the profits to the original entrepreneur will be large and justly so. But when, for instance, fifty years have elapsed since the original investment, is it not understandable that the people of the country concerned should make a political issue of local control and ownership of that particular natural resource? Is it not logical for them to believe that the reward to the foreign entrepreneur has been fully paid and that the successors of the latter have no sacrosanct right indefinitely to own and operate that particular resource? Failure to recognize political reality and to take suitable steps in a spirit of business statesmanship to anticipate it under relatively favorable conditions have been regrettable facts of life in some countries of the hemisphere, though in others a peaceful, fair, and cooperative "disinvestment" process has been pursued.[1]

Similarly, in the case of public utilities a generation or so of foreign control ought to be enough to satisfy the most avid operator and investor. In both the fields we have been considering, legitimate discrepancies about the valuations at which assets should be transferred from foreign to local ownership may be great. The United States government should come into the picture only after its nationals have exhausted all of their legal remedies in the country where they are operating and then, if it decides to espouse the case, should not do so in the context of a threat of some specific action in a field unrelated to that in controversy. The possibility of special financing for the transfer to local control of certain politically obsolete and hence vulnerable American investments should be actively explored.

It is to the interest of the people of the United States that American influence in Latin America recover from its present level. It is to the interest of the people of the area that the influence of the strongest and most powerful member of the inter-American community recover from that level. That influence will grow to the extent that the United States once more adapts its foreign policy to its capacities and turns its energies away from Asiatic warfare to the solution of its domestic problems in social and educational fields. That influence will also grow to the extent that the policy of the United States in Latin America is seen to be oriented toward the creation of conditions that will affirm the responsibility of the governments and the people of the Latin American countries for their own destinies. The United States should take whatever role the other members of the community may wish it to take in the protection of the area from foreign intervention—but should defer to community judgments in this most sensitive matter.

Notes on the Cuban Background

INTRODUCTION

CUBA's modern history has not stimulated a Cuban sense of control over Cuban destinies. Skepticism as to the purpose and the efficacy of Cuban political institutions was a factor in the rapid and relatively unopposed destruction of the Cuban social structure in 1959 and 1960. Even Castro's admittedly phenomenal talents would have been unsuccessful in subverting a self-reliant and cohesive society with a leadership that had a will to defend itself and sufficient acceptance in the society to make defense feasible.

Cuba's problems of political and social development were aggravated by the working of three external factors. These were: first, the impact of wide, eccentric, and unpredictable fluctuations in the market for sugar, Cuba's major product, generally equivalent to one-third of the country's total output of goods and services and 90 percent of which is exported; second, the nature of the relations, political and economic, between the governments of Cuba and the United States; and third, the role of private American interests in Cuba. Sugar in its broadest aspects lends itself to separate treatment, but the relations between the Cuban and the American governments and the influence exercised by American corporations with Cuban investments upon the American government and upon political and economic conditions in Cuba are closely intertwined. I have therefore divided these notes into two sections: "Cuba and Sugar" and "Cuban American Relations and the Dynamics of Cuban Politics." Sugar will, of course, recur in both sections; it is and has been the chief source of Cuba's wealth, of its prosperity or the lack of it and a major factor in an ironic and undynamic providentialism among many of its people especially at elite levels.

My treatment of Cuban politics under the Republic will emphasize those matters least pleasing to the patriotic sentiment of the people of Cuba and, indeed, to all those who, like myself, have affection and admiration for Cuba and faith in the potential of its people. I do not claim to give a detailed description of the developments, the final outcome of which I summarize. I have, to some extent, neglected the too often unsuccessful labors

229

of the many Cubans who tried to realize the ideals of the great José Martí. I am, however, aware of the life and work of Martí and of those men who made Cuban independence possible after a struggle of thirty years. I have enjoyed friendship and association with many of the most distinguished figures in the modern history of Cuba, men and women who fought the tendencies in the political life of Cuba which it will be my duty to record. I am confident that their vision of a better, freer, more democratic Cuba has only temporarily been frustrated by the bankruptcy of the Republic and the Castro interlude.

CUBA AND SUGAR

For the past century and a half sugar has dominated the island's economic, political, and social life. Sugar exports (over 90 percent of production) during the latter decades of the republic (1930–1959) represented over 30 percent of the total national product. In earlier times the percentage was even higher.

The President of Cuba, on the threshhold of the Great Depression of the 1930s, remarked that the price of sugar affected the lives of four-fifths of the population. He was understating the matter. Before Castro, while only 10 percent of the population was actually engaged in the production and handling of sugar, the entire economy of the country rested on the volume and the price of what could be sold abroad. Government revenues, local purchasing power, the level of domestic business and employment, as well as the ability of the nation to import consumer or developmental goods and to engage in serious economic planning were all dependent on the amount and the terms of Cuban sugar exports. Those exports have fluctuated violently throughout Cuban history because of factors which neither Cuban producers nor the Cuban government has been able to influence. Today, Castro's frenzied attempts to increase sugar production have increased rather than diminished the vulnerability of the island's economy in this respect.

The Nineteenth Century

The first real boom in Cuban sugar began early in the nineteenth century during the years in which Spain's other Latin American dominions were finding and following the road to independence from the mother country. That boom followed the bloody slave uprisings in Haiti and Santo Domingo and the failure of Napoleon's generals to reduce the rebellious blacks and to call them to account for the hideous excesses with which the conquest of their freedom had been accompanied. Hundreds of former plantation owners and overseers from the devastated lands fled to Cuba and resumed the cultivation of sugar and coffee. They brought with them hor-

---

The statistics in this section (compiled from the most reliable official sources) have been taken from the tables in José Álvarez-Díaz, ed., *Un Estudio Sobre Cuba* (Coral Gables, Fla.: University of Miami Press, 1963).

rible tales of the consequences of servile insurrection. In an atmosphere of near hysteria the presence of Spanish military forces seemed the only protection available against a repetition in Cuba of the tragic events in Hispaniola. This sentiment was a powerful element in keeping Cuba from following the revolutionary example of the rest of Latin America.

This early sugar boom in Cuba coincided with the firming up of opinion in the Atlantic world that snatching blacks from their African homes (even with the collusion of their rulers) and bringing them to the American continent as slaves was wrong. The United States Constitution in 1787 made the trade illegal as of 1808. The Congress of Vienna decided against the trade. In 1817 Spain and Great Britain signed a treaty declaring the trade unlawful and committing the parties to its prevention.

This treaty was awkward for the old, the new, and the would-be planters in Cuba. It came at a time of greatly increased demand for slaves because of the high prices and the brilliant prospects of sugar (and coffee). The existing slave population was inadequate to meet expanding needs in part because of the high death rate of the existing bondsmen. The situation was only "saved" through massive illegal importations in spite of all the British Navy could do to stop them. These contraband transactions were carried out with the connivance and to the great personal profit of high officials of the Spanish colonial and home administrations. The illicit trade brought an estimated 300,000 Africans to Cuba between 1817 and 1865.

Two unhappy patterns were thus established. One was the reliance of a considerable part of the Cuban elite—including both local and Spanish planters—upon an outside force, the Spanish army, for security, protection, and law and order. The other was the existence of and broad tolerance by that same elite for systematic corruption at the higher levels of government.

With the outcome of the Civil War in the United States, slavery in Cuba was doomed. Abolition was hastened by the revolt against Spanish authority known as the Ten Years' War (1868–1878) in which it was one of the issues. The revolt was mainly centered in the eastern part of the island where sugar cultivation was not yet of major significance. Escaped slaves furnished an important contingent of the insurgent forces.

The end of slavery with its real and fancied impact on the cost of producing sugar was only one of the problems with which the industry was now faced. Rapid technological advances were concentrating and industrializing what had been a business composed of as many as 2,000 integrated and self-sufficient units. Steam had been applied to the grinding of cane as early as 1819. Progressive mechanization, especially in the latter half of the century, had given the industry the structure with which we have become familiar in this century; it consists of between 150 and 175 large *centrales* or mills, each possessing a dominant influence in its surrounding area through its ownership of cane lands and through its ability to control cane planters, whether tenants or owners in the area.

Also during the latter half of the nineteenth century, especially after 1884, the modern relationship of Cuban production to world markets developed. Earlier, Cuban mills had produced various grades of sugar largely in final form for consumers. With the rapid development of the beet-sugar industry and with the competition of beet sugar in markets formerly the province of tropical cane producers, the latter found it expedient to enter into alliances with the cane-sugar-refining industry (a large-scale operation usually enjoying tariff protection) in the major importing countries. Thus the pattern was established which has since prevailed between Cuba and its principal customers. The Cuban producer ships raw sugar (with a polarization of ninety-six degrees) for refining and marketing by large processing interests in the importing country. These manufacturers have a vested interest in the movement of as great a volume as possible of raw sugar from their tropical suppliers—at the lowest possible prices.

The year 1884 marked the beginning of a steady decline in the price of sugar, a decline that seriously affected the Cuban sugar industry, although total production was moving to higher levels. Cuba was temporarily bailed out of the consequences of this decline by tariff action in the United States and by the trade agreement which that action forced upon a reluctant Spanish government.

Since the end of the American Civil War, the United States had been the major market for Cuban exports, including sugar. The Spanish government, however, with a lack of realism worthy of a more quixotic cause, had endeavored, through the tariffs it prescribed for Cuba, to preserve the Cuban import market for Spain. Discrimination of as much as 800 percent in favor of Spanish products was embodied in the Cuban tariff. American flour shipped via Spain to Cuba as a Spanish product cost the Cuban importer much less than if that flour had been imported directly from the United States and had paid the duty applicable to American flour.

In 1890 the McKinley Tariff Act put sugar on the free list as part of a series of measures designed to reduce government revenues considered excessive. But the Aldrich Amendment provided that the benefits of the act would not be granted to the products of foreign countries that discriminated in their own tariff legislation against American goods. This amendment was obviously directed against Spain. The Spanish government surrendered to the facts of life and to the pressures from Cuba and negotiated with the United States an agreement that radically improved the access into Cuba of the products of the United States.

The benefits of this agreement for a Cuban sugar industry now almost entirely dependent on the American market under conditions of increasing world-price weakness proved ephemeral. Cuban production topped one million Spanish long tons in 1894 for the first time. That same year the Democratic administration in Washington, reversing the then usual roles of our two major parties in tariff matters and seeking new revenues to compensate for the decline resulting from the depression of those years, reimposed duties on Cuban sugar entering the United States and did so to the tune of 40 percent ad valorem (the Wilson Tariff Act). This was a heavy blow to Cuba. Many historians have given the resulting economic stagnation as one of the causes contributing to the outbreak of the final Cuban struggle for liberation from Spain in 1895.

As that struggle deepened in intensity and in savagery on both sides, sugar production declined rapidly as sugar mills were paralyzed or destroyed by the opposing armies. But the rapid falling off in Cuban production did not have a compensatory effect on prices; they continued to decline throughout the war. This was due to a disturbing development in the policy of major European nations toward their beet-sugar producers. Not only did they take steps to protect the home markets of those producers, they subsidized their exports so as to permit them to enter new markets. Thus quantities of German and Austrian sugar entered the United States and readily made up for decreased availabilities from Cuba.

The Cuban Sugar Industry Americanized After 1898

During the war years, from 1895 through 1898, Cuban production was reduced to one-fifth of what it had been in 1894. A first task after the cessation of hostilities was the rebuilding of the industry on which the welfare of the island had traditionally depended. Some Cuban writers of the revisionist and antiimperialist school have gone to the lengths of making a grievance against the United States of the restoration of the Cuban sugar industry largely with American capital.[1] They have argued that the island could have achieved a greater degree of economic independence and a more diversified and industrialized economy had the destructive work of the insurgents been left untouched and Cuba's sugar industry left to its reduced state. While it is true, as will be developed in these pages, that massive American investment in mills and in the purchase of cane lands produced some unfavorable results for Cuba and had an important and often corrupting effect on Cuban politics, one might as well have contemplated freeing Alabama from cotton or Kansas from wheat as Cuba from sugar under the conditions of the early 1900s. Even today, as Castro has rediscovered, sugar remains the essential factor in the island welfare, undesirable as some of the consequences may be.

Once Spanish rule had been eliminated, the task of rehabilitating the sugar industry as well as other productive activities in Cuba was urgently undertaken. The United States government stimulated the process by creating favorable conditions for investment in the rebuilding and the repair of mills and the construction of new mills. The Platt Amendment (see the next section) appeared to insure to American investors—and others—a degree of political and economic stability.

In order to give Cuban sugar an assured position in the American market, tariff preference was deemed essential. The tariff philosophy of the times demanded that such preference involve reciprocal preferences on American goods entering Cuba. These were achieved on both sides, though with some delays and with opposition in both countries, by means of an agreement that became effective in 1903.

It was also considered essential to remove the destructive competition of subsidized beet-sugar exports. This was accomplished with the powerful assistance of the United Kingdom's concern for its West Indian and other sugar-producing colonies; the Brussels Agreement of 1902, one of the first international sugar agreements, put an end to subsidized beet exports. (American tariff legislation as early as 1897 had discouraged these by applying a surcharge to them equivalent to the amount of the subsidy.)

At the same time, of course, the Philippines and Puerto Rico were following in the wake of Hawaii and securing free access to the American market as parts of the expanding American empire; annexationist sentiment in Cuba was fueled by the prospect of a place for Cuba inside the American

tariff wall almost as much as it was by the attraction of the American political system and by the hope of eventual statehood under the Stars and Stripes.
(I believe, however, that majority sentiment in both countries opposed Cuban membership in the American Union.)

Cuban production did not again reach the 1-million-ton level attained
in 1894 until 1904. Larger crops coincided with an improvement from the
generally depressed prices at which the much lower crops of the intervening
years were sold. The 1904 product was worth about the same as that of 1894.
During the American intervention, sugar had briefly yielded first place to
tobacco; it now permanently recovered leadership.

The first decade in the new century was one of the most stable in the
history of Cuban sugar. There was a steady expansion of the industry's production with prices remaining in the range of two to three cents. Production
moved toward the 2-million-ton mark (reached in 1913) and prices toward
the end of the decade were close to three cents a pound. The preference
granted Cuban raw sugars in the United States gave Cuban sugar a competitive advantage over sugars from other foreign countries entering the American market. The Cuban producer reaped the full advantage of the preference;
when he sold at the world price in New York, his return was superior by the
amount of the preference to that of the foreign supplier.

As this first decade came to an end, however, Cuban sugar had more and
more displaced its full-duty-paying competitors. The price received by the
Cuban producer now tended to be that resulting from the interplay of market forces in the United States. To the extent that the American refiner
could buy Cuban sugar at a price minus the full duty that was less than what
he would have had to pay for other sugars, he got the benefit of the preference rather than the Cuban producer. During this period practically all exportable Cuban sugar went to the United States, and after 1910 United
States sugar imports came primarily from Cuba.

In the year 1913 Cuba produced a record of nearly 2.5 million Spanish
long tons of sugar, the first time the crop had exceeded 2 million tons.
Owing, however, to the fact the price had dropped by a significant fraction
from what it had been in the immediately preceding years, the value of this
record crop was less that that of the 1.9 million ton crops of 1910 and 1912
and only eleven million dollars more than the crop of 1911 which was under
1.5 million tons.

Cuban Sugar and World War I

After 1913 there was a continued rapid expansion with four million tons being produced for the first time in 1919. This expansion was stimulated by the European conflict and by American participation in that struggle beginning in 1917. The United States negotiated for the entire Cuban crop during the war years and arranged for its distribution. Cuba accepted the arrangement because of its closeness to the United States, its participation in the struggle against the Central Powers, and the obvious need of careful coordination of available shipping and of essential Cuban imports if the industry was to keep on producing and disposing of its product.

During the war years the trend of prices and of costs was steadily upward. In 1919 the average price received by the Cuban producers was in excess of five cents per pound as against a maximum of just over three before the war. Controls were then removed; the war was over and "normalcy" was the spirit of the times.

Conditions were, however, far from normal. The war on the western front had been fought on the beet fields of France. The other European countries had suffered serious losses in capacity for sugar production. There was a tremendous actual demand for sugar and an even greater speculative fever in the markets and in Cuba. These were the months, sadly famous in Cuban annals as the "Dance of the Millions," during which raw sugar changed hands at over twenty cents a pound.

During this sensational year—1920—a Cuban crop of less than four million tons achieved a value of over one billion dollars—the first and last time any such result has been achieved in the annals of Cuban sugar. (In the event that Castro ever makes his ten-million-ton crop and can sell half of it to the Russians at a premium price of six cents a pound and the rest at over three cents on the world market, he would approximate the one-billion-dollar figure—in much depreciated dollars and Russian goods—but his total crop would be two and a half times as large as that of 1920.)

In spite of the painful bursting of the postwar bubble, the outlook for Cuban sugar still seemed favorable in view of the relative slowness of European recovery and of steadily increasing world consumption of sugar. Even after the shock of the crash of 1920, there continued to be optimism as to

Cuban prospects. American investors made large new commitments in Cuba. The crops of 1921 and 1922 sold at comparatively depressed prices and grossed under $300 million. There was a recovery in 1923 when a comparatively short crop of under four million tons brought an average of over five cents a pound and grossed $425 million. But, thereafter, world production tended increasingly to outstrip consumption. Prices fell to under three cents after 1924. The European producers again supplied their traditional markets, and Java loomed larger and larger as a formidable claimant for a growing share of a shrinking market. Cuba ran into serious trouble even before the worldwide depression knocked the bottom out of the prices and the demand for other basic commodities.

In 1925 Cuba made what was up to that time a record crop of over five million Spanish long tons. But its total value of just under $300 million compared unfavorably with the $373 million obtained the previous year for a crop of four million tons. With the exception of the crop of 1929, Cuba did not again make over five million tons of sugar until 1947 and it was only in 1944, the last full year of World War II, that the value of what was produced again exceeded the $300 million mark. For most of the intervening twenty-year period, volume and value were about half those of 1925.

Cuban Sugar and the Great Depression

The story of attempts after 1925 by Cuban sugar producers, with the help of their friends in New York, to introduce some rationality into the world sugar market makes pathetic reading. Seldom have energy, ingenuity, and good intentions been so frustrated. Cuban crops were restricted in 1926 and 1927; restrictions were abandoned in 1928. All sorts of arrangements were tried; there were gentlemen's agreements, there were Chadbourne Plans, but nothing really worked or even gave hope of working for very long. Production of sugar outran consumption on an increasingly major scale. And, as prices sagged, the existing protective devices in the countries that imported tropical cane sugar for part of their requirements and produced sugar (mostly beet) for the balance became increasingly burdensome and absorbed ever higher proportions of the sinking duty-paid prices.

During most of the decade the American duty on Cuban sugar was slightly over 1.75 cents per pound (the Fordney-McCumber Act of 1922). It was raised by the Hawley-Smoot Act of 1930 to 2.0 cents. The Cuban cost of production may have averaged just below 2.0 cents a pound. When duty-paid sugar in the New York market brought over 5.0 cents a pound, as it did during much of the early twenties, the return to the Cuban producer was somewhere in the neighborhood of 2.5 cents after he had paid the duty and his freight, insurance, and other costs. But when the prices declined to 3.0 cents a pound, duty paid, in New York, the return to the Cuban producer dropped below 1.0 cent a pound or less than half his cost of production.

At the same time American producers behind the tariff wall were receiving 3.0 cents a pound. Under depression conditions the result was greatly to stimulate production in the insular territories of Hawaii, the Philippines, and Puerto Rico; these areas then secured, at the expense of Cuba, positions in the American market from which they were never dislodged—nor could they have been as a matter of practical politics. Parallel situations confronted Cuba in some of its other markets.

After 1929 the sugar crisis was engulfed in the steadily deepening world economic crisis that put such a somber finis to the expansiveness and the optimism that had characterized most of the twenties, especially in the United States. All the world suffered from depressed conditions, which were worsened by the desperate efforts at self-preservation at the expense of the rest that characterized the behavior of most of the victims whether governments or private individuals and corporations. But Cuba, because of its one-crop economy, suffered more than most.

A comparison of the Cuban sugar industry in 1925, a year representative of relatively normal, or average, conditions in the twenties, with the year 1933, the trough of the depression, is dramatically illustrative. In the latter year, of the 183 mills that had been active in 1925, only 125 were still grinding. The average days of work afforded during the crop season had dropped from 123 to 57. Production had fallen from over 5 million Spanish long tons to just under 2 million; the value of the crop had shrunk from nearly $300 million to $54 million, that is, it was little more than one-sixth the value of that of 1925.

It is worth noting that Cuba's loss of sales and the depressed level at which sales were made in the United States coincided with only relatively small decreases in the consumption of sugar in the United States. The total dropped from nearly 7 million short tons in 1929 to about 6.25 million in 1933, a decrease of less than 11 percent and, thereafter, moved upward, though slowly.

One effect of the depression and of curtailed Cuban production and prospects was to arrest growth or change in the structure of the industry. This was partly due to an aroused social consciousness in Cuba, which demanded that the burdens and the rewards of sugar be divided more or less equally throughout the country and that the socioeconomic factors involved in the operation of each unit in its own particular area be given priority in the establishment of public policy. No new mill was built after 1927, and the major investment in new and modern mills and equipment was completed in the early twenties. After 1930 the installation of a new mill became subject to prohibitive taxation. The industry was confined both by circumstances and by law to its major existing physical components—though there were, of course, constant changes and reorganizations of the ownership of these components.[2]

This rigid socioeconomic principle was firmly maintained to the end of the Republic. I recall that in 1943 an American-owned mill burned down. The owners did not wish to rebuild. They had the support of the American Ambassador, though not of the Department of State. The Cuban government maintained its position; the mill was rebuilt under Cuban ownership. While the social reasons for the policy in question are clear, it did result in a monopoly position for those already in sugar and protected them from competition at the same time that it discouraged research and development.

World War II Comes to Cuba's Rescue

Cuba's rescue from the depths to which the depression had plunged it depended on the interest and the will of Cuba's principal customer, the United States. The United States in 1934 granted Cuba a portion of the American market a little more than half what Cuba had enjoyed prior to the depression and signed with Cuba a reciprocal trade agreement cutting the duty on Cuban sugar entering the United States by more than half. The amount that Cuba could ship to the United States was no longer dependent on the demand for sugar that could be satisfied by Cuba in spite of the tariff; it was now fixed by the unilateral action, at first administrative and then legislative, of the government of the United States.

Cuban exports to the United States now became stabilized at around 2 million short tons per year at a price which, partly because of the reduced duty, was a remunerative one. The total Cuban crop rose from the low figure of just under 2 million Spanish long tons in 1933 to a range between 2.7 and 2.9 million toward the end of the decade. The average price received by the producers for their total output to all markets, however, remained well below 2.0 cents and often below 1.5 cents. The industry was going through hard times with the number of crop-work days hovering around 60 as compared with over 100 prior to 1930.

During these years Cuba exported an average of just over 500,000 Spanish long tons of sugar to the United Kingdom and about 200,000 tons annually to other traditional customers. But prices in the world market continued at depression levels. The International Sugar Agreement negotiated in 1937 had no opportunity to prove its worth; it was to become effective on September 1, 1939—the day Hitler moved into Poland. The annual average price for world sugar ready for shipment from Cuba remained at about one cent for the entire period of the thirties and hovered below that figure during the middle years of the decade. Assuming the cost of producing sugar in Cuba to be in the neighborhood of two cents it becomes apparent that the premium price in the United States kept the industry afloat and allowed the Cubans to continue to produce for the world market; that premium price probably strengthened the Cuban bargaining position in world-market negotiations so far as the setting of the Cuban export quota was concerned.

This Cuban state of shabby gentility as compared with the expansive twenties came to an end with the opening of World War II. Again the disasters and the follies of the rest of the world had come to the rescue of Cuba. The Cuban crop which amounted to less than two and a half million tons in 1941, worth $130 million, rose in 1944 to over four million tons with a value of $330 million. The crops from 1942 through 1947 were bought by the United States at negotiated prices which began at 2.65 cents per pound during the first three years with the average in 1947 a shade below 5.0 cents a pound. Cuba cooperated with the war effort, and the war effort cooperated with Cuba in the sense of making available to Cuba the shipping needed to move the sugar, the supplies and the fuel needed to produce it, and the commodities required as a minimum to keep Cuba a going concern.

During the period Cuban production moved steadily upward registering a total in excess of 5 million Spanish long tons in 1947 and nearly 5.7 million in 1948. It is worthy of note, however, that the 1948 crop brought $20 million less than the one for the previous year in spite of the fact that it was larger by over 300,000 tons than the latter. The era of fluctuating prices had come again after the years of wartime controls.

Following the war there was a general expectation in Cuba that the demand for sugar would tend to revert to the levels of the previous decade—or at least that it would be below the wartime figures. The boom-or-bust psychology which Cubans had inherited from generations of their predecessors influenced the behavior of hundreds of thousands of them including most of those in positions of authority and influence. Nevertheless a much greater stability in Cuban outlets for sugar at more satisfactory price levels than ever before experienced was the lot of Cuba in the postwar years through 1960. It is lamentable that confidence-inspiring institutions and leadership were not available to convert this prosperity into the foundations of a more solid and coherent national community.

Sales to the United States at premium prices after 1947 fluctuated between 2.4 and 3 million Spanish long tons. The basic upward trend from the increase in American consumption was distorted by the windfalls arising from Cuba's statutory share in supplying the American market with amounts needed to cover the deficits of other producing areas. In the world market Cuba seldom sold less than 2 million tons as against the average of 700,000 tons before World War II. Average prices on the world market remained in excess of 4.0 cents per pound through 1952 and during the Korean crisis in 1951 and 1952 they reached 4.98 and 5.67 cents respectively. The net American price for the Cuban producer was in the neighborhood of 5.0 cents per pound—even when the price on the world market was higher, the Cubans made a point of filling their American quota.

After 1952 the Cuban industry was once more obliged to restrict production; the lush years of the immediate postwar period had ended. But the situation by no means deteriorated in a fashion comparable to earlier experience. The Suez crisis in 1956 drove average prices up again, although they stayed below 3.5 cents during most of these years, and indeed in 1959 the average was only 2.97 cents.

The Outlook When Castro Came to Power

This relatively favorable picture was due to the unilateral American legislation, to the aggressive efforts of the Cubans themselves to expand their markets, to windfall purchases by the Soviet Union, and to conditions created first by the Korean War and then by the Suez crisis. The negotiation of an international agreement in 1957 setting export quotas was helpful. Yet Cuba was not achieving a normal, steady development with a progressive rise in the general welfare, in part because of the population increase.

The Batista administration inspired confidence in business circles. That confidence was expressed in significant private investment which diversified the agriculture of the country (especially in rice and cattle) and led to the establishment of a number of new industries (petroleum refining, mining, and miscellaneous factories). The government conducted a lavish public works program designed to absorb the chronic and large-scale unemployment that was such a blemish on Cuban society (8 percent during the sugar crop and 20 percent during the so-called dead season which covered eight or nine months of each year). But the country's export earnings plus available credit were insufficient to meet the demands of the development program—and of the frenzied pace of consumer imports. During the six years of Batista's rule Cuba's gold reserves were reduced from a net of over half a billion dollars to the point that when Batista fled the country on January 1, 1959, the balance available, considering liabilities incurred but not yet liquidated, was negative.

Cuba's problem was succinctly set forth in a United States Department of Commerce booklet entitled *Investment in Cuba* published in 1956 for the benefit and encouragement of Americans who might be interested in Cuba. After describing Cuba's dependence on exports which "contribute between 30 and 39 per cent of the national income," the report adds that these "play a role of considerably greater magnitude [than the percentages would indicate] since almost all the activities of the island are geared to the rise and fall in the volume and value of export crops. Sugar and its by-products account for 86% of total exports." The booklet continues:

> The decade ahead should witness a substantial increase in the tempo of economic diversification. It would be foolhardy, however, to gloss over or underestimate the extent of the problem confronting Cuba in its efforts to maintain, let alone increase, the standard of living of its people.[3]

The publication refers to a study by the National Bank of Cuba, an organization then staffed by economists of the highest professional competence, indicating that "the Cuban gross national product, in 1948–54, grew sufficiently to permit the maintenance of the 1947 standard of living in only five of the seven years included in that period and was sufficient in only two years (1951 and 1952) to permit a 2 per cent annual increase over the 1947 standard of living level." The conclusion drawn from all this, on the basis of a population in 1947 of 5,283,000 and of an estimated population in 1965 of 6,677,000, is as follows:

> The National Bank of Cuba pointed out that the sugar crop in 1965 would have to reach 9,395,000 short tons valued at 793 million pesos to give the 1965 population the living standards enjoyed by the 1947 population, or a crop of 14,763,000 short tons valued at 1,246 million pesos to permit of an annual increase of 2 per cent in the standard of living between 1947 and 1965.[4]

As the Batista regime came to an end the Cuban economy, if orderly and steady development was to be achieved, was desperately in need of a constant, moderate increase in the gross national product and of an improvement in the balance of payments and the use of exchange earnings that would sustain a substantial investment program on the order of the one the Batista government had been conducting. Hopefully, this program would be less corrupt and would be accompanied by the reforms that moderate nationalist opinion in Cuba had come to believe were essential. The prospects for the needed increase, which could come only from sugar or from the development of alternate resources, seemed less than promising in 1958. The outlook for sugar both in the premium American market and in the highly competitive world market was not hopeful so far as major increases were concerned. In fact, the tendency in the United States since 1951, accentuated in 1956, had been to curtail Cuba's share in the slow but steady increase in American consumption. Russia was a promising but an enigmatic prospect for modest sales. The world market seemed to have settled into a pattern in which Cuba could not hope to do more than maintain current levels of sales at comparatively low prices.

Castro thus inherited an admittedly unpromising situation. In 1960 the Russians took over the American responsibility for the Cuban economy. Whether the Russian purchases at six cents, with only 20 percent in free exchange, were the equivalent of the previous American purchases at premium cash prices is hardly worth discussion; the state of the Cuban economy

today is sufficient answer. The Russians have had to supplement their purchases of sugar with credits now over the two-billion-dollar mark. It should,
however, be noted that a limiting factor here has been Cuba's inability under
Castro to produce even half the sugar for the Russian market that the Russians have contracted to take.

In the world market Castro has experienced the traditional alternatives
of brief periods of feast followed by long years of fasting. During the first
four years of his rule the world market averages stayed below 3.0 cents. Then
in 1963 and 1964 there was a boom due to scarcities resulting partly from
Cuban short crops and from American purchases from countries that consequently had less available for the world market. At one point in 1963 the
price was over 12.0 cents, double what the Russians were paying largely in
Russian goods. In 1964 it reached a peak of over 11.0 cents, although in these
two years the averages were respectively 8.48 cents and 5.46 cents. By the end
of 1964 the price had dropped below 3.0 cents and in the next four years the
average was to remain below 2.0 cents—the lowest level to which it had
plunged since the depressed thirties. This was the situation that led Castro
in the fall of 1968 to sign an international agreement limiting the amounts
he would sell on the world market. While his sales to Russia were not restricted in the agreement, the Soviet Union did agree to limit its sales to that
market.

The 1968 agreement has to some extent caused, and to some extent coincided with, an improvement in world-market conditions. Sugar sold briefly
at over 4.0 cents in 1969, although the average for the year was just below 3.5
cents. During the latter half of 1970 the average was about 4.0 cents and by
the end of the year was approaching 4.5 cents with doubts as to the Cuban
potential for production, a factor in rising prices.

CUBAN AMERICAN RELATIONS AND THE
DYNAMICS OF CUBAN POLITICS

The Platt Amendment

AMERICAN participation in Cuban and Caribbean affairs dates from the earliest days of our republic and even before. For example, the British unsuccessfully besieged Cartagena in what has become Colombia in 1741; they took Havana in 1762. American colonial contingents were present at both actions.

I do not propose to rehearse American attitudes toward Cuba in the nineteenth century. The political-gravity theory of Jefferson and John Quincy Adams, Manifest Destiny, the attempts to buy the island under Polk and Pierce, the Ostend Manifesto of 1854 with its outrageous doctrine that a Spanish refusal to sell would justify armed action by the United States, the filibustering expeditions in the Southern slaveholding interest, the efforts made to commit the United States on the insurgent side in the Cuban revolt of 1868 to 1878—all these are familiar tales.[1] During most of the century, American official policy upheld Spanish control of the island and hoped for an orientation of Spanish rule acceptable to the people of the island.

The United States was, however, generally pessimistic as to Spanish power and wisdom in Cuba and was hostile to the possibility that some other colonial power, such as Britain or France, might succeed Spain in the Pearl of the Antilles. Nor did the prospect of Cuban independence and the consequent addition of another turbulent republic to those that had ruled the area since the expulsion of the Spaniards have great appeal to responsible policymakers in Washington. Eventual annexation of Cuba (and of other Latin American territories) was viewed enthusiastically by some and fatalistically by other elements in the American establishment.

As the century wore on trade relations with Cuba became increasingly important. The selfish policies of Spain, especially in tariff matters, led commercial interests in Cuba and in the United States to make common cause. But, until well after the beginning of the final struggle for Cuban independence in 1895, American official policy, in spite of the opinion and the interests arrayed on the side of activism toward the solution of the island's problems, remained one of wait and see. That policy did not change until the frustrations and the atrocities of the fighting on the island, coupled with the impetus given an already aroused compassion and bellicosity, forced a reluctant McKinley into war with Spain.

A widely held Cuban belief, not confined to Castroites or to radical nationalists, is that at the outbreak of the Spanish-American War the Cuban insurgents were about to drive the Spanish army into the sea. The more extreme form of the legend is that the United States, perceiving this, intervened to avoid a purely Cuban victory. The leaders of the Cuban rebels, Máximo Gómez and Calixto García, together with the extraordinarily brave and able Antonio Maceo, killed in action in December 1896, had indeed fought the Spanish armies to a standstill and had generated in Spain a war-weariness that weighed against a continuance of the struggle. But it is quite possible that, if left to themselves, the Spaniards and the Cubans, who were also war-weary, could have worked out a patchwork arrangement in the framework of autonomy, denying the insurgent leadership the complete independence it sought at least for a few more years.

The American military victory over Spain truly cut a Gordian knot which neither Cubans nor Spaniards of various political complexions had been able to unravel in the course of an active grappling with an exploding problem during more than thirty years. The American intervention was due, in my judgment, to the decision of the American people no longer to tolerate on their doorstep a spectacle so repugnant to the humanitarian sentiments and the desire for freedom for all peoples traditional with Americans. The expansionists and the naval strategists, the Mahans and the Roosevelts, the Pulitzers and the Hearsts—all with axes to grind—were incidental in the majority decision to go to war. After the Spaniards were thrown out of Cuba, however, the larger public's interest in the island subsided.

Cuban detractors of the United States have made much of the fact that the United States government declined, in spite of frenzied and indelicate lobbying in the Congress by and on behalf of the Cuban Revolutionary Junta in New York, to recognize the insurgents as the government of Cuba.[2] Washington insisted on a period of pacification and reorganization before turning the administration of the island over to Cubans duly elected by their fellow citizens to govern them. In this the United States had the approval of Máximo Gómez, the Dominican military genius who led the soldiers of the "Cuban Republic in Arms"; he had a poor opinion of the insurgent political organization.[3] The death of José Martí in an early skirmish in the insurrection he had fathered left the Cuban independence movement with a civilian leadership that proved less than effective in the circumstances of the times.

Before allowing the Cuban Republic to inaugurate its first President, the United States imposed upon the new state what has been known as the Platt Amendment.[4] It curtailed the sovereignty of the Republic in a number of ways. Its text follows:

ARTICLE I. The Government of Cuba shall never enter into any treaty or other compact with any foreign power or powers which will impair or tend to impair the independence of Cuba, nor in any manner authorize or permit any foreign power or powers to obtain by colonization or for military or naval purposes, or otherwise, lodgment in or control over any portion of said island.

ARTICLE II. The Government of Cuba shall not assume or contract any public debt to pay the interest on which, and to make any reasonable sinking fund provision for the ultimate discharge of which, the ordinary revenues of the Island of Cuba, after defraying the current expenses of the Government, shall be inadequate.

ARTICLE III. The Government of Cuba consents that the United States may exercise the right to intervene for the preservation of Cuban independence, the maintenance of a government adequate for the protection of life, property, and individual liberty, and for discharging the obligations with respect to Cuba imposed by the Treaty of Paris on the United States, now to be assumed and undertaken by the Government of Cuba.

ARTICLE IV. All acts of the United States in Cuba during its military occupancy thereof are ratified and validated, and all lawful rights acquired thereunder shall be maintained and protected.

ARTICLE V. The Government of Cuba will execute, and, as far as necessary, extend the plans already devised, or other plans to be mutually agreed upon, for the sanitation of the cities of the island, to the end that a recurrence of epidemic and infectious diseases may be prevented, thereby assuring protection to the people and commerce of Cuba, as well as to the Southern ports of the United States and the people residing therein.

ARTICLE VI. The Island of Pines shall be omitted from the boundaries of Cuba specified in the Constitution, the title thereto being left to future adjustment by treaty.

ARTICLE VII. *To enable the United States to maintain the independence of Cuba, and to protect the people thereof, as well as for its own defense, the Government of Cuba will sell or lease to the United States lands necessary for coaling or naval stations, at certain specified points, to be agreed upon with the President of the United States.*

These articles became a part of the Cuban Constitution and were incorporated in a treaty signed in 1903 between Cuba and the United States. The limitation on the Cuban government's financial transactions (Article II), the right of the United States to intervene in Cuba (Article III), together with the obligation to sell or lease lands to the United States for naval or coaling stations (Article VII) were the clauses that then aroused the most opposition in Cuba and have been over the years the theme of the diatribes of Cuban nationalists.

The Amendment must, however, be placed in the context of the circumstances prevailing at the time. Its major clauses were an early expression of the thinking later embodied in the Roosevelt Corollary of the Monroe Doctrine. The concept was that the countries of the Caribbean area—an area of vital importance to the United States—were inept in the handling of their affairs, that there were predatory imperialisms (the Kaiser's Germany was the one most in the minds of McKinley, Roosevelt, and Root) ready to take advantage of this ineptness to the detriment of the independence of these countries, and that consequently it was necessary for the United States to assume broad responsibilities that would protect these states from themselves and would safeguard the security of the United States. By acting as a benevolent policeman, the United States government would encourage the private investment (largely American) and promote the trade needed for the well-being of these countries and of the United States. There was also implicit in the Corollary and in the Amendment the generous if, in my judgment, mistaken belief that the threat of the restraining hand of the United States and, if necessary, the hand itself would develop the capacity of these peoples for self-government and accelerate their progress toward political maturity.[5]

There were Cubans in high positions in the new Republic to whom Mr. Root's concept as embodied in the Amendment had a definite appeal. They accepted the necessity for the Cuban Constitutional Assembly to approve the Amendment in order to put an end to the American military occupation of their country and to insure the establishment of the reciprocal trade relationship with the United States then deemed essential to the welfare of Cuba. They believed that the document made sense in Cuban terms. As these Cubans, men of undoubted patriotism, surveyed conditions in the independent Caribbean and Central American republics in 1901, they could plausibly conclude that their own infant republic would have better prospects of insuring the happiness of its inhabitants under the protection of its powerful and, at the time, generally admired neighbor than if left to its own devices. The purposes and the hopes with which the Amendment was justified in the minds of its American proponents were thus shared to some extent in Cuba.

Additionally, the Platt Amendment had been made more palatable and more politically acceptable to the Cubans by the Root interpretation precluding its use as a basis for constant interference and intermeddling in Cuban domestic affairs by the United States. Mr. Root promised the Cubans that intervention by the United States would not take place until the Cubans themselves had created the situation that made it necessary for the United States to comply with its Platt obligations.[6]

In spite of the allegedly discouraging effect of the Amendment on Cuban politics, there developed a two-party system of some vigor and significance beyond the personalities of the leaders. The Liberals had much of their strength in the smaller towns and in the countryside. They claimed a close identification with the struggle against Spain. Their appeal was to the common man in town and country. In contrast the Conservatives, briefly known as *Moderados*, derived much of their support from the capital and from the traditional sources of power in the island's planter society and governing bureaucracy. The Conservatives affected to regard the Liberal leaders as demagogues playing in a most dangerous and irresponsible fashion on the passions and the appetites of the unlettered mob, while the Liberals scoffed at the Conservatives' claim that they were to be considered responsible statesmen and pilloried them as the reactionary and corrupt guardians of entrenched wealth and privilege.

The first President of the new Republic, Tomás Estrada-Palma, was a man of the highest character and of complete personal integrity.[7] He had for a time been chief executive of the insurgent "Republic in Arms" during the Ten Years' War a quarter of a century earlier. He had spent twenty years as the headmaster of a school in rural New York state. He had presided over the Cuban Revolutionary Junta in New York City after Martí's death in 1895. When Máximo Gómez refused the presidency, Estrada-Palma was the choice of the people of Cuba in the election of 1902. He was, however, out of touch with the personalities and the happenings of his native land. He viewed the populist-nationalist platforms of the Liberal politicians with alarm and distaste. He did not consider that the Liberals had rights he was bound to respect; to this ex-schoolmaster they were simply bad boys. In the counting of votes midway through his term as well as in the elections in which he was reelected for a second term, he condoned the wholesale frauds perpetrated by the Moderados with whom he had become affiliated. The Liberals concluded that a recourse to arms was the only remedy available to them.

The Root interpretation of the Platt Amendment had been so well observed by American representatives in Havana that when civil war threatened on the island in the summer of 1906 President Theodore Roosevelt found that his diplomats not only had not meddled in the internal affairs of Cuba but were indeed not very knowledgeable about those affairs.[8] The President sent the Secretary of War, William Howard Taft, and the Acting Secretary of State, Robert Bacon (the Secretary, Elihu Root, was on a goodwill tour of South America), to Cuba to investigate and report.

The American commissioners found that a serious state of civil conflict existed on the island, that the government of Estrada-Palma was unable to cope with the rebellion against its authority, that the principal cause of the trouble was the suppression by the governing party, the Moderados, of the opposition Liberals by means of widespread electoral fraud and intimidation, and, finally, that the government had not only rejected a formula of constitutional continuity worked out by the commissioners and accepted by the opposition but had taken steps to decapitate itself and to leave the country without a government. Intervention under the Platt Amendment was considered unavoidable; it lasted over two years and then handed the government over to a duly elected Liberal president.[9]

That the United States government had circumvented his constitutional authority and had supported the rebellion was a devastating blow to President Estrada-Palma; he had been confident of an intervention that would crush the enemies he could not suppress.[10] He had believed that the Platt Amendment should have led the United States to thwart those wretched Cubans who, in his opinion, would convert his beloved Cuba into merely another Central American or Caribbean republic.

Future Cuban presidents learned to buttress their internal security apparatus so as to avoid the situation in which Estrada-Palma had found himself. To the Liberals the fact that the United States had intervened to right the wrongs they had suffered at the hands of their domestic opponents was most welcome. The hope that the United States would intervene on the side of the oppressed in the Cuban political arena encouraged rebellions in later years. American policy was, however, altered in practice after the Estrada-Palma episode of 1906. The rationale for the judgments of Taft and Bacon did not establish a precedent.

The two formal interventions of the United States in Cuba are identified with General Leonard Wood (1899–1902) and with Governor Charles Magoon (1906–1909). They conferred, thanks to the dedication and the industry of many able Americans and Cubans, constructive benefits in a number of fields such as electoral legislation, public health, administration, education, and so forth. But on the whole intervention was considered politically undesirable in Washington and was seriously desired by Cubans only on those not too infrequent occasions when they believed themselves to be the victims of intolerable wrongs at the hands of their fellow Cubans.

In order to avoid the necessity for further formal interventions the United States now tacitly changed its policy toward Cuba in two respects. In the first place, the criteria under which the United States would intervene were in practice modified. The 1906 intervention had been decided upon when Taft and Bacon concluded that the Estrada-Palma government was unable to maintain law and order, including the protection of foreign properties, and that the rebel cause was a just one in the sense that the rebels had been the victims of oppression and violation of the democratic liberties of the Cuban people. Henceforward, and to the disappointment of the rebels of 1917 and 1921 who were indeed the victims of electoral fraud, the American government dropped the second of these criteria and based its policy on the ability of what it accepted as the legitimate or constitutional government to protect the property of foreign investors, now predominantly American. After 1906 abuses in the electoral process no longer motivated American intervention, although American official efforts were made, without much success, to reduce such abuses.

This change of policy was not announced in so many words. It did not alter the Cuban conviction that intervention was an ever-present possibility. In fact there grew up a companion conviction that an absence of intervention was a reflection of approval in Washington of whatever Cuban group held the reins of power.

My father, Stephen Bonsal, visited Cuba in 1912 as President Gómez was ending his term. Father was disappointed at the failure of the high hopes for Cuba he had entertained at the time of the Spanish-American War. He gives an illuminating, if discouraging, definition of the American role in Cuba from which I quote the following:

> He [President Gómez] lights matches and plays with fire apparently quite confident that, should a conflagration ensue, we should have to intervene and put it out at our expense. Our role, in the eyes of the professional Cuban politicians, would seem to be that of an insurance company such as never existed in this selfish, grasping world; one that would employ fire-fighters without cost, never ask clients for premiums, and make good all losses promptly and with thanks for the opportunity of altruistic service.[11]

One can readily agree that the Platt Amendment was hardly a character builder in Cuba.

The second major change in American policy after the second, or Magoon, intervention of 1909 involved the abandonment of the Root interpretation of the Amendment. Washington now embarked on a course of calling the Cuban government's attention to situations which the Department of State believed would produce effects that might oblige the United States to intervene in accordance with its rights and obligations under the Amendment. This so-called preventive policy prevailed for the next fifteen years, ending in 1924.[12] Although this policy was a reflection of the American desire to avoid formal intervention, it stimulated Cuban belief in the possibility of intervention. Many of the steps taken under it seemed to fearful or hopeful Cubans possible precursors of all-out intervention.

The preventive policy led the United States government to give pressing advice to President Gómez on how to handle the threatening protest of the Cuban Veterans' Movement (1911), on the urgency of subduing a menacing Negro uprising (1912), and on how to draft an amnesty bill (1913). Concessions and contracts were a favorite target for the exercise of the policy. American pronouncements were well intended and generally, though not always, judicious. At times they were clear and decisive, at others vague and ambiguous. They thwarted powerful interests in Cuba and in the United States and exacerbated nationalistic feeling in Cuba instead of promoting that passion for integrity they reflected. They sometimes invested unconscionable schemes against the Cuban public interest with a patriotic aura that concealed their imperfections.

In spite of the conscientious pursuit of the preventive policy the United States government had to recognize at the time of the postwar crash in 1920 and 1921 that corruption and frivolity in fiscal matters appeared endemic in the Cuban regime. In spite of American preachments, civic virtue seemed to be less of a favorite than it had been ten years earlier. There was a huge floating debt. Government payrolls were not being met nor were the government's suppliers being paid. The Cuban economy was in a deplorable shambles after the sensational bursting of war-induced prosperity.

Washington's answer was the dispatch to Cuba of that truly eminent public servant, General Enoch Crowder, with his credentials of successful work in Cuba during the Magoon intervention fifteen years earlier and the great prestige of his outstanding record in setting up the selective service system in the United States during World War I. Crowder's title was Special Representative of the President; he was the next thing to a formal intervention. With full Washington backing he imposed a lengthy and detailed series of reforms in a variety of fields, even to the point of demanding that President Zayas appoint Cabinet Ministers of whom the General approved. All of these demands were conditions precedent to the granting by an American bank of a substantial loan that would enable the Cuban government to put its disorderly fiscal house in shape and settle the floating debt that reflected the improvidence of Cuban administrations past and present.[13]

When all of Crowder's demands had been met, the Cubans got their loan, and the creditors were paid off. The "honest Cabinet," on whose appointment Crowder had insisted, was then junked, and the reforms rapidly unraveled. The General's industry and dedication appeared to have been sterile. There was nothing to be done about it, short of the formal intervention Washington was determined to avoid. General Crowder now became Ambassador and abandoned his efforts to run the government of Cuba.

American Investment in Cuba

The very rapid growth of American investment during the first two decades of the century rehabilitated the island economy and contributed to the progress and increasing well-being of important sectors of the population. From only fifty million dollars when the Spaniards departed, the American stake in the island had risen to over a billion and a quarter dollars by 1925. Americans controlled the more modern sugar mills, half of the railways (the other half were British), and the major utilities plus an impressive list of miscellaneous assets.[14]

This influx of investment and the problems to which it gave rise profoundly affected the Cuban political scene. Cubans and Americans with interests in capital ventures established constructive relations with both major parties. Liberal politicians vied with the Conservatives in representing these new interests. In the case of American companies a process began in which Cuban lawyers and politicians, rather than the Platt Amendment or the prevailing view about the responsibility of the American government for the protection of American private investment abroad, became the first line of defense for American interests. (The American government remained, however, the court of appeal in these matters.)

The opportunities presented by American investment produced a new breed of Liberal leaders—men who, while maintaining on the hustings and in the Congress the populist-nationalistic platform of the party, also worked for foreign and domestic business interests. Like their Conservative colleagues, they acquired stock. They sat on boards of directors. They developed a way of life that required a continuation of the relationship. The change in the character of the political leadership, especially on the Liberal side, had transferred to the Cuban political system by 1925 much of that role in the protection of foreign-property interests on the island, which the Platt Amendment and the practice of dollar diplomacy by Washington were supposed to provide. The rapid influx of American capital and the activity to which it gave rise tended to drain the local political system of its function as advocate of the national interest dealing at arm's length with the business community.

The growth of the sugar industry, due largely to American investment, had an unfortunate impact on social conditions in the Cuban countryside in spite of the wealth it created and the employment it supplied. The large American corporations not only invested in modern mills and machinery, they also bought up land on a major scale. This was particularly the case in the eastern provinces of Camagüey and Oriente where the greatest expansion of the industry after 1900 took place. Wide areas of these provinces were relatively sparsely populated. Their development became largely the responsibility of American or Cuban corporations rather than of a multitude of independent Cuban pioneers with their homesteading families.

In his influential book, *Sugar and Population in the West Indies*, first published in 1927, Dr. Ramiro Guerra remarks:

> When all this toil of centuries [by generations of Cubans] seemed to be almost completed and the fruits could at last be enjoyed by their children, the sugar latifundium, which had ruined the West Indies with its two formidable instruments, foreign capital and imported cheap labor, invaded the island. Its appearance marked the beginning of the wholesale destruction of our small and medium-sized properties and the reduction of our rural landowners and independent farmers, backbone of our nation, to the lowly condition of a proletariat being stifled by that economic asphyxiation which afflicts the country today from one end to the other.[15]

Dr. Guerra recalls that the proposal of a Cuban military and political leader, Manuel Sanguily, formulated in 1903, to prohibit land sales to foreigners was so scorned by his colleagues in Congress that it was not even debated by them. Sanguily's fame has been posthumous on this issue. Dr. Guerra estimated in 1927 that as much as 40 percent of Cuba's total area was dominated by a few corporations, largely American.

Before 1920 and the great crash that ended the "Dance of the Millions," Cuban lawyers and politicians having lucrative connections with banks, sugar mills, or other major enterprises represented appreciable national and non-American concerns. But with the transfers of bankrupt properties in the liquidation of the crash and the replacement of the largely defunct Cuban banking system by American and Canadian banks which now owned or controlled many assets previously Cuban, the profitable representation of business was to a major extent that of American business.

In 1920 Cuban banks had deposits of 352 million pesos; these fell to just below 25 million in 1921. The corresponding figures for foreign banks were 88 million and 55 million. The bursting of the speculative bubble caused a shrinkage in total deposits on the order of 80 percent and the transfer of a major share of the remainder to the foreign banks. In 1927 the totals were 177 million for the foreign banks and 62 million for the Cuban institutions. Cuban control of the sugar industry and of the banking system was only established after 1950, although in both these fields American interests remained significant and influential.

The Era of Machado

In 1924 Cuba, as seen from Washington and New York, appeared to be entering on a period of relative prosperity and political stability. American interests dominated the economy and were intrenched in the political system. Those interests were happy with the newly elected President, Gerardo Machado. The Department of State now rapidly lost its enthusiasm not only for renewed efforts at reform in Cuba but also for intervention in the Caribbean and in Central America under the Roosevelt Corollary of the Monroe Doctrine. With the Allied victory in World War I the danger of predatory imperialisms seemed to have vanished so far as the Western Hemisphere was concerned. American interventions in Haiti, the Dominican Republic, and Honduras had not convinced their objects that such interventions were helpful steps on the road to a confidence-inspiring political maturity and economic responsibility. They were causing the United States increasingly serious problems with its own public opinion and with public opinion in Latin America which the United States was anxious to conciliate for political and economic reasons. The right of intervention was not formally renounced until 1933, but, after the mid-twenties, it was only exercised with the greatest reluctance in the very special circumstances that prevailed in Nicaragua.[16]

The election of Machado as President of Cuba on the Liberal ticket in 1924 coincided with and probably hastened the disposition in Washington to abandon the preventive policy in dealing with Cuba. It also represented a culminating point in the business orientation of Cuban politics.[17] Machado was very close to the electric light and power interests of what later became the American & Foreign Power group. His accession was greeted with enthusiasm by the business community; one exuberant New York banker in those days of exuberant New York bankers publicly expressed the hope that the

Cuban people would find a way to keep Machado in office indefinitely.[18] The denunciations of the Platt Amendment in which Machado had indulged during his electoral campaign to show that he was true to the Liberal tradition did not bring down upon him the admonitions and representations which his predecessors would have incurred.

As Machado's term opened the Cuban internal security forces appeared capable of guaranteeing law and order and thus of making it most unlikely that it would be necessary to contemplate further recourse to the Amendment to protect the properties of Americans on the island. In that era of optimism and complacency so rapidly drawing to a close, the Amendment no longer seemed the vital element in the State Department's policy toward Cuba it had been only five years earlier.

With the help of his American bankers Machado embarked on a major public works program that included both the Central Highway the length of the island (over 700 miles)—a major breakthrough in Cuba's economic development—and the National Capitol in Havana, a model of ostentatious extravagance. Authoritarian and self-confident by nature, Machado lapped up the waves of flattery from local and American sources that convinced him of his infallibility as a man of destiny. (A flatterer in Cuba is known as a *guataca*—a term which also describes the hoe used to spread manure in the fields.) A large part of the political establishment demonstrated its frivolity and its materialism by surrendering its normal role in the political system. Machado successfully downgraded the political process through a scheme known as *cooperativismo* which made it possible for the leaders of opposition parties to participate in the swelling spoils of office in return for their cooperation in Machado's plans and particularly in his determination to extend his term of office from four years to ten years.

If Zayas, Machado's predecessor, had even proposed to extend his term of office beyond the constitutional four years, General Crowder would have rushed to the Palace in a desk-pounding mood. When Machado actually did it, there was no more than an expression of neutrality from President Coolidge—an expression which in Havana was readily transformed into an endorsement of the action.

Washington policy had indeed changed. Throughout Machado's rule, even when the going became very rough, the Republican administration took a position equivalent to a denial that it had any responsibility for internal conditions in Cuba. This was in sharp contrast to the policies both Democrats and Republicans had followed from 1909 to 1923.[19] The prevailing mood in Cuba, however, continued to be *plattista*: no interference from Washington was the equivalent of its approval, without which, it was believed, no Cuban regime could survive. Machado and his friends, Cubans and Americans, made the most of this ingrained attitude.

Machado soon ran into political problems made more acute by a weakness in the sugar market that antedated the world economic crisis by a number of years and was greatly intensified by that crisis. His own autocratic temperament was soured by adversity. Early in his administration he is said to have ordered the murder of the editor of a paper that had attacked his family. He pleased some and alarmed others by his arrests and deportations of labor agitators, including Communists.

As his rule moved beyond the four-year term for which he had been originally elected into the additional six years which many of his fellow citizens believed represented a flagrant violation of the Cuban Constitution, Machado's image at home and abroad became more and more that of a tyrannical despot. Terrorism by the opposition was met by the counterterrorism of the government's security apparatus. There was a steady escalation of killings on both sides. The intellectual classes represented by the faculty and the student body of the University of Havana became completely alienated from the Machado establishment. In 1931 the President's efficient military machine snuffed out a rebellion in which Menocal, the Conservative whom Machado had defeated in the elections of 1924, and Mendieta, the unsuccessful candidate for the Liberal nomination in that year, were involved. The army also thwarted an invasion attempt under the leadership of Carlos Hevia.[20]

Throughout all these trials Machado persisted in servicing Cuba's foreign obligations, although to do so he was forced to float fresh loans with the American bankers who had become so deeply involved with his administration. He did not hesitate to cut government payrolls to the bone, to reduce the pay of those who remained, and to default on the salaries due these wretchedly paid employees. He failed to meet a whole series of domestic obligations, including those to hard-pressed suppliers. He seems to have believed that the only thing that could bring about American intervention in his affairs would be a failure to service the country's foreign debt.[21]

I have earlier summarized the problems that faced the Cuban sugar industry in these years. I will here only recall that in Machado's first year in office (1925) Cuba produced 5,189,347 tons of sugar valued at $295 million, while in 1933, when Machado was driven from the presidency, the comparable totals were 1,994,200 tons and $53 million.

In 1930 the United States took action that aggravated Cuba's crisis. The Hawley-Smoot Tariff Act raised the duty on Cuban sugar entering the United States from the 1.76 cents per pound of the Fordney-McCumber Tariff Act of 1922 to 2.0 cents per pound. To the desperate Cubans the action was comparable to that of a drowning man's best friend who pushes his head under water when he comes up for the third time. All but forgotten in the United States, it has remained green in Cuban memories.

The American tariff, both before and after Hawley-Smoot, favored American producers and particularly the so-called offshore domestics, including Puerto Rico, Hawaii, and the Philippines. These areas permanently increased their share of the American market at the expense of Cuba since the fall in the price inflated the protection of the tariff and depressed Cuban production thanks to the pitifully small return left the Cuban industry after the tariff had been deducted.

By 1933 the Machado administration faced truly desperate circumstances in the political, social, and economic fields. Eight years earlier it had reflected the verdict of the Cuban people at the polls. Now the traditional political parties were profoundly divided. New and untested extremist elements were working underground for a violent overthrow of the regime. Eight years earlier the country had rejoiced in a prospect of economic progress; now, unemployment, misery, and even starvation were the lot of many. World depression had sapped the foundation of the nation's economy. The United States, Cuba's traditional friend and protector, paralyzed and bewildered by its own tribulations, had helped the process along. Eight years earlier most Cubans had rejoiced at the conclusion of a period of thoroughgoing interference in their domestic affairs by the United States; now many looked to American intervention as the way of salvation for Cuba.

A New Deal for Cuba Too

The administration that took over in Washington in March 1933 changed American policy toward Cuba as radically as had its predecessor in 1924.[22] President Roosevelt was anxious to clean up the mess on the island and to improve the economic conditions and prospects of its people. American public opinion was increasingly hostile to the Machado regime. Indeed popular sentiment was in some ways reminiscent of that which had prevailed in 1898, thirty-five years earlier. The numerous and bitter opponents of Machado in Cuba and in the United States argued fervently that intervention under the Platt Amendment was both a necessity and a duty.

The President and his choice as Ambassador to Cuba, Sumner Welles, saw the problem as one of rescuing the Cuban people without helping Machado. It soon became apparent to Welles that the elimination of Machado was essential to a solution. The mediation, or round table, conference of Cuban leaders over which Welles presided, did not find a formula for a peaceful transition. But the operation in itself further weakened the shaky regime. The threat of an American intervention—believable in Cuban terms —hastened the process of disintegration.

Although Machado's position, even in the medium run, was clearly untenable, two developments determined his departure from Cuba on August 12, 1933. He had made a deal with the Cuban Communist leaders whereby the latter would break up a crippling general strike with political overtones in return for the legalization of their party; the Communists couldn't deliver and the strike went on. Soon after, Machado received an intimation from his armed forces that they were withdrawing their support. The Cuban Secretary of Defense, a general, had been convinced that the failure of Machado to depart would lead to an American intervention to restore order. This was the conventional wisdom of the times; Welles may have encouraged it since it served his purposes, even though the new administration in Washington would have been extremely reluctant to intervene formally in Cuba.[23]

Ambassador Welles exaggerated only slightly when he reported that the fall of Machado represented "the expression of the volition of very nearly the totality of the Cuban people." But he soon found that there was not even an approach to a consensus as to the nature of the regime that should follow the departed tyrant. He has, I think, been unfairly criticized because he confined his own contacts largely to traditional politicians and to the business establishment, both Cuban and American, and failed to deal with the forces of revolutionary renovation that had played a major part in the underground opposition to Machado. Most of the latter, however, refused to have anything to do with him. They regarded him as the symbol of an intolerable American meddling in the affairs of Cuba. The Cuban Left was bitterly critical of the new administration in Washington, roughly representative of the Center-Left in the American political spectrum, for doing what the previous administration, symbolizing the right wing in Washington, had steadfastly refused to do.

Furthermore, Ambassador Welles was not in Cuba to make a revolution or to promote the elimination or the disintegration of the extensive American interests on the island as advocated by so many of the extremists. His task was that of engineering within a framework of legality as representative as possible a governing apparatus. He was, as I know from my own association with him, fully imbued with the liberalism and the social consciousness of the New Deal. But he was convinced of the importance of Cuban and American private capital in the sociopolitical structure of the island.

It was soon demonstrated to the Ambassador that the government he had put together under the leadership of the holder of a most eminent name in Cuban history (Carlos Manuel de Céspedes) was not viable. Céspedes's materials for government-building were too slender and the onus of American interference too heavy a burden. The professionals who had gone along with Machado and *cooperativismo* were obviously unavailable. Menocal and the Conservatives who had opposed Machado would have none of the new formula. Most of the radical opposition forces remained in conspiratorial and revolutionary attitudes. All Céspedes could count on were two anti-Machado splinters of the old Liberal party and the conservative wing of the ABC, a subversive organization of generally right-wing and nationalistic tendencies. The regime also had the nominal support of the army leadership, Machado's bulwark until the eve of his fall.

Stenographer-Sergeant Fulgencio Batista had been a member of the clandestine ABC; he now stepped upon the stage where for the next quarter of a century he was to play a prominent and indeed, for most of the time, the leading role in Cuban political life. More of a pragmatist than an ideologue, he sensed that the position of the armed forces, until recently the mainstay of the hated Machado, was precarious unless it could be brought into line with the renovationist spirit of the times. The existing officer corps was a hindrance to that objective. Grievances were not lacking among the noncoms and the enlisted men centering around such items as pay, housing, and treatment by their officers. The latter had backed Machado and were now backing Céspedes, plausibly pictured as an American creation. Batista's natural talent for leadership soon drew him to the attention of the radical civilian leaders who had refused to participate in the Welles mediation and in the Céspedes formula. Batista's temporary alliance with these radicals created the instrument for the overthrow of Céspedes.

The Revolutionary Committee, in whose name the bloodless expulsion of Céspedes was achieved on September 5, 1933, twenty-four days after the flight of Machado, included Sergeant Batista as the only military figure and Professor Ramón Grau-San Martín and Carlos Prío-Socarrás, both of whom were to be Presidents of the Republic and both of whom were to be ejected from office by Batista—Grau early in the following year and Prío in 1952. (On the other hand, in 1944 Grau defeated Batista's candidate for the presidency, Carlos Saladrigas of the ABC who had been a member of Céspedes's Cabinet in 1933.)

Ambassador Welles was chagrined at the overthrow of the governing formula he had sponsored and at the ease with which it was accomplished. He was deeply worried at the prospect now opening before the country. Alarmist reports of all kinds flowed into his office in the Embassy; Americans and Cubans begged for American intervention as the only thing that could save them from the chaos, the confusion, the bloodshed, and the destruction to be anticipated from those they saw as the extremists, the hysterical students, and the mutinous and probably licentious soldiery who had turned against their officers. Anarchy, amid the most savage of excesses, appeared imminent.

For a brief period Welles favored the armed intervention called for by so many Americans and Cubans in Havana.[24] He was not supported by President Roosevelt or by Secretary Hull; they were determined to avoid intervention and the consequent stultification of the policy of the new administration toward Latin America. They were understandably more philosophical about developments in Cuba than their man on the spot possibly could be.

An impressive naval force was, however, sent to Cuban ports or cruised in Cuban waters so as to be in a position promptly to evacuate American citizens should the situation further deteriorate. That force represented in the eyes of many in Cuba and elsewhere a continuing threat of intervention, and it influenced the course of events in Cuba even though Roosevelt and Hull, with the later concurrence of Welles, were determined not to intervene.

Though he rapidly recovered from his extreme alarm about Cuban developments, Welles maintained consistently that the government presided over by Dr. Grau-San Martín was incompetent, inefficient, and so burdened with anti-American extremists that it could not be considered representative of the will of the Cuban people and so entitled to American recognition. The combination of intellectuals, academics, and students over which Grau presided was not considered to be Communist infiltrated; it was, however, demonstrably unable to control the Communists who were taking advantage of the prevailing disorder to set up soviets in sugar mills and perform other acts that threatened the established organization of society.

At the same time Welles discovered that Batista was no ignorant mutineer at the head of an undisciplined rabble. Instead, as he witnessed the performance of the forces loyal to Batista in a number of the critical emergencies of those troubled times, he began to regard Batista as the only hope of order. The latter had started on his public career only a few weeks earlier with a strong prejudice against American interference in Cuban affairs and had made clear to Welles that the force at his command would fight any American troops that might be landed on the island. Batista, however, soon achieved a conviction of the importance of the establishment of a Cuban government which could count on American recognition. Cuba desperately needed a favorable access for its sugar to the American market, including a trade agreement that would lower the American tariff. Batista, the pragmatist, soon shared the views of Welles and of his successor, Jefferson Caffery, as to the incompetence and the folly of the people who surrounded Grau and over whom Grau's authority was thought to be little more than nominal.

The changed view of Batista now held by Welles and Caffery also became that of Cubans "with a stake in their country." Their reliance on American influence and eventually on American intervention became compatible with an acceptance of Batista as the strong man who would defend interests threatened and indeed injured by the revolutionary thrust of Grau's followers. The incident that occurred that fall when a group of Havana society people abandoned their tables at a fashionable night spot rather than tolerate the presence of the upstart sergeant represented a most ephemeral frame of mind.[25] Batista was not the only pragmatist.

During the late fall of 1933 and the early weeks of 1934, most Cubans were living under desperate conditions. Widespread unemployment, poverty and near famine, uncertain future prospects, the constant daily emergencies, acts of violence, strikes and threats of strikes, and the wild rumors that flew about produced unbearable tensions. Batista's decision to remove Grau in January 1934 was greeted with relief by important sectors of the population, perhaps even by a majority. The possessing classes were delighted. They realized that Batista had found the formula for American recognition of a Cuban government that would defend an establishment endangered by the atmosphere of revolutionary excess that had prevailed.

In describing the fall of Grau, the *New York Times* correspondent wrote with an accurate irony, "Cuba has again recognized the United States."[26] The United States, for its part, promptly recognized Grau's successor, Carlos Mendieta.

A New Deal for Cuba followed quickly; it included a share in the American sugar market (less by half what Cuba had enjoyed before the depression), a reciprocal trade agreement that reduced the duty on Cuban sugar to less than half what it had been under the Hawley-Smoot Tariff Act, and the abrogation of the Platt Amendment. The latter action, in spite of the significance given it by official circles on both sides of the Florida Straits, does not seem to have greatly mollified the revolutionary Left in Cuba, nor did it alarm the possessing classes with the notion that the United States, which had saved them from Grau, was now about to abandon them. The Amendment had in fact become irrelevant. The American economic positions in Cuba, the American alliance with the old, and new, Cuban establishment, and Cuba's dependence on the goodwill of the American government for even the reduced well-being of the island population made the continuance of the explicit curtailment of Cuban sovereignty contained in the Amendment neither necessary nor expedient.

The reciprocal trade agreement, besides reducing the duty on the amount of Cuban sugar now permitted to enter the United States under the Sugar Act of 1934 and its successors, established a new modality in the commercial relations between the two countries. Heretofore, the tariff preferences they had granted each other had been independent of the actual rates in the schedules of each country. Thus the United States lowered its tariff on sugar in 1913 and raised it in 1921, 1922, and 1930; Cuba, throughout, enjoyed a discount of 20 percent on the rate, whatever it might be.

The Cuban tariff was mainly for revenue purposes. When the first President decided in 1903 that he needed to raise more revenue, he upped the rates and found that he had inadvertently laid the foundations for the Cuban beer industry (shades of Tropical, Polar, Hatuey, and all the rest).[27] But he had not violated his agreement with the United States, since he had not altered the percentage preferences to which American imports were entitled on Cuban duties whatever they might be. Similarly, in 1927 President Machado introduced comprehensive modifications with protective overtones into the Cuban schedules, but he respected the percentage preferences guaranteed American imports under the agreement. Contrary to the assertions of some Cuban writers, the agreement of 1903 did not of itself preclude the adoption by the Cuban government of protective tariffs, although the unavailability of alternate sources of revenue and the hope that adherence to moderate free-trade principles would help sugar had a deterrent effect on Cuban protectionists until 1927.

The agreement of 1934 changed the system from one of percentage preferences on independently established tariff schedules to one of specific duties mutually agreed upon and incorporated into a binational contractual arrangement. The Hull trade-agreements program justified itself in Congress and to special interests in the United States by claiming that in the course of negotiating agreements no American duties were lowered except in return for concessions by the other party. This tended to preclude unilateral lowerings of American duties even when warranted by the economic facts and by the needs of the developing or underdeveloped countries with which most of them were negotiated. The supplementary agreements with Cuba in later years and even the special arrangement under GATT in 1947 failed to give Cuba the latitude professionally competent Cuban economists and experts deemed was required. In 1955 the American government turned down a Cuban request for renegotiation. An affirmative American position on this issue was not arrived at until 1959, when nothing was further from Castro's mind than a trade agreement with the United States.

The Sugar Act of 1934 and Its Successors

In terms of sugar the new American program in 1934 permanently reduced Cuba's share of the American market (a share which for generations had been about 50 percent) to a range near 30 percent except when quotas were suspended as they were from 1942 to 1947.[28] The gains which the American insular territories had made owing to the low prices and the high tariffs of the depression years were preserved. But Cuba did reap a price and quantity stability that were powerful factors in the steadying of the island's politics and represented a substantial gain from the trough of the depression. The world market, however, continued for most of the decade of the thirties in the doldrums of the depression years.

The Sugar Act of 1934 was an outgrowth of the Roosevelt program for the rationalization of farm crops and marketing in the United States. Production was to be restricted in return for certain benefits to producers. Total consumption of sugar in the United States was estimated annually by the Secretary of Agriculture at a level that would result in prices equitable for producers at home and abroad and for consumers in the United States and designed to stimulate the export trade of the United States. Quotas for domestic production and for imports (98 percent of which came from Cuba) were established in 1934 by the Secretary of Agriculture on the basis of past performance. The base years he selected were those of the depression when Cuban production had been strangled by low prices and high tariffs. In later sugar acts quotas were fixed by Congress; this gave rise to the feverish lobbying by rival producers with which we have become familiar.

Foreign producers for the American market—of which Cuba was by far the most important—paid the American duty, reduced substantially from the Hawley-Smoot rate (Cuba enjoyed a discount from this full duty), and did not receive the benefits enjoyed by domestic producers in return for their acceptance of crop restrictions. In relation to the Cuban cost of production, the Act was deemed fair to the Cuban producer. It raised the island from the depths to which it had been plunged in the depression. The policy of the Act was part of an enlightened and progressive New Deal for agriculture in the United States.

The Sugar Act, however, had serious drawbacks from the Cuban point of view—drawbacks which, even without the distortions of the professional antiimperialists, contributed to growing pessimism as to Cuban responsibility for Cuban destinies. Through the Act Cuba permanently lost nearly half the share of the American market it had enjoyed prior to the Great Depression. During the five years beginning with 1935, Cuba sold a little over seven million Spanish long tons of raw sugar to the United States. The comparable figure for the five years beginning in 1925, a decade earlier, had been nearly seventeen million tons. Consumption of sugar in the United States varied little during these two periods.

A second Cuban grievance was that the American Congress set the

Cuban quota and varied it from time to time without reference to the Cuban government. The quota was a unilateral American decision. The fact that the Congress, at least until 1951, resisted demands advanced at quota time by other producers at Cuba's expense, was not an adequate answer to the Cuban sense of inferiority or to the Cuban belief that the sugar quota should be embodied in a bilateral agreement, as were the concessions Cuba granted American trade in Cuba in return for Cuba's access to the American sugar market.

Under the new sugar system adopted in 1934, the Department of State was Cuba's indispensable friend, protector, and supporter when, as happened every few years, American sugar legislation was reconsidered by the Congress. In the course of the lobbying for increased quotas by the politically potent mainland beet and cane producers and the offshore producers under the American flag (Puerto Rico, Hawaii, and the Philippines), the Department of State was the major advocate of the Cuban cause. Fair treatment for Cuba was a sound tenet of American foreign policy. But the Congress had to be convinced that Cuba deserved such treatment: in this judgment many voices could play significant roles one way or the other.

In devising and coordinating strategy for the defense of Cuba's quota in the United States, American investors in Cuban sugar production were logically prominent. They were supported by the east coast refiners anxious to process as much cane sugar as possible. (In several cases mills in Cuba and refineries in the United States were under common ownership.) The participants in the business of Cuban sugar were backed up by a well-organized group of American exporters enjoying preferential positions in the Cuban market and vitally interested in the maximization of Cuban purchasing power. Then there were American investors in Cuban activities other than sugar production, including the important utilities companies (telephone and electric light and power).

All of these interests, with their capacity for "educating" legislators and policymakers in Washington, preached in Havana the importance for Cuba of putting its best foot forward at quota time. That best foot was defined as the course of conduct most acceptable to the business-minded community in Cuba and in the United States. American views, political and economic, were constantly conveyed to the Cuban government and to the Cuban establishment by the highly paid and efficient representatives maintained in Washington by the Cuban Sugar Stabilization Institute—an industry organization with Cuban government representation. The battle for the quota was an arduous one. All the combatants, including the Cuban government, had to be under strict discipline if victory was to be achieved or at least too grievous a setback avoided.

The Sugar Act of 1937 represented for Cuba little more than a confirmation by Congress of the quota worked out by the Secretary of Agriculture, although a change in the handling of the Philippine quota produced a sense of grievance in Cuba. Quotas were suspended during the war and its immediate aftermath, through 1947.

World War II meant greatly increased sugar production in Cuba. The Cuban crop which amounted to less than 2.5 million long tons of raw sugar in 1941, worth $130 million, rose by 1944 to over 4 million tons with a value of $330 million.[29] The demands of the war, including those arising from the initial, almost catastrophic, success of the German submarine campaign, were met by the closest sort of cooperation between the Cuban and American governments. The Cuban sugar crops were bought at prices deemed equitable by the United States and accepted by Cuba as its contribution to the war effort—a contribution which demonstrated once more the strategic value of the industry to the United States.[30] In turn the United States saw to the provision of the shipping needed to move Cuban sugar and to supply Cuba with a minimum of the scarce goods and commodities required to keep the Cuban economy turning over at an acceptable rate. This added up to price controls in Cuba. The island was fortunate in being able to call on Carlos Hevia who handled a difficult and unprecedented situation with integrity, firmness, and a considerable degree of success. Cuba cooperated in the antisubmarine campaign and furnished the sites for two large American wartime air bases.

Cuba had demonstrated the value to the United States of her nearby, flexible, and readily expandable sugar resources. Recognition that this required from the United States reciprocity of a kind was embodied in an exchange of notes in December 1941 between the American Ambassador in Cuba, George S. Messersmith, and the Cuban Foreign Minister, José Manuel Cortina, at the time of the first intergovernmental sugar transaction in World War II.[31] The United States government committed itself to make all possible and appropriate efforts to protect the position of Cuba as a supplier of sugar to the United States, at least in the proportion established in the American Sugar Act of 1937. (Quotas under this act had been suspended during the war emergency.) The Cuban aim was to secure, in recognition of the value of Cuban sugar in times of stress and scarcity, a commitment that would protect Cuba's access to the American market from the hazards of periodical quota changes by the American Congress.

With the return to more normal conditions government-to-government sugar transactions were abandoned and quotas were reimposed. The Sugar Act of 1948 complied generally with the Messersmith-Cortina exchange of notes. Indeed it opened new prospects for Cuba by giving Cuba for the first time a participation in the amounts of sugar which certain other areas might but were failing to produce under their quotas.[32] But it also contained a clause which, though it was never applied, aroused much bitterness in the breast of Cuban nationalists and underlined the unilateral character of the relationship between the two countries. That clause, Section 202(e) of the Act, read as follows:

If the Secretary of State finds that any foreign country denies fair and equitable treatment to the nationals of the United States, its commerce, navigation or industry, and so notifies the Secretary [of Agriculture], the Secretary shall have authority to withhold or withdraw any increase in the share of the domestic consumption requirements provided for such country by this Act as compared with the share allowed under Section 202(b) of the Sugar Act of 1937; Provided, That any amount of sugar so withheld or withdrawn shall be prorated to domestic areas on the basis of existing quotas for such areas and the Secretary shall revise such quotas accordingly; Provided further, That any portion of such amount of sugar which cannot be supplied by domestic areas may be prorated to foreign countries other than a country which the Secretary of State finds has denied fair and equitable treatment to nationals of the United States.[33]

This provision was designed to strengthen the foreign debt collecting and claims adjusting function which American business interests, as well as official opinion in general, believed to be a part of the duties of the Department of State and of the American Foreign Service. There were legitimate claims of American citizens which the Cuban government—for this clause was aimed at Cuba—had neglected in the confusion and the corruption of the times. Some of these claims—and in the discussion of the clause in question the administration had made it clear that it would apply only to them—had been confirmed by decisions of the Cuban courts. Nevertheless the clause was a serious irritant in Cuba, even though it was never invoked and later disappeared from the statute book.

The episode of Section 202(e) underlined the impact in Cuba—actual and potential—of American sugar legislation and of the circumstances surrounding its passage. The whole process involved American judgments based upon actions or nonactions of the Cuban authorities in matters only indirectly if at all related to the export of sugar from Cuba to the United States. These judgments were formed in terms of the interests of Americans doing business in Cuba rather than in terms of the exigencies of the Cuban political and social situations—exigencies on which different views might well honestly be held by concerned citizens of the two countries. The conclusion seems to me unavoidable that the periodical renewals of American sugar legislation and the prospect of such renewals effectively if not explicitly limited Cuban sovereignty.

Congressional modifications of American sugar legislation in 1951 and 1956 were considered in Cuba to represent a violation of the commitment contained in the Messersmith-Cortina exchange of notes and a further watering down of the traditional relationship between the two countries. They gave domestic producers first call on the filling of the deficits of domestic areas. They were held once more to demonstrate Cuban impotence in dealing with the United States.[34] In effect these changes reduced the extent to which Cuba might expect to share in increased sugar consumption in the United States.

A definitive judgment as to the actual impact of the changes is hard to make in view of the complexities of deficit reallocations when some producing areas failed to fill their quotas. But the sense of injury in Cuban circles was real. Knowledgeable Cubans in the National Bank held that the situation of Cuba in the face of rising population and more or less stagnant living standards was truly desperate. They believed that Cuba required a significantly higher sugar quota in the United States if the living standards of the growing Cuban population were to be, not raised, but maintained. The Department of State's refusal in 1955 even to negotiate on the quota reinforced the Cuban sense of helplessness. The administration in Washington took the position that to negotiate on this point with the Cubans would invade the quota-setting function of the Congress. Reluctance to rock this particular boat was understandable in political terms. At the same time, it is difficult to quarrel with the conclusion of the authors of the monumental *Study on Cuba* who, after describing the 1956 modifications of American sugar legislation, write, "This change in the sugar legislation which took place in mid-1956 once again brought into high relief the helpless position of Cuba in the United States sugar market and the necessity for her to guarantee her participation in that market by means of a treaty."[35]

Cuba Free of the Platt Amendment

Some Cubans heartily applauded and others bitterly resented the expulsion of Grau in January 1934. Most concurred that Batista's decision reflected his education in the realities of Cuban American relations by Ambassadors Welles and Caffery. Grau's supporters in general maintained attitudes of sullen and conspiratorial resistance to the regime headed by Carlos Mendieta, Batista's choice.[36] The frustration of the revolution of 1933 was blamed on Batista and on the United States. The sense of dependence on the United States was strengthened among Cubans who welcomed that dependence as well as among Cubans who detested it. The abrogation of the Platt Amendment that spring did not really alter the situation.

The new American Ambassador was Jefferson Caffery, a most able man who was to retire in 1955 after having served as Chief of Mission in six countries over a period of thirty years. He maintained with Batista the most cordial and confidential of relationships. The two men saw eye to eye as to conditions in Cuba. Both were pragmatists. The American Ambassador influenced the course of Cuban affairs. He believed the Mendieta administration to reflect the will of the Cuban people; he did not include in the determination of that will the whims of the "ignorant masses" misled by specious demagoguery.

The new Cuban President, Carlos Mendieta, had a bluff, straightforward personality representative of an earlier, simpler Cuba. His popularity had been enhanced by his opposition to Machado. His administration, politically speaking, represented little more than the Céspedies formula which had been so ignominiously repudiated. It enjoyed the support of the same Liberal fragments and the continued opposition of Menocal's Conservatives. But its military backing, instead of the discredited, repressive apparatus identified with Machado, was now the disciplined armed force loyal to Batista, the new star in the Cuban sky. Mendieta had the earnest support of the business community thoroughly frightened by the Grau experience. American approval was emphasized by Ambassador Caffery's conduct of his mission and by his frequent informal meetings with Batista who continued to be nominally no more that the commander of the army but who was the real power in the country.

The serious opposition to Mendieta's government was of an underground and subversive nature; it was not responsive to Mendieta's assurances of a determination to return to normal electoral procedures as soon as possible. Public order left almost as much to be desired as it had in the final months of Machado or under Grau. The latter's political partisans, known as the *Auténticos*, and the student elements affiliated with them regarded the Mendieta administration with its military complexion and its reputation as an American imposition to be one with which they could not engage in a political dialogue. Subversion and terrorism continued unabated. Mendieta and Batista faced a general strike with revolutionary implications in March of 1935.

The "economic royalists" in Cuba and their American allies fully supported Mendieta, Batista, and Caffery—not for them the attitude of their confreres in the United States shown in Peter Arno's famous cartoon on their way to the movies to hiss "that man in the White House!" Roosevelt haters from the north became Batista admirers in Cuba.

Conditions slowly improved during Mendieta's administration, although remaining far below the levels of well-being reached in the previous decade. Weariness, disillusionment, and frustration helped restore a semblance of stability. Mendieta and Batista felt able to conduct elections for the presidency and the Congress in January 1936. The presidential candidates were Miguel Mariano Gómez for the Liberals and General Mario Menocal for the Conservatives. Gómez was the son of the Liberal leader who had been President twenty-five years earlier. Menocal was the former President (1913–1921) not yet reconciled to Batista whom he regarded as an upstart and mutinous sergeant. Gómez won; popular participation in the elections was limited. The curse of Machadoism lay heavy on many politicians. The Auténticos and other anti–*status quo* elements sullenly abstained.

President Gómez thought, with a logic divorced from reality, that now that he was the first properly elected chief executive in a dozen years, it was time to terminate the quasi-military rule that had prevailed in the thirty months since the fall of Machado. Batista, on the other hand, with his taste of real power and the American support on which he counted, had no intention of retreating to Camp Colombia and becoming a mere soldier. The two men soon clashed. Gómez vetoed a law establishing a tax on sugar for the benefit of the system of rural schools under military auspices in which Batista was interested. Batista was furious. The Congress, in order to avoid a military coup that would have destroyed its participation in public affairs, followed Batista's suggestion that the President be impeached, not for having vetoed the law but on the charge of having used improper pressures on the congressmen to get them to vote against it. In December 1936 Gómez was duly impeached, convicted, and driven from office. No one lifted a finger on his behalf.

Gómez had tried desperately to get the United States at least to make a statement that would amount to a "moral intervention" against what he regarded, not unreasonably, as a fracturing of the Cuban Constitution at the hands of the military. President Roosevelt allowed it to be said informally that in his opinion Gómez had done no more to press views on the legislators than was normally done in the United States in similar cases. The impact of this in Cuba was nil. Most people in Havana firmly believed that Batista would not have done what he did without Ambassador Caffery's approval. Some went so far as to credit the Ambassador with thinking up the impeachment scheme.[37]

Gómez was perhaps as ineffective and impractical as Ambassador Caffery seems to have considered him or as reactionary in his social views as Batista, anxious to identify himself with renovationary currents in Cuba, described him. Nevertheless his summary expulsion, though a highly successful political maneuver, produced unfavorable currents of opinion in Cuba and in the United States. Washington decided on a change of ambassadors which would introduce a different style into the relations between the two countries. Caffery was soon on his way to Brazil where he was to serve in a distinguished and effective manner for seven years. Batista, after a few months of going it alone in the political field, accepted the need for a less dictatorial approach to the political process in Cuba.

Cuba was fortunate in Gómez's successor as constitutional President, Federico Laredo-Bru, the former Vice President. Laredo-Bru had a good record in the War for Independence, had been a Cabinet member twenty years earlier and had been identified in the early twenties with a fighting movement for political reform. Although he lacked the flamboyance of personality and the conspicuous wealth of other Cuban presidents, he was certainly one of the most patriotically dedicated men to occupy the presidential office. When Batista decided to undertake the revival of the politics of the country, he found in Laredo-Bru a most effective coworker.

Batista's decision was hastened by evidences of public apathy in the partial elections of 1938. With the active help of Laredo-Bru, Grau and Batista became reconciled and made a deal of which the initial element was a broad amnesty to restore the civil rights, cancel the sentences, and permit the return to Cuba of thousands implicated in the turbulence of the preceding years. Batista yielded to Grau's demand that the first elections to be held should be for an assembly that would draw up a new constitution to replace the one which had been drafted in 1901 during the American military government. In return Grau agreed that his party would abandon revolutionary activity and would participate in the elections, scheduled for November 1939, to select delegates for the Assembly.

Neither Ambassador Caffery's activist style of diplomacy nor his intimate relationship with Batista were emulated by his successor, J. Butler Wright, also an able professional and a man of great charm, energy, and common sense. (I had the privilege of serving under him.) There was, however, no change in American support for Batista or in its overt expression.

Late in 1938, in his capacity as chief of the Cuban armed forces and at the invitation of the American Chief of Staff, Batista visited Washington. Following conversations at the politico-economic rather than the military level, he returned home with the prospect of a further reduction in the sugar tariff and a loan from the Export-Import Bank. He was acclaimed the "Messenger of Prosperity" by his local followers.

The United States government, however, made it bluntly clear to the Cuban government that the benefits promised Batista were contingent on the payment of claims amounting to over $80 million in which American citizens were interested and which had mostly originated in the extravagant and allegedly corrupt days of the repudiated Machado. A commission, appointed by President Mendieta in 1934 and made up of highly respected Cubans, had found this indebtedness, so far as it pertained to the Machado public works program, to have been illegally contracted. The commission became aware of corruption and laxity as well as, in some cases, of collusion between debtor and creditor in the case of some of the expenditures involved.

It recommended settlement on ethical grounds with those who held Cuban bonds they had bought in good faith. Washington, however, was adamant that payment of all the evidences of indebtedness be made at face value. The Cuban Congress reluctantly yielded and approved the highly unpopular bond issue underwritten by an American bank to pay off the debt.

In so doing, the Congress allegedly approved bonds to be distributed to the legislators to compensate them for their cooperation in a matter hardly likely to endear them to the electorate. The lawmaker charged with the distribution of this compensation was reported not to have given satisfaction to his colleagues. The manner in which the affair was conducted left a bad taste in the mouths of Cubans sensitive to the dignity and the good name of their country.[38]

On the other hand, the concerned officials of the United States government (of whom I was one at a modest level) believed they had no choice other than to insist on full payment of claims contracted by a legal Cuban government and owing to creditors whose actions had not been impugned by Cuban courts. These creditors were a highly vociferous lot. A failure to satisfy them either by not pressing the Cuban government sufficiently hard or by getting snarled up in an interminable debate about the legitimacy and the ethics of the acts of the Machado regime could have had unfortunate repercussions on the support in the United States for the administration's policy toward Cuba in particular and Latin America as a whole.

The leverage of the United States government on this issue arose not only from the prospect of the immediate benefits mentioned above. It drew strength also from the general and continuing belief among realistic Cubans in the need to follow Washington directives on major matters.

The Constitution of 1940

The election of delegates to the Constituent Assembly in November 1939 was an opportunity for demonstrating renewed vitality in the Cuban political system. For the first time in fifteen years all of the major components in the political spectrum had agreed to participate. Though the purpose of the voting was to select a body that would frame a new constitution for the country and would then give way to a newly elected executive and legislature, the struggle was envisaged by most of the voters as a contest between Colonel Batista and Ramón Grau-San Martín for control of a majority of the votes in the forthcoming assembly. The voters were being asked to judge the performance and the records of these two men since the fall of Machado six years earlier.

As the date for the elections approached both leaders maneuvered to broaden the base of their popular support by attracting as many as possible of the parties in the field to their respective coalitions. Grau had to counter fears inspired by the radicalism of some of his Auténticos and the recollection of their associations and terroristic activities. Ready to join his team were both General Menocal's Conservatives with their leader's continued aversion to Batista and Miguel Mariano Gómez's Liberal splinter. (Gómez was the man who had beaten Menocal for the presidency in 1936 and had a few months later been impeached and expelled at Batista's behest.)

Batista's problem was to temper the reputation he had achieved as the favorite of the traditional establishment and of the United States and to identify himself with the renovationary and socially progressive ideas in which he was sincerely interested at the time. He made a deal with the Cuban Communist party involving, in exchange for its support, the legalization of the party and the right for it to publish a daily newspaper. This appears today a more radical move than in fact it was. In those days the Nazis and the Fascists were the enemies of the democratic world while the Soviet Union had been helping a Spanish Republic that many in Cuba and elsewhere regarded as a beleaguered outpost of that world. The Cuban Communists had control of many labor unions and were able to induce the membership to vote not so much for the Communist ticket as for tickets supporting Batista rather than Grau.

Only 57 percent of the electorate went to the polls in November 1939, an alarming manifestation of popular apathy. The two coalitions divided the total ballots almost evenly, but Grau captured a majority of forty-three delegates to thirty-five for Batista. The Auténticos turned out to be the largest single party, with about one-fifth of the total votes cast. If, however, the various splinters of the Liberal party had held together, that traditional party would have controlled one-third of the electorate. The Communists polled under 10 percent of the votes. The Constituent Assembly organized itself on the basis of these results with Grau in the chair.[39]

The unimportance of the expressed preferences of the voters was soon given a dramatic demonstration. The verdict of the electorate on the Grau versus Batista issue was promptly reversed. Batista made a deal with General Menocal transferring the latter's fifteen Conservative delegates elected on an anti-Batista ticket to the Batista column. Grau lost his chairmanship of the Assembly. He was replaced by a well-known Cuban politician who, though he, too, had been elected on an anti-Batista ticket, had quarreled with the chief of his party, and had changed sides.[40] Menocal's son, with Batista's support, won the election for the coveted mayoralty of Havana, generally considered the second most important political plum in Cuba.[41] These developments were hardly calculated to stimulate the faith of the ordinary voter in the political process or in the responsiveness of its manipulators to the electorate.

Meanwhile, amid impassioned debate often in the presence of packed and noisy galleries, the work of constitution-making was completed by the many able statesmen and legal experts among the delegates. The final product was generally considered enlightened and progressive. It reflected a serious consideration of Cuba's experience and of Cuba's problems. It embodied the hopes and aspirations of many. Some of its clauses may have been, as alleged particularly by conservatives, unworkable. It contained a number of provisions requiring implementing legislation from the Congress. That legislation, in certain matters affecting the propertied classes and their American allies, was either not forthcoming or was delayed to the very end of the twelve years during which the constitution was in force, from 1940 until Batista's coup in 1952.

In spite of the political maneuvers I have described, the adoption of the new constitution was a positive forward step. It gave promise of popular participation in government within a moderate-progressive framework. Its provisions paved the way for the apparent triumph of democracy in the elections of 1944.

Thanks to his pact with the Conservative Menocal and with the continued support of the Communists, Batista handily won the election of 1940. His four years in office coincided with the unfolding of the drama of World War II in which Cuba was the faithful and helpful ally of the United States. Batista ruled with the emergency powers Congress had granted him. He tried unsuccessfully to get Grau to join in a government of national unity. He managed to lure a couple of the smaller parties away from Grau's coalition and rewarded their leaders with Cabinet jobs. In the atmosphere created by the circumstantial alliance of the United States and the Soviet Union, he gave Cabinet posts to two Communists both of whom today occupy posts of importance in the Castro regime.

Following Butler Wright's lamented death in November 1939, George Messersmith served ably and effectively as American Ambassador to Cuba. When he was transferred to Mexico he was succeeded in Havana by Spruille Braden, a dedicated, industrious, and forceful promoter of American interests in Cuba as he saw them. His sensitivity to Cuban susceptibilities was not great. Batista, who was also strong minded and autocratic, resented the Braden style and tried to get rid of him. He was finally persuaded by his Ambassador in Washington, Aurelio Fernández-Concheso, who discussed the matter at length with Secretary Hull and with me, that for Batista to declare Braden *persona non grata* would be an inappropriate episode in the wartime relations of two such firm allies as the United States and Cuba.[42] (In due course Braden was transferred to Argentina where he had opportunities on a wider stage for the practice of his diplomatic method.)

A few weeks before the elections of 1944 Ambassador Braden issued a public call for American firms doing business in Cuba to refrain from contributions for the benefit of Cuban political factions. Illustrative of the Cuban mood was the fact that many judged the Ambassador's request to be motivated not so much by a desire to keep American business out of Cuban politics as by a wish to hurt the campaign of Batista's choice for the presidency who was running against Grau-San Martín. The reasoning was that with or without the ambassadorial injunction American firms were hardly likely to help Grau, a man who had so threatened them and frightened them a decade earlier.

Though Batista could not succeed himself he was confident that his follower, Dr. Carlos Saladrigas, would win handily over Grau's Auténticos and their allies. The election of Grau, even though the Batista coalition kept control of Congress, came as a stunning surprise to the outgoing President and to most observers. It was reported that Batista was restrained from forcibly disregarding the people's choice by a personal message from President Roosevelt.[43] However that may be, Batista departed in a blaze of glory for having accepted the verdict of the polls in exemplary fashion. What a pity his career in Cuban politics did not end at this point!

The Auténticos in Power, 1944–1952

Grau was inaugurated in an atmosphere of hope and enthusiasm not duplicated until the arrival of Castro in Havana fifteen years later.[44] A new era seemed to be dawning, one in which Cuban politics, freed from military domination, would achieve a new vitality. The United States was praised not only for having accepted but even for having smoothed the way for Grau, the man who eleven years before had been denounced as an incompetent extremist by the United States and had been forced by the refusal of the United States to recognize him to step down ignominiously from the presidency to which the revolution of September 1933 had elevated him. The defeat of Batista's candidate was believed to promise a decrease in the influence exercised by the American Ambassador in Havana and by the Department of State in Washington on the course of Cuban affairs.

The state of the economy was most favorable to the plans of a government pledged to use Cuban resources for the benefit of the Cuban people. Although there had been some inflation, the rise in government revenues from 78 million pesos in 1940 to over 150 million in 1945 and to more than 200 million the following year represented a substantial real increase in the government's income. Grau did not have control of Congress, but he had retained the executive's wartime powers. His major asset was popular faith in his campaign pledges to renovate the administration and to eliminate the corruption generally believed to have disfigured the previous regime.

Unfortunately for him Grau's coalition was far from homogeneous. It included conservative anti-Communists who had voted against Batista's candidate because of the latter's continuing alliance with the Communists. Many of the Auténtico legislators were recent deserters from more traditional groupings; they were not renovators at all but primarily seekers after personal power and profit. Among the hard core Auténticos of the revolutionary days of 1933 and earlier, there remained extremists identified with terrorist methods and veterans and their disciples from the years of the underground struggle against Machado and Batista prior to the elections of 1939. This heritage of clandestinity and violence bore sinister fruit then and later.

Hardly was Grau in the presidential chair than he took action to give his administration a thoroughly pro-Grau complexion. He made a complete purge of Batista followers in the higher echelons of the army. He operated a ruthless spoils system throughout the civil bureaucracy, setting aside the legal provisions which had been designed, in the spirit of the Constitution of 1940, to set Cuba on the road to a modern and efficient career civil service. He went so far as to direct one of his decrees at removing from office those public employees who, ten years before, had disregarded the call for a revolutionary strike issued by his then clandestine party.[45]

The Grau administration quickly destroyed the illusions of those who hoped that a new day in Cuban political life had dawned. Such belief in genuine popular participation as had been generated by the political pacification for which Batista and Laredo-Bru were responsible, by the adoption of the Constitution of 1940, and by the emancipation from the restraints of the Batista era resulting from Grau's election was almost immediately undermined. Instead of the upward path that seemed so fairly to open before it, the new rulers soon chose to follow the worst practices of the politics of previous decades. Faith in the ability of the political process to contribute to the general welfare rather than to that of the professionals and their friends received a number of heavy blows. The extraordinary reputation for corruption earned by the Grau and the Prío administrations was a major factor in the disillusionment that made Batista's coup in 1952 so easy.

This matter of corruption is an unpleasant one which must, however, be discussed in order to understand political life in the Cuban Republic. It cannot be dismissed with the statement that corruption in government is found everywhere—even in the United States. I know of no country among those committed to the Western ethic where the diversion of public treasure for private profit reached the proportions that it attained in the Cuban Republic. Most of the presidents were rightly believed by their fellow citizens to have accumulated for themselves and their near relatives massive fortunes which their legitimate activities never would have won for them. This seems to have been true particularly and spectacularly in the cases of Batista, Grau-San Martín, and Prío-Socarrás who ruled the country from 1940 to 1959. Hundreds of their supporters followed their example.

This corruption did not, in my judgment, proceed from any special flaw in the Cuban character. It was rather a reflection of the failure of Cuban society as a whole to achieve a valid sense of responsibility for Cuban destinies and hence a responsibility for the Republic considered in the classic sense as the "public thing." Corruption was not a cause of public apathy about politics; it was public apathy that encouraged the corruption though there was, of course, a secondary vicious-circle effect. The belief that major favorable or unfavorable developments in Cuba depended largely on external factors led logically to a depreciation of the importance of Cuban actions except as they affected the fortunes of individual Cubans. Many wealthy citizens whom one would have thought of as having a stake in the growth of responsible government avoided direct participation in politics themselves, although they encouraged corruption in such matters as the determination of the taxes they owed.

Grau's philosophy of government was expressed in his aphorism: "To govern is to distribute." And distribute he did, though not with equity or with foresight. He was later sued for having misappropriated 174 million pesos. Not all of this was alleged to involve the conversion of public funds to private profit; much of the total represented expenditures for public purposes without what the complainants considered to have been legal authorization. The Congress failed to pass national budgets during the entire period of the presidencies of Batista and Grau from 1940 to 1948; the executive was forced to rule by decree under special wartime powers, the constitutionality of which could be and was impugned. The fact, however, that the offices of the court where the suit against Grau was to be tried were attacked and the documents removed by persons unknown and never recovered would seem prima facie evidence that Grau and his followers had much they did not wish discussed before a court of law.[46]

The opportunities for illicit gain were many. There were barter deals with other countries where favored insiders profited at the expense of legitimate traders. The "sugar differential" or compensation for increased price levels received from the United States government as purchaser of the sugar crop and supposed to be divided among the producers was impounded by the government and some of it seems to have found its way into hands not entitled to it. Then there was the notorious "Item K" in the budget of the Ministry of Education fed by funds derived from a constitutional provision regarding the minimum percentage of the national revenues to be devoted to educational purposes. In a time of rapidly rising revenues, this item reached considerable proportions; it seems to have functioned as a slush fund for political and other purposes rather than, as intended, to finance additional educational activities beyond those included in the ordinary budget of the Ministry.

There were also less sophisticated methods of getting at the public funds. The Minister of Education was generally reputed to have drawn large amounts in bills from the treasury, which he carried in suitcases to Miami for investment in Florida real estate for the benefit of himself and family. He is reported to have been touchingly generous to his friends; for example, after a visit to the sickbed of one of these it was found that the Minister had discreetly left 100,000 pesos of the people's money under the patient's pillow. The Congress once voted to bring the Minister before it for questioning. On the afternoon when he was due to appear, the Capitol was machine-gunned from a passing car; the session was suspended, and it was never possible to put together the necessary votes to call the Minister before the legislators again.[47]

By his flirtations with the Communists, Grau disillusioned those who hoped that his anticommunism had justified their voting for him instead of for Batista's Communist-supported candidate. Not until the last year of Grau's term did the Auténticos move against the Communist control of the labor unions which had been one of the dividends of Communist cooperation with Batista since 1938.[48]

In the matter of violence and gangsterism in politics, a field into which the youthful Fidel Castro was now moving, the Grau administration not only proved itself quite impotent but even gave the impression that it was hand in glove with such activities. Grau's Chief of Secret Service was murdered when the administration failed to release from prison a number of individuals in whom a group of Grau's followers was interested. Grau promptly freed the men in question; the killers were never found.

Under Grau political gangsterism flourished with impunity especially in the University where groups, called *bonches*, adopted high-sounding labels to cover their depredations and their murders. Castro belonged to one of these gangs and was believed to have participated in a couple of particularly cowardly killings. President Grau thought to develop a sense of responsibility in some of the gang leaders by appointing them to high posts in the national security apparatus. Soon there was a pitched battle finally broken up by the army; it was caused by the attempt of the Chief of Grau's Bureau of Investigation, a notorious gangster, to arrest a confrere who rejoiced in the title of Chief Instructor in the Police Academy.[49] This sort of thing went on through both the Grau and the Prío administrations and caused many to welcome Batista's coup in 1952 as giving promise that at least this intolerable state of affairs would be suppressed.

284   *Notes on the Cuban Background*

In outlining Grau's dreary story mention must be made of the *Cayo Confites* expedition. This was a Bay of Pigs type of operation clandestinely mounted by Grau's notorious Minister of Education. Weapons and funds were provided from government sources. When the fact of the expedition was discovered by the man against whom it was to be directed, the disreputable Trujillo of the Dominican Republic, international pressures, largely American, were brought to bear. The operation was disowned by the Cuban government and broken up by the Cuban army. Fidel Castro was a member; he is said to have made a heroic escape from the remote key on which the expedition was surrounded, swimming ashore carrying a machine gun.[50]

Faith in the possibility of successful popular government in Cuba received a blow from the Grau experience from which it was never to have a chance to recover. Grau was the man who had been regarded in 1944 by many as the redeemer of the Cuban people from all the ills of the past including local militarism and corruption as well as alleged interference and exploitation by the United States. Some Cuban writers have detected in the abysmal loss of prestige of the Cuban political system in those years a deep-laid Communist smear campaign; there is no doubt the Communists used the situation for their purposes, but they did not create it.[51]

Grau's record had alienated a segment of his party which, under the leadership of Eddy Chibás, a vigorous and single-minded anticorruptionist, proceeded to form a new opposition group. The new party members were known as the *Ortodoxos*. In spite, however, of the vigor of the Chibás campaign and of the dismal record of the Auténticos, the latter and their presidential candidate, Carlos Prío-Socarrás, won handily in 1948. Their victory reflected the efficient political machine of the ruling party and the support of a spinter of the old Conservative party, one of whose members became Vice President. Chibás ran a poor third behind a coalition of the traditional Liberals and Conservatives; their candidate was a distinguished surgeon, Ricardo Núñez-Portuondo, the son of one of the heroes of the struggle for independence.

The traditionalist ticket headed by Núñez-Portuondo won for that coalition the generous minority representation in the Cuban Senate provided in Cuban law for the runner-up party. A Senator so elected was former President Batista. He had remained in his Florida home during the campaign but returned to Cuba at the end of the year to participate actively in the political system which, less than four years later, he was to destroy.

Prío, like Grau before him, entered upon his presidency with the best of prospects so far as the material resources needed for constructive government were concerned. The anticipated postwar slump in sugar had not materialized. The crop which in the early years of Grau's term had amounted to 4 million tons worth from $250 million to $400 million rose in 1947 and 1948 to 6 million tons valued for the first time in twenty-five years at over $600 million. Though there had been some price inflation, there was a very real advance in the revenues available to the government. It is sad to have to record that the results achieved, in spite of the efforts of many men of goodwill and ability, were well below the minimum a not too exigent community would have demanded in order to maintain its faith in the politics of the times and in the desirability of active participation in those politics.

The new President had won his victory to some extent on his record as Minister of Labor when Communist control of the unions was smashed. He was remembered as an outstanding student leader and as a member of the Revolutionary Committee of 1933. He had become an industrious politician with a flair for the combinations of the professionals while at the same time maintaining a popular revolutionary image. He acquired a lot of money and spent it lavishly. He did not do his party's reputation for integrity in the handling of public funds any good, although his warm amiability and his handsome presence led many to hope that he would be able to redeem the party promises so neglected by his predecessor.

Prío quarreled bitterly with Grau over unpaid bills and other matters. He conducted a purge of the armed forces to remove those he thought of as Grau partisans. (Neither Grau's nor Prío's conduct with the army materially diminished its nostalgia for Batista.) Prío was fearful of a Communist conspiracy in view of the revival of Moscow's interest in the international movement. He had his labor problems. His government often found itself obliged temporarily to take over enterprises refusing to grant what their managements considered exorbitant worker demands. These take-overs did not endear him to the business community.

Prío did not boost the ethical standards of the public administration in the estimation of the public. He emerged from his years in power with a very considerable personal fortune. He was generous with his followers. He and his brother, who served for a time as Minister of Finance, were said to have been involved in a scandalous manipulation of worn-out currency bills supposedly turned in for incineration and replacement.[52]

The prevailing mood was one of feverish self-enrichment. Though the expected postwar slump in sugar had not taken place, the notion that in Cuba periods of prosperity are invariably followed by acute depressions because of external factors in the operation of which Cuban decisions and actions are irrelevant led the majority in positions to do so to adopt the policy of getting theirs while the getting was good. This was a factor in the frittering away under Grau and Prío of the real opportunity that existed to put Cuban wealth to work for the long-range welfare of Cuban society as a whole. (Sugar production had risen from 16 million Spanish long tons worth $750 million in the six years [1936 through 1941] that preceded American entrance into World War II to nearly 32 million tons worth $3.6 billion [somewhat depreciated dollars] in the six years [1946 through 1951] that followed the conclusion of hostilities.)

Prío also dabbled in the politics of the Caribbean area as had his predecessor. The Caribbean legion with Cuban governmental assistance in the shape of weapons, financing, and hospitality played a significant part in the successful overthrow by José (Pepe) Figueres of an allegedly dictatorial-plus-Communist regime in Costa Rica. Then Prío decided that President Arévalo of Guatemala needed help to counter the threats of reactionary elements in his country. In violation of his constitutional obligation not to leave the country without congressional approval he made a clandestine trip to Guatemala to survey the situation.[53] He seems to have accomplished nothing except to lose prestige in his own country.

The midterm elections of 1950 showed Prío that the electorate was becoming disenchanted with his administration and with his party. His brother, the somewhat tarnished Minister of Finance, lost the race for Mayor of Havana to the incumbent, a defector from the government party. Eddy Chibás, the Ortodoxo leader, won a Senate seat formerly occupied by an Auténtico. There were other losses. Batista was again active in politics; his decade or more in power seen through the prism of six years of Auténtico rule gave him a political magnetism that alarmed Prío and his friends.

The President was roused to take vigorous though belated steps to redeem the fame of his administration and to improve the prospects of his partisans. He announced a policy of *Nuevos Rumbos* ("New Directions"). Though initially discounted much as a profligate's New Year's resolution would be—after all it had been six years since the Auténticos had made their empty promises to give the electorate a genuine new deal—Prío's new orientation did in fact give a more constructive thrust to his government. He persuaded some good men to join him and he gave them scope. Both Ernesto Dihigo and Jorge Mañach, men of unblemished reputations and high abilities, served as foreign ministers in this period. In the financial field José (Pepín) Bosch, a business man of energy and ideals, and José Álvarez-Díaz, a brilliant practical economist and professor, responded to the President's call. (Álvarez-Díaz, during the early years of his post-Castro exile in the United States, was the guiding spirit of the monumental *Study on Cuba* at the University of Miami, an invaluable, well-organized compendium of information on the politico-economic and social history of Cuba from the days of Columbus through the first years of Castro.) Prío's new policy also brought about, at long last, the establishment of a central bank with the distinguished and able Felipe Pazos at its head. This was an essential step toward the economic independence of Cuba, one complemented by the founding of a series of related planning, development, and financing institutions.

Nor did Prío neglect electoral politics. Faced with the growing opposition of Batista and his new party and with that of Chibás and his Ortodoxos, he managed to conclude a pact with the coalition of traditional Liberals and Conservatives that had opposed him in 1948; in that year the alliance Prío now arranged had polled 75 percent of the votes. (Batista had turned his back on the traditional parties to which he owed his election to the Senate in 1948 and was engaged in organizing the personal following which he hoped would return him to power.)

Meanwhile Chibás was continuing his strident opposition and apparently gaining many converts in spite of, or perhaps because of, the fact that his platform was limited to a single plank, "Turn the rascals out!" What he would have amounted to as a responsible executive and administrator remains wrapped in mystery. His end came dramatically and absurdly. He shot himself at the end of one of his immensely popular radio broadcasts and, after lingering for a few days, died. He had made some accusations of corruption he had been unable to substantiate in spite of his repeated promises to do so. The fatal shot was supposed to demonstrate his own integrity and to be a final warning to the guilty parties. His successor in the leadership of the party was Roberto Agramonte, a distinguished professor of sociology at the University of Havana.

Batista's coup in March 1952 put a violent and squalid end to the period of constitutional government which had been inaugurated in 1940. The loss of democratic momentum resulting from the acute disillusionment of wide sectors of the Cuban people because of the Auténticos' conduct in power had fatally weakened the country's political muscle and made the triumph of Batista, as he himself boasted, bloodless and unresisted. The tragedy was compounded by the fact that the movement toward more reputable government that took place in the last two years of Prío's presidency might well have been consolidated and strengthened by either one of the candidates deemed to have a chance of victory in 1952.

I am conscious that in these notes I have neglected many constructive developments identified both with the years when Batista dominated the scene after the expulsion of Grau in 1933 through Batista's presidency ending in 1944 and with the administrations of the two Auténtico presidents. Able and patriotic Cubans made notable achievements in legislation and administration. But the disillusionment of the people with the political process continued for the reasons I have sketched. It was to be given a dramatic illustration by Batista in 1952 and by Castro in 1960.

As I contemplate this historical background, I am led to agree with the eminent Cuban authors of the *Study on Cuba* to whom I am indebted for so much information and enlightenment when they attribute the success of Batista's barracks coup in 1952 to "the insufficient level of public morality, of a community political consciousness and of citizen responsibility in the face of collective problems."[54] That seems to me a fair if painful statement.

Notes

Chapter 2: Batista Paves the Way for Castro

1. For the immediate antecedents of Batista's coup, see the section "The Auténticos in Power" in "Notes on the Cuban Background."
2. "Recurso de Inconstitucionalidad" presented to the Supreme Court, April 3, 1953—over a year after Batista's coup. There were thirty-eight signers, and a number of individuals and institutions publicly expressed support for the argument against the constitutionality of Batista's legislation.
3. R. Hart Phillips, Cuba: Island of Paradox (New York: McDowell Obolensky, 1959), pp. 260–61.
4. Fulgencio Batista, The Growth and Decline of the Cuban Republic (Greenwich, Conn.: Devin-Adair, 1964), p. 39.
5. The Cuban Communists, Batista's allies and supporters as recently as the partial elections of 1950, went underground after Batista's coup and his break with the Soviet Union in March 1952. They and their Russian mentors disapproved of Castro's attack on the Moncada barracks; in fact they opposed violence against Batista up to the summer of 1958. They made a deal with Castro only when the success of his movement seemed assured.
6. Eduardo Suárez-Rivas, Un Pueblo Crucificado (Coral Gables, Fla.: Service Offset Printers, 1964), pp. 335 ff. The author at this time was a follower of Grau and one of the Senators resulting from the arrangement he describes in his book.
7. Phillips, Cuba: Island of Paradox, p. 324, quotes Batista as remarking, "I'm glad Ambassador Gardner approves of my government but I wish he wouldn't talk about it so much."
8. Carlos Márquez-Sterling, Historia de Cuba Desde Colón Hasta Castro (New York: Las Américas Publishing Company, 1963), p. 377. See also Nathaniel Weyl, Red Star Over Cuba (Greenwich, Conn.: Devin-Adair, 1960), p. 148.
9. Suárez-Rivas, Pueblo Crucificado, p. 347; and Rufo López-Fresquet, My Fourteen Months with Castro (New York: World Publishing Company, 1966), p. 160.
10. Phillips, Cuba: Island of Paradox, pp. 284–85. The reporter was Ernestina Otero.
11. López-Fresquet, My Fourteen Months with Castro, p. 35.
12. See Márquez-Sterling, Historia de Cuba, p. 428, for a description of Matthews's pro-Castro activities in 1958.
13. Suárez-Rivas, Pueblo Crucificado, p. 354; Márquez-Sterling, Historia de Cuba, p. 390; and Bohemia, May 28, 1957.
14. Earl E. T. Smith, The Fourth Floor: An Account of the Castro Communist Revolution (New York: Random House, 1962), p. 5.
15. Jules Dubois, Fidel Castro: Rebel, Liberator, or Dictator? (Indianapolis, Ind.: Bobbs-Merrill, 1959), p. 174, quotes Secretary Dulles's statement on Ambassador Smith. See also Smith, Fourth Floor, p. 24.
16. Dubois, Fidel Castro, p. 188.
17. Ibid., p. 280.

289

18. Theodore Draper, Castroism: Theory and Practice (New York: Praeger, 1965), p. 25.
19. Smith, Fourth Floor, p. 23.
20. Ibid., p. 37
21. Márquez-Sterling, Historia De Cuba, pp. 395, 430–37; Phillips, Cuba: Island of Paradox, p. 380; Suárez-Rivas, Pueblo Crucificado, pp. 364–69; and Smith, Fourth Floor, pp. 152–57.
22. Smith, Fourth Floor, pp. 90–91.
23. Draper, Castroism, pp. 26–34.
24. Smith, Fourth Floor, p. 91.
25. Ibid., p. 155.
26. Ibid., pp. 166–68, quotes from Pawley's testimony before the Internal Security Sub-committee of the Senate Judiciary Committee on September 2, 1960.
27. Ibid., p. 160.
28. Ibid., p. 174.
29. Interview with Spruille Braden, Police Gazette, August 1958; see also Márquez-Sterling, Historia de Cuba, p. 433.

Chapter 3: The United States Recognizes Castro

1. See New York Times editorial, May 10, 1957.
2. There is extensive American and Cuban backing for this thesis that Castro could have been denied power had the lower echelons of the Department of State been properly motivated and illuminated. It reflects, in my judgment, a total misconception of American power and responsibility for Cuban affairs in 1958.
3. An excellent summary of this American position is contained in a series of speeches made in 1955 by Henry Holland, then Assistant Secretary of State for Inter-American Affairs and published in pamphlet form by the Department of State.
4. For the evolution of American policy, see William Rogers, The Twilight Struggle (New York: Random House, 1967), pp. 3–25.
5. R. Hart Phillips, The Cuban Dilemma (New York: Ivan Obolensky, 1962), p. 28.
6. A Castro speech made in February or March 1959.
7. Federal Register, March 1958.
8. Castro's virulent speeches on this subject coexisted with the failure of the Cuban government to present any extradition requests under the existing treaty between Cuba and the United States.
9. Herminio Portell-Vilá, Historia de Cuba en Sus Relaciones con los Estados Unidos y España, 4 vols. (Havana: Jesús Montero, 1938–1941).

Chapter 4: Cuba Seen from the American Embassy

1. José Álvarez-Díaz, ed., Un Estudio Sobre Cuba (Coral Gables, Fla.: University of Miami Press, 1963), pp. 642–56, describes the Law of Sugar Coordination adopted in 1937.
2. Rufo López-Fresquet, My Fourteen Months with Castro (New York: World Publishing Company, 1966), pp. 84–87, gives an account of Law Number 40.

Chapter 5: First Contacts with Castro

1. *Time*, March 16, 1959, quoted Castro as saying of the new American Ambassador, "Friendly, cordial and knowledgeable about Cuba—a good Ambassador." Andrés Suárez, *Cuba: Castroism and Communism, 1959–1966* (Cambridge, Mass.: M.I.T. Press, 1967), p. 47, recalls Castro's remark on his television show about the "cordial and friendly conversation" he had had the previous day with the new American Ambassador.
2. In my opinion the best work on the subject is still Theodore Draper, *Castroism: Theory and Practice* (New York: Praeger, 1965).
3. U.S., Congress, Senate, Committee on the Judiciary, "Communist Threat to the United States Through the Caribbean: Testimony of Robert C. Hill," 87th Cong., 1st sess., June 12, 1961. See especially pp. 803–06.
4. Paul P. Kennedy, "US Envoys Split on Castro's Cuba," *New York Times*, April 12, 1959, p. 26.

Chapter 6: Castro Visits the United States

1. The fate of Cuban sugar in the Great Depression is discussed in "Notes on the Cuban Background."
2. Rufo López-Fresquet, *My Fourteen Months with Castro* (New York: World Publishing Company, 1966), p. 110, confirms my recollection.
3. See, for example, R. Hart Phillips, *The Cuban Dilemma* (New York: Ivan Obolensky, 1962), p. 71.
4. López-Fresquet, *My Fourteen Months with Castro*, p. 177.
5. From Castro's speech of January 8, 1959, at Camp Colombia—renamed Campo Libertad.
6. Boris Goldenberg, *The Cuban Revolution and Latin America* (New York: Praeger, 1965), p. 182. On May 25 the Congress of Sugar Workers passed a resolution censuring *Hoy*, the Communist daily, for its reports of their proceedings. The hope that the PSP was in eclipse was furthered by the announcement that Che Guevara was to go abroad on a long trip.

Chapter 7: Land Reform at Home and Intervention Abroad

1. The full text of the note is to be found in U.S., Department of State, *Bulletin*, June 29, 1959; and in the *New York Times*, June 12, 1959.
2. The *New York Times*, June 13, 1959, commented editorially as follows: "The American note to Havana is courteous and within the legitimate bounds of friendly relationship. It will surely be treated as such."
3. Quoted by Sen. J. William Fulbright, *The Arrogance of Power* (New York: Random House, 1967), p. 100; the newspaperman in question was Herbert Matthews, whose credulity concerning Castro was proverbial in Cuba.
4. Leovigildo Ruíz, *Diario de una Traición* (Miami: Florida Typesetting, 1965), pp. 113–14, 116–17.
5. The so-called Declaration of Santiago on Representative Democracy.

Chapter 8: *July and August of 1959*

1. Rufo López-Fresquet, *My Fourteen Months with Castro* (New York: World Publishing Company, 1966), pp. 116–21.
2. It is estimated that new American investment in Cuba in 1959 was higher than that in some earlier years of the decade.
3. López-Fresquet, *My Fourteen Months with Castro*, pp. 141–43.
4. President's press conference, July 15, 1959.
5. The announcement was made on July 17, 1959.
6. A front-page story in the *New York Times*, July 16, 1959, datelined Havana over Matthews's by-line. Matthews's assurances to me came both orally and in writing.
7. Leovigildo Ruíz, *Diario de una Traición* (Miami: Florida Typesetting, 1965), p. 163, under the date of September 1.
8. Mrs. Phillips is the author of *Cuba: Island of Paradox* and *The Cuban Dilemma*, both cited in the section, "Principal Books Consulted."
9. Walter Lippmann, "Cuba and Communism," *New York Herald Tribune*, July 23, 1959. This column was considered so friendly by the then fanatically pro-Castro *Bohemia* that it appeared in translation in the August 9, 1959, issue of that publication. Castro took no notice of the words of this most influential public philosopher.

Chapter 9: *A New Foreign Minister and an Interview with Castro*

1. I have lost the clipping from a San José, Costa Rica, paper in which this very apt description appeared in August 1960.
2. Jose Martí, *Obras Completas* (Havana: Editorial Lex, 1953), pp. 1816–18 (Martí's letter of January 18, 1892, to Fernando Figueredo).
3. "La concreción viscosa de todas las excrescencias humanas."
4. Raúl Roa, *En Pié, 1953–1958* (Santa Clara: University of Las Villas, October 1959). In his concluding pages and after describing the Castro movement and the struggle in the hills, he remarks, "It is not immaterial to point out that the communists, as a party, remained absent from the preparation, the development and the outcome of these happenings."
5. Ibid., p. 192.
6. This calumny was a favorite in revolutionary circles. It appeared in the weekly, *Bohemia*, soon after the fall of Batista. I had occasion to deny it indignantly in my first interview (in March) with the late Manuel Quevedo, the editor of that popular, influential, and often unscrupulous magazine.
7. Lee Lockwood, *Castro's Cuba, Cuba's Fidel* (New York: Macmillan, 1967), p. 141.

Chapter 10: *An Uncertain Interlude*

1. Leovigildo Ruíz, *Diario de una Traición* (Miami: Florida Typesetting, 1965), p. 164.
2. Rufo López-Fresquet, *My Fourteen Months with Castro* (New York: World Publishing Company, 1966), p. 142.
3. Ruíz, *Diario de una Traición*, p. 174, under September 29, 1959.
4. Richard M. Nixon, *Six Crises* (New York: Doubleday, 1962), p. 379.
5. *New York Times*, October 17, 1959.

Chapter 11: The Arrest of Matos and the "Bombing of Havana"

1. On April 21 in the course of a press conference at the United Nations, Castro had remarked, "The Revolutionary Government plans to make of tourism the principal industry of the country." Quoted in "Guía del Pensamiento Político Económico de Fidel," Diario Libre, Summer 1959, p. 91.
2. For the Matos episode, see R. Hart Phillips, The Cuban Dilemma (New York: Ivan Obolensky, 1962), pp. 112 ff.; Rufo López-Fresquet, My Fourteen Months with Castro (New York: World Publishing Company, 1966), p. 147; Boris Goldenberg, The Cuban Revolution and Latin America (New York: Praeger, 1965), pp. 188 ff.; and André Suárez, Cuba: Castroism and Communism, 1959–1966 (Cambridge, Mass.: M.I.T. Press, 1967), pp. 76–77.
3. López-Fresquet, My Fourteen Months with Castro, p. 130.
4. For the Matos letter and statement and Castro's reply and oratory, I have relied on Leovigildo Ruíz, Diario de una Traición (Miami: Florida Typesetting, 1965), pp. 182–88.
5. My account of the bombing is based on personal recollection confirmed by Goldenberg, Cuban Revolution, p. 190, and Phillips, Cuban Dilemma, p. 114.
6. U.S., Congress, Senate, Events in United States-Cuban Relations: A Chronology, 1957–1963 (Washington, D.C.: U.S. Government Printing Office, 1963), p. 12. The entry for March 20, 1960, describes the indictment by a United States grand jury in Florida of two persons who arranged and participated in such flights "for acting as agents of the Cuban Government without filing the registration statements required by law."
7. My recollection confirmed by Phillips, Cuban Dilemma, pp. 114 ff.; Goldenberg, Cuban Revolution, pp. 190 ff.; and New York Times, October 27, 1970.
8. This was the account current in Havana at the time; it is confirmed by López-Fresquet, My Fourteen Months with Castro, p. 60.
9. U.S., Department of State, Bulletin, November 16, 1959, carries the Department of State press release of October 27.

Chapter 12: What Course for the United States?

1. U.S., Department of State, Bulletin, November 16, 1959, carries the Department of State press release of October 27.
2. Statement dated October 26, 1959.
3. This so-called Fernandina expedition of three ships was seized by United States authorities on January 10, 1895. Herminio Portell-Vilá, Historia de Cuba en Sus Relaciones con los Estados Unidos y España, vol. 3 (Havana: Jesús Montero, 1938–1941), pp. 125–26; Jorge Mañach, Martí el Apóstol (Buenos Aires: Espasa Calpe, 1942), pp. 241–42; and Walter Millis, The Martial Spirit (Boston: Houghton Mifflin, 1931), p. 25.
4. Frederick Funston, Memories of Two Wars (New York: Charles Schribner's Sons, 1911), pp. 3–14.
5. See n.6, chap. 11.
6. Andrés Suárez, Cuba: Castroism and Communism, 1959–1966 (Cambridge, Mass.: M.I.T. Press, 1967), pp. 73–74.

7. General Cabell's statement was made to the Senate Internal Security Subcommittee.
8. I recall a prevalent rumor that Guevara, in the course of his jaunt abroad from May to September 1959, had made a secret trip to Moscow.
9. *Revolución*, November 3, 1959.
10. U.S., Department of State, *Bulletin*, February 1, 1960, carries the Department of State press release of January 11, 1960.
11. Castro made his speech on January 21, 1960.

Chapter 13: *The American Commitment to Nonintervention Reaffirmed*

1. U.S., Department of State, *Bulletin*, February 15, 1960, carries the White House press release of January 26, 1960.
2. Bryce Wood, *The Making of the Good Neighbor Policy* (New York: Columbia University Press, 1961), p. 28.
3. For example, Tad Szulc's dispatch from Rio to the *New York Times* at the end of January cited in R. Hart Phillips, *The Cuban Dilemma* (New York: Ivan Obolensky, 1962), pp. 149–50.
4. Amoedo's supposedly secret interview with Castro was reported in the press and in the news magazines; it had been leaked in Washington.
5. Of interest are articles by Theodore Draper and Julio Amoedo, *New Leader*, April 27, 1964, dealing with aspects of this matter. I believe the Department of State made a clarifying statement.
6. Roa's note of February 11, 1960.

Chapter 14: *The Castro-Mikoyan Deal, February 1960*

1. José Álvarez-Díaz, ed., *Un Estudio Sobre Cuba* (Coral Gables, Fla.: University of Miami Press, 1963), p. 966, table 368.

Chapter 15: *Nonintervention Abandoned, March 1960*

1. U.S., Congress, Senate, *Events in United States-Cuban Relations: A Chronology, 1957–1963* (Washington, D.C.: U.S. Government Printing Office, 1963), p. 11.
2. R. Hart Phillips, *The Cuban Dilemma* (New York: Ivan Obolensky, 1962), pp. 170 ff.
3. *New York Times*, April 21, 1960.
4. Dwight D. Eisenhower, *Waging Peace* (New York: Doubleday, 1960), p. 533; and Richard M. Nixon, *Six Crises* (New York: Doubleday, 1962), p. 379.
5. Phillips, *Cuban Dilemma*, p. 179—as an example.
6. Roa's television interview was in March.
7. Guevara made his statement on March 2.
8. Phillips, *Cuban Dilemma*, p. 209.
9. Andrés Suárez, *Cuba: Castroism and Communism, 1959–1966* (Cambridge, Mass.: M.I.T. Press, 1967), p. 102, has an illuminating comment on the PSP's dilemma in accepting Castro's leadership.
10. Ibid., p. 91.

Chapter 16: American Sanctions: Oil and Sugar

1. Fulgencio Batista, The Growth and Decline of the Cuban Republic (Greenwich, Conn.: Devin-Adair, 1964), p. 188.
2. U.S. Congress, Senate, Events in United States-Cuban Relations: A Chronology, 1957–1963 (Washington, D.C.: U.S. Government Printing Office, 1963), p. 12, states that the first shipment of Soviet crude oil arrived in Cuba on April 19.
3. This document was made public on August 10 and was transmitted to the Organization of American States.
4. A. E. Hotchner, Papa Hemingway (New York: Random House, 1966), p. 235.
5. Decree of July 5, 1960.
6. Quoted from a letter I received from a Department official in June.
7. Proclamation dated July 6, 1960. According to Events in United States-Cuban Relations, p. 15, the grounds for the action were that "Cuban commitments to pay for Soviet goods with Cuban sugar have raised serious doubts as to whether the United States can depend on Cuba as a source of sugar." In my judgment there was no justification for such a view. The full text may be found in U.S., Department of State, Bulletin, July 25, 1960, and in contemporary press reports.

Chapter 17: Revolutionary Progress and American Frustration

1. Andrés Suárez, Cuba: Castroism and Communism, 1959–1966 (Cambridge, Mass.: M.I.T. Press, 1967), p. 102.
2. My impression at the time—based on information from sources I believed reliable. Castro, of course, soon made the best of the fact that he had been made a satellite; he had no other choice in view of the destruction by the United States of the major Cuban American economic bond—a destruction he warmly welcomed since it forced the Russians into his arms from the economic point of view.
3. On December 16, 1960, President Eisenhower set the Cuban quota at zero for the first quarter of 1961, and on March 31, 1961, President Kennedy fixed the quota for the entire year at zero. See U.S., Congress, Senate, Events in United States-Cuban Relations: A Chronology, 1957–1963 (Washington, D.C..: U.S. Government Printing Office, 1963), p. 19.
4. Ibid., under September 17 and October 24, 1960.
5. Inter-American Institute of International Legal Studies, The Inter-American System: Its Development and Strengthening (Dobbs Ferry, N.Y.: Oceana Publications, 1966), p. 12, gives the text of this resolution, dated August 29, 1960.
6. A French text of the "Declaration of Havana" of September 2, 1960, may be found in Fidel Castro Parle, Cahiers Libres Num. 24–25 (Paris: François Maspero, 1961), pp. 202 ff.
7. Roa had made a point of this at San José in August.

Chapter 18: The End of My Mission and Electoral Politics at Home

1. U.S., Congress, Senate, Events in United States-Cuban Relations: A Chronology, 1957–1963 (Washington, D.C.: U.S. Government Printing Office, 1963), p. 18.

2. I recall two major cases: one in June involved the arrest and expulsion of two FBI men who had been in contact with enemies of the regime; the other in September was the discovery of the bugging by the CIA of the China News Agency office in Havana. The equipment for the latter operation had been installed in the apartment of an embassy secretary. Those arrested who had diplomatic immunity were promptly expelled, but their local coworkers drew long prison sentences.

3. Carlos Olivares turned out to have been an old-time Communist. He later became Castro's ambassador to Moscow. He once refused to receive one of my protest notes because in it I had described the language used in an expropriation decree as being reminiscent of Communist propaganda.

4. R. Hart Phillips, *The Cuban Dilemma* (New York: Ivan Obolensky, 1962), p. 254; see also the New York press for the period of the Assembly session.

5. John F. Kennedy, *Strategy of Peace*, edited by Allan Nevins (New York: Harper and Row, 1960), pp. 167–68.

6. The quotations from the campaign speeches of the candidates are derived from *The Speeches of Senator John F. Kennedy—Presidential Campaign of 1960; The Speeches of Vice-President Richard M. Nixon—Presidential Campaign of 1960;* and *The Joint Appearances of Senator John F. Kennedy and Vice-President Richard M. Nixon—Presidential Campaign of 1960* (Washington, D.C.: U.S. Government Printing Office, 1961). These texts were compiled at the behest of a Senate committee.

7. *The Speeches of Senator John F. Kennedy*, p. 1168.

8. Ibid., p. 510.

9. *The Joint Appearances of Senator John F. Kennedy and Vice-President Richard M. Nixon*, p. 432.

10. *The Speeches of Senator John F. Kennedy*, p. 608. Speech made on October 15.

11. Ibid.

12. Arthur M. Schlesinger, Jr., *A Thousand Days: John F. Kennedy in the White House* (New York: Houghton Mifflin, 1965), quotes this on p. 72.

13. *The Joint Appearances of Senator John F. Kennedy and Vice-President Richard M. Nixon*, p. 147.

14. Ibid., p. 265.

15. Ibid., p. 266.

16. *The Speeches of Senator John F. Kennedy*, p. 726. See the telegram dated October 23.

17. Richard M. Nixon, *Six Crises* (New York: Doubleday, 1962), p. 381, quoting Senator Kennedy.

18. Ibid., pp. 380 ff.

Chapter 19: President Kennedy, the Bay of Pigs, and the Missile Crisis

1. Arthur M. Schlesinger, Jr., *A Thousand Days: John F. Kennedy in the White House* (New York: Houghton Mifflin, 1965), p. 248.

2. Ibid., p. 243.

3. Ibid.

4. Especially the exile edition of the *Diario de la Marina*.

5. Theodore C. Sorensen, *Kennedy* (New York: Harper and Row, 1965), p. 302.

6. Schlesinger, *Thousand Days*, p. 233.

7. Ibid., pp. 72–73.

8. Ibid., p. 251. For the text of Senator Fulbright's memorandum of March 29 opposing the Bay of Pigs operation, see Karl E. Meyer, ed., *Fulbright of Arkansas* (Washington, D.C.: Robert B. Luce, 1963).
9. Schlesinger, *Thousand Days*, p. 262; see also Haynes Johnson, *The Bay of Pigs: The Leaders' Story of Brigade 2506* (New York: W. W. Norton, 1964), p. 72.
10. In an interview years later Mr. Richard Bissell, the CIA project manager, said that he and others had perhaps been overoptimistic as to the degree to which American participation could be concealed (*Washington Evening Star*, July 20, 1965, interview with Mr. Bissell headlined "The Bay of Pigs Revisited—Former CIA Aide Tells What He'd Do Differently").
11. Johnson, *The Bay of Pigs*, p. 76.
12. Ibid., p. 153; Schlesinger, *Thousand Days*, p. 278.
13. Ellis O. Briggs, *The Anatomy of Diplomacy* (New York: David McKay, 1968), p. 199, n. 7.
14. Schlesinger, *Thousand Days*, pp. 275–76.
15. Article by Jean Daniel in the *New Republic*, December 11, 1963; see also Schlesinger, *Thousand Days*, p. 795.

Chapter 20: Cuba and the United States, 1970 and Beyond

1. Lee Lockwood, *Castro's Cuba, Cuba's Fidel* (New York: Macmillan, 1967), p. 128.
2. In none of the accounts of the Missile Crisis that I have read does this noninvasion pledge figure as the concession that our hawks and Castro would like to make of it. See, for a recent example, Robert F. Kennedy, *Thirteen Days: A Memoir of the Cuban Missile Crisis* (New York: W. W. Norton, 1969).
3. Richard M. Nixon, *Six Crises* (New York: Doubleday, 1962), p. 379.
4. Richard M. Nixon, "Cuba, Castro, and John F. Kennedy," *Reader's Digest*, November 1964, pp. 285–300.
5. Emilio Núñez-Portuondo et al., *Diario de las Américas* (of Miami), Fall 1968 and Winter 1969.
6. Full text in the *New York Times*, February 19, 1970.
7. See, for example, U.S., Department of State, *Bulletin*, May 2, 1966, for a statement by a Department official dated March 23, 1966.
8. William Attwood, *The Reds and the Blacks* (New York: Harper and Row, 1967).
9. The spectacular harassment of the Swiss diplomats occupying the premises of the former American Embassy in Havana by Castro's mob following the recent kidnapping of Cuban fishermen by Cuban exiles is an example of such tactics.

Chapter 21: Future Economic Relations Between Cuba and the United States

1. Statistics derived from José Álvarez-Díaz, ed., *Un Estudio Sobre Cuba* (Coral Gables, Fla.: University of Miami Press, 1963).
2. These and other statistics are derived from ibid. This document, in turn, took them from standard sources such as the publications of the International Sugar Council, the World Bank, and the Food and Agriculture Organization of the United Nations.
3. Boris Goldenberg, *The Cuban Revolution and Latin America* (New York: Praeger, 1965), p. 280, quotes Guevara's remarks on July 14, 1963, to this effect.

4. For quotes from Castro's speeches, see Angel J. Sierra, *Azúcar Comunista* (Miami: Royal Palm Printers, 1967).
5. Ibid., p. 49, for Castro's speech of November 27, 1963.
6. It seems a reasonable speculation that the all-out effort in 1970 to produce 10 million tons in one crop-year will have had an impact on human, natural, and material resources resulting in relatively short crops over the next two or three years.
7. Based on imports from Cuba by the USSR in International Sugar Council, *Sugar Year Book*, 1969, p. 261.
8. Statistics of the International Sugar Council covering Soviet production for 1964 and subsequent years in the annual *Sugar Year Books*.
9. Ibid.
10. Lamborn & Co., *Lamborn's Chart of World Sugar Prices, 1931–1969* (New York: Sugar Institute, January 1970).
11. See quotations in the *New York Times*, mid-1968.
12. The text of the agreement was published by the United Nations. It is well summarized in Food and Agriculture Organization, *Monthly Bulletin of Agricultural Economics and Statistics*, 17, no. 12 (December 1968). I am also indebted to Miss Gertrud Lovasy of the World Bank for much information and insight into the agreement and into conditions in the international sugar trade; her expertise is widely recognized. (Any errors of fact or of interpretation, however, are mine alone.)
13. Information supplied by Miss Lovasy. See n. 12 above.
14. The European Economic Community is not a signatory to the Sugar Agreement of 1968, although it is granted a basic export quota of 300,000 metric tons in that agreement. At the time of the Geneva meetings in 1968, it was reported that the EEC aimed to produce 117 percent of the consumption requirements of its membership. This would have meant an export availability in excess of 1 million metric tons per annum. Current plans appear more modest.

Chapter 22: Conclusion

1. As current illustrations, I suggest Peru's expropriation of the International Petroleum Corporation (Standard Oil of New Jersey) as a case which business statesmanship a generation ago could have averted; the Bolivian government's seizure of the Gulf Oil properties as a case of shortsighted and mistaken governmental action (after all, Gulf did not come to Bolivia until 1956 and then did so on the basis of legislation designed by the Bolivian revolutionary government to attract investors to develop the country's oil resources); and the arrangements between the Chilean government under President Frei and the copper companies established there before World War I as an example of a hopefully successful, if belated, harmonizing of foreign private and public national interests. To those wishing to pursue the subject, I recommend Albert O. Hirschman, *How to Divest in Latin America and Why*, Essays in International Finance, no. 76 (Princeton, N.J.: Princeton University, November 1969).

Cuba and Sugar

1. See, for example, Herminio Portell-Vilá, *Historia de Cuba en Sus Relations con los Estados Unidos y España*, vol. 4 (Havana: Jesús Montero, 1938–1941), pp. 129–35.

2. See José Álvarez-Díaz, ed., *Un Estudio Sobre Cuba* (Coral Gables, Fla.: University of Miami Press, 1963), pp. 642–65, for a summary of the Ley de Coordinación Azucarera of 1937.
3. U.S., Department of Commerce, *Investment in Cuba* (Washington, D.C.: U.S. Government Printing Office, 1956), p. 7.
4. Ibid.

Cuban American Relations
and the Dynamics of Cuban Politics

1. See, for example, Samuel Flagg Bemis, *The Latin American Policy of the United States* (New York: Harcourt, Brace, 1943).
2. It is hard to avoid the conclusion that some $2 million in bonds of the future Cuban republic were issued by the Revolutionary Junta in New York (issue of 96/97) and wound up, through an intermediary, in the hands of unknown persons in a position to work for the recognition of the insurgent government by the government of the United States at the time of the declaration that a state of war existed between the United States and Spain. See Herminio Portell-Vilá, *Historia de Cuba en Sus Relaciones con los Estados Unidos y España*, vol. 3 (Havana: Jesús Montero, 1938), pp. 351 ff., where he cites the minutes of the Revolutionary Junta in 1897 and 1898 and a memorandum on the subject forwarded to the Department of State by the Legation of the United States in Havana in 1904. These bonds were paid off.
3. For details on Máximo Gómez's attitude in 1898 and 1899, see Orestes Ferrara, *Mis Relaciones con Máximo Gómez*, 2d ed. (Havana: Molina y Cía, 1942), pp. 207–33; and Rafael Martínez-Ortiz, *Cuba: Los Primeros Años de Independencia*, 2d ed., vol. 1 (Paris, 1921), pp. 32–54.
4. The Platt Amendment was the creation of Elihu Root. See Philip C. Jessup, *Elihu Root* (New York: Dodd, Mead, 1938), pp. 313–15. For the history of the Amendment from the American point of view, see Dana G. Munro, *Intervention and Dollar Diplomacy in the Caribbean, 1900–1921* (Princeton, N.J.: Princeton University Press, 1964); and Leland Jenks, *Our Cuban Colony*, American Imperialism Series (New York: American Fund for Public Service Studies in American Investments Abroad, 1928). For the Cuban side of the story the best source still seems to me to be Martínez-Ortiz, *Cuba*, vol. 1, pp. 195-294.
5. Munro, *Intervention and Dollar Diplomacy*, pp. 113–14, quotes the following from a speech made by Elihu Root in 1907: "I think the key of our attitude toward these countries can be put in three sentences. First: We do not want to take them for ourselves. Second: We do not want any foreign nation to take them for themselves. Third: We want to help them. Now, we can help them—help them govern themselves, help them to acquire capacity for self-government, help them along the road that Brazil and the Argentine and Chile and Peru and a number of other South American countries have travelled—up out of the discord and turmoil of continual revolution into a general public sense of justice and determination to maintain order." The countries Mr. Root had in mind were those of the Caribbean and Central America, the republics to which the Roosevelt Corollary of the Monroe Doctrine was deemed applicable.
6. Ibid., p. 26; Martínez-Ortiz, *Cuba*, p. 258.

7. Martínez-Ortiz, a Liberal, gives what seems a fair portrait of Cuba's first President, a Conservative or Moderado. Martínez-Ortiz, Cuba, pp. 313–14, for example.
8. Munro, Intervention and Dollar Diplomacy, p. 129.
9. Ibid., pp. 129–33; Martínez-Ortiz, Cuba, pp. 613–750.
10. Martínez-Ortiz, Cuba, p. 639; see also a letter from Estrada-Palma to an old friend dated October 10, 1906, and quoted in ibid., pp. 810–15. The last sentence of that letter reads as follows, in translation, "I have never hesitated to say—and I'm not afraid to say it aloud—that it is a hundred times preferable for our beloved Cuba to be submitted to a political dependence that insures to us the fruitful gifts of freedom rather than [to have] the independent and sovereign republic discredited and wretched because of the sinister impact of periodic civil wars."
11. Stephen Bonsal, The American Mediterranean (New York: Moffat Yard & Co., 1913), p. 44; see also Martínez-Ortiz, Cuba, p. 760.
12. Munro, Intervention and Dollar Diplomacy, pp. 469–529; and Jenks, Our Cuban Colony, pp. 104–37.
13. Munro, pp. 469–529; and Jenks, pp. 246–65.
14. See Jenks for a picturesque description of the growth of American investment.
15. Ramiro Guerra, Azúcar y Poblacion en las Antillas (Havana, 1927), quotation taken from translation Sugar and Society in the Caribbean (New Haven, Conn.: Yale University Press, 1964), p. 74. Dr. Guerra's work had great influence in Cuban opinion and was reflected to some extent in the legislation on sugar during the depression years and in the provisions of the Constitution of 1940 on landholding.
16. Bryce Wood, The Making of the Good Neighbor Policy (New York: Columbia University Press, 1961), pp. 6–7, describes the United States in the late twenties as "moving toward a general policy of non-intervention."
17. Jenks, Our Cuban Colony, p. 288.
18. New York Times, April 29, 1927, quoted in Robert F. Smith, The United States and Cuba: Business and Diplomacy, 1917–1960 (New York: Bookman Associates, 1960), p. 116.
19. The Platt Amendment was now held to be applicable only in the event of serious danger to American lives and property on the island. The Root interpretation pledging no interference or intermeddling—in other words, no preventive policy—was once more adopted by Washington to the distress of anti-Machado Cubans and Americans.
20. See R. Hart Phillips, Cuba: Island of Paradox (New York: McDowell Obolensky, 1959), pp. 5–14, for many dramatic details illustrative of the atmosphere of the times.
21. José Álvarez-Díaz, ed., Un Estudio Sobre Cuba (Coral Gables, Fla.: University of Miami, Press, 1963), p. 591.
22. Wood, Making of the Good Neighbor Policy, is my major authority for the events described in this section.
23. Ibid., p. 65. Welles had a confidential talk with the Minister of Defense within hours prior to the latter's ultimatum to Machado. The Minister may well have achieved the impression that unless the President departed, the United States would intervene, although Welles may not have wished to convey such an impression—or at least not in black-and-white terms that would have risked having his bluff called. A Cuban belief in the imminence of intervention might well have coexisted—as it had earlier and did later—with an American determination to avoid intervention.

24. Ibid., pp. 72–75. On the basis of a careful examination of the documents, Wood says of Welles that "on three occasions he asked fruitlessly that American troops be landed in Cuba." These three occasions took place during the three days from September 5 to September 8 and reflected the impact on Welles and on his Cuban and American contacts in Havana of the drastic events that followed the fall of Céspedes.
25. Edmund Chester, *Un Sargento Llamado Batista* (Havana: Editorial Arocha, 1954), p. 109.
26. Phillips, *Cuba: Island of Paradox*, p. 150.
27. Martínez Ortiz, *Cuba*, pp. 428–29.
28. For details of sugar legislation, see Álvarez-Díaz, *Estudio Sobre Cuba*, pp. 631–35 (Sugar Acts of 1934 and 1937), pp. 946–48 (Sugar Act of 1948), pp. 952–53 (modification of 1951), and pp. 982–85 (modification of 1956). I have also relied on the legal texts and on a pamphlet entitled *What Is the United States Sugar Program*, rev. ed. (Washington, D.C.: United States Sugar Beet Association, March 1966).
29. Álvarez-Díaz, *Estudio Sobre Cuba*, p. 942, table 366.
30. The average prices at which the United States government bought the Cuban crops during the war period were as follows: 2.65 cents per pound in 1942, 1943, and 1944; 3.10 cents in 1945; 4.1816 cents in 1946; and 4.9625 cents in 1947. Taken from Lamborn & Co., *Lamborn's Chart of World Sugar Prices, 1931–1969* (New York: Sugar Institute, January 1970).
31. Álvarez-Díaz, *Estudio Sobre Cuba*, p. 937.
32. War damage in the Philippines had caused major curtailment of sugar production there; the Sugar Act of 1948 gave 95 percent of the Philippine deficit to Cuba—a significant plus for Cuba until the Philippine industry was rehabilitated several years later.
33. U.S., Congress, *Sugar Act of 1948*, 80th Cong., 1st sess., August 8, 1947, p. 919.
34. Álvarez-Díaz, *Estudio Sobre Cuba*, pp. 952, 983, gives the Cuban judgments on these modifications.
35. Ibid., p. 985.
36. Wood, *Making of the Good Neighbor Policy*, pp. 104–17, gives a clear and concise account of the Mendieta and Gómez administrations.
37. Eduardo Suárez-Rivas, *Un Pueblo Crucificado* (Coral Gables, Fla.: Service Offset Printers, 1964), pp. 104–05. The author, then a leader of the Gómecista Liberals in the lower house gives an illuminating account of his interview with Ambassador Caffey at this time—illuminating in terms of an understanding of the Cuban mood. He concludes, "I left convinced of the Embassy's support for Batista's maneuver [the impeachment of Gómez]." In 1950 the Cuban Congress annulled the impeachment—a posthumous reparation.
38. There were, in reality, two sets of public works obligations: the Machado regime's public works bonds underwritten by an American bank and distributed to the general public, and the certificates of indebtedness held by Warren Brothers and Purdy and Henderson who had performed some of the work involved.
39. Phillips, *Cuba: Island of Paradox*, pp. 196–97; Márquez-Sterling, *Historia de Cuba*, pp. 324–26; and Suárez-Rivas, *Pueblo Crucificado*, pp. 121 ff.
40. Suárez-Rivas, *Pueblo Crucificado*, p. 125.
41. Ibid., p. 180. In 1944 Menocal's son abandoned the Batista coalition and joined a

splinter group of Conservatives who went over to the Auténticos and were a significant factor in the victory of Grau in that year. General Menocal had died in 1941, the year after his pact with Batista.

42. This episode remains green in my memory. Braden and Batista later became reconciled.

43. This is a personal recollection of hearsay at the time.

44. For the chronology and the salient events of the Grau and Prío presidencies, I have drawn on Phillips, *Cuba: Island of Paradox;* Suárez-Rivas, *Pueblo Crucificado;* and Márquez-Sterling, *Historia de Cuba.* The statistics are derived from Álvarez-Díaz, *Estudio Sobre Cuba.*

45. Suárez-Rivas, *Pueblo Crucificado,* p. 207. Suárez-Rivas was president of the Senate and a member of the Liberal party at the time; consequently he was a member of the opposition to Grau.

46. Phillips, *Cuba: Island of Paradox,* pp. 253–54; this occurred on July 4, 1950.

47. Suárez-Rivas, *Pueblo Crucificado,* pp. 270–76, gives most of the specifics I have cited. See p. 216 for the attempt to question the Minister of Education.

48. Phillips, *Cuba: Island of Paradox,* pp. 240–41.

49. This was the so-called battle of Orfila Street on September 15, 1947.

50. Phillips, *Cuba: Island of Paradox,* p. 242; Suárez-Rivas, *Pueblo Crucificado,* p. 216; and Márquez-Sterling, *Historia de Cuba,* p. 346.

51. Throughout his work on the history of Cuba, Carlos Márquez-Sterling expounds his theory of the *amalgama.* This he defines as a system of purely destructive attacks having as their objective the denigration and the undermining of any existing political system. He gives a prominent role in its execution to the Communists. He concludes that the non-Communist politicians who fall for this tactic and utilize it in their own maneuvers to overthrow their opponents will promote "the disappearance of the democratic regime and the imposition of communism" (Márquez-Sterling, *Historia de Cuba,* p. 292). After making allowances for the extravagance of political struggle in Cuba (and elsewhere) and recognizing the passionate and unscrupulous level at which political debate was often conducted, I venture the belief that Márquez-Sterling has confused cause with effect. The generally agreed loss of prestige of the Cuban political process was not so much the work of a malevolent Communist conspiracy as it was the result of the irresponsibility, the corruption, and the illegality that characterized the functioning of the system. For this Batista, Grau, Prío, and again Batista share responsibility during the final two decades of the republic. The Communists—and others—took advantage of this loss of prestige, but they did not create it.

52. Suárez-Rivas, *Pueblo Crucificado,* p. 275.

53. Ibid., p. 235.

54. Álvarez-Díaz, *Estudio Sobre Cuba,* p. 1275.

Principal Books Consulted

In the course of this attempt to communicate my own experiences in Cuba and the thinking to which those experiences gave rise, I have had occasion to read widely, to become familiar with much of the literature on Castro and his Revolution, and to renew my acquaintance with the background that made the Revolution possible. I am listing below, in alphabetical order by author, the major works which I have consulted. My awareness of what has been written about Cuba, however, is not confined to these works. Hugh Thomas's monumental book, *Cuba: The Pursuit of Freedom* (New York: Harper & Row, 1971), appeared after my manuscript was completed. I had the pleasure of reading it while my work was at the printer's.

Álvarez-Díaz, José, ed. *Un Estudio Sobre Cuba.* Coral Gables, Fla.: University of Miami Press, 1963.
The editor and a team of Cuban economists at the University of Miami, including Roberto González Cofiño, Roberto E. Hernández-Morales, Jose M. Illan-González, Rafael Miquel-Zayas, Raul Shelton-Ovich, and Mrs. Ofelia Tabares Fernández-Díaz, cover the economic, political, and social development of Cuba from the days of the colony through the Republic to Castro's current Marxism-Leninism. It is an essential and thorough reference work, well organized, a mine of important information on all aspects of the Cuban society and economy. In its 1,700 pages the reader will find answers to most conceivable questions on Cuban history in these fields. This is a work of true scholarship and lasting value. An abridged English translation was published in 1965, also by the University of Miami Press.

——— et al. *Cuba: Geopolítica y Pensamiento Económico.* Miami: Colegio de Economistas de Cuba en el Exilio, 1964.
A valuable and stimulating interpretation of the Álvarez-Díaz book listed above.

Batista, Fulgencio. *The Growth and Decline of the Cuban Republic.* Greenwich, Conn.: Devin-Adair, 1964.
This is one of several books published over the former dictator's signature and presumably at his expense. These publications have not altered the adverse verdict of most Cubans and of almost all foreign observers.

Chester, Edmund A. *A Sergeant Named Batista*. New York: Henry Holt, 1954.
This work by Batista's long-time public relations man and apologist provides much fascinating detail about its hero and his contemporaries. It was published in Spanish in the same year by Editorial Arocha in Havana.

Draper, Theodore. *Castroism: Theory and Practice*. New York: Praeger, 1965.

———. *Castro's Revolution: Myths and Realities*. New York: Praeger, 1962.
These two volumes are essential to an understanding of the Castro phenomenon. I consider them to be the best available on the subject.

Dubois, Jules. *Fidel Castro: Rebel, Liberator, or Dictator?* Indianapolis, Ind.: Bobbs-Merrill, 1959.
The late Jules Dubois rushed into print with this book early in 1959 while he was still under the Castro spell—a spell from which, unlike Herbert Matthews, he soon freed himself. The book is valuable today chiefly for the pre-1960 documentation and the quotations that gave such an erroneous view of the policies Castro was to pursue.

Ferrara, Orestes. *Mis Relaciones con Máximo Gómez*. 2d ed. Havana: Molina y Cía, 1942.
Military and political recollections of the period 1897 to 1905 by one who became an outstanding figure in the Cuban Republic. Ferrara, a young Italian student, suspected by some Cuban rebels of anarchistic tendencies, came to Máximo Gómez's camp in the bush during the War for Cuban Independence, attained the rank of colonel in the insurgent army, went on to become a leader of the Liberal party and an important figure in the legal and business worlds. His identification with Machado destroyed his political career. He has lived in Spain and Italy for the last thirty years and has written a number of scholarly and combative works on episodes in the histories of those countries. An extraordinarily able and many-sided man. Had he been born in Cuba, he might well have become President.

Goldenberg, Boris. *The Cuban Revolution and Latin America*. New York: Praeger, 1965.
An important study by a European and former Marxist who lived for many years in pre-Castro Cuba.

Guerra, Ramiro. *Azúcar y Población en las Antillas*. Havana, 1927.
Often reedited, this work has had great influence on the develop-

ment of Cuban thinking on sugar and on land tenure. An English translation entitled *Sugar and Society in the Carribbean* was published in 1964 by Yale University Press.

Jenks, Leland. *Our Cuban Colony*. American Imperialism Series. New York: American Fund for Public Service Studies in American Investments Abroad, 1928.
Mr. Jenks's work is a valuable record of American Cuban relations up to 1927, especially in the economic field. Two of his comments seem to me worth reproducing. On page 6 he remarks that the facts he is about to relate "will tell a story of excellent intentions, of ineptitude and misunderstanding, of meddlesome helpfulness, and of a somewhat pettifogging support of American 'interests' on the part of Washington." He adds, "In the hopes and fears engendered by the credit system there are sanctions which do not require cruisers for their enforcement."

Jessup, Philip C. *Elihu Root*. New York: Dodd, Mead, 1938.
A model biography of one of the most important of American public servants who was the brains of our Cuban and Latin American policies during the first decade of the century.

Johnson, Haynes. *The Bay of Pigs: The Leaders' Story of Brigade 2506*. New York: W. W. Norton, 1964.
A lively account of that fiasco based on the stories of the leaders of the expeditionary force: Manuel Artime, José Pérez-San Roman, Eneido Oliva, and Enrique Ruíz-Williams.

Lockwood, Lee. *Castro's Cuba, Cuba's Fidel: An American Journalist's Inside Look at Today's Cuba*. New York: Macmillan, 1967.
A marathon interview with Castro lavishly illustrated with excellent photographs by the author. The subtitle raises in the mind of this reader the question of how unconditional an admirer of Castro's does an American journalist have to be to get the attention and the facilities required for this type of publication. Sold at the reactionary price of $9.95!

López-Fresquet, Rufo. *My Fourteen Months with Castro*. New York: World Publishing Company, 1966.
A perceptive and illuminating account of what it was like for a liberal, progressive economist to work for Castro. The author was Cuban Minister of the Treasury from January 1959 to March 1960.

Mañach, Jorge. *Martí el Apóstol*. Buenos Aires: Espasa Calpe, 1942.
Often reedited, this is a splendid biography of Cuba's great leader by a noted Cuban man of letters.

Márquez-Sterling, Carlos. *Historia de Cuba Desde Colón Hasta Castro.* New York: Las Américas Publishing Company, 1963.
This work by a well-known Cuban politician is enlightening both in what it records and what it omits. The author was the leader of a splinter party that was willing to fight the elections of 1958 in opposition to Batista's candidate at a time when most Cuban politicians in general and Castro in particular were refusing to have anything to do with the political process as long as the dictator maintained his hold on the power he had usurped.

Martí, José. *Obras Completas.* Havana: Editorial Lex, 1953.
This complete edition of Martí's writings—articles, essays, speeches, letters, poetry, drama, fiction—runs to some four thousand pages. It gives even the casual reader some conception of the many-sided genius whose death at the age of forty-two in a skirmish with the Spaniards was such a blow to the prospects of the republic "of all Cubans for all Cubans"—the republic he had dreamed of, worked for, fought for, and almost brought to life.

Martínez-Ortiz, Rafael. *Cuba: Los Primeros Años de Independencia.* 2d ed. 2 vols. Paris, 1921.
This standard history by a Liberal politician is objective and thorough. It is a painstaking narrative of the events it describes and of contemporary opinion about those events. It covers the period from the end of the Spanish-American War to the end of the second American intervention in Cuba (March 1909). It is well documented and rich in revealing anecdotes and in quotations from the utterances of contemporary personalities.

Munro, Dana G. *Intervention and Dollar Diplomacy in the Caribbean, 1900–1921.* Princeton, N.J.: Princeton University Press, 1964.
This carefully researched, well-organized work includes a full account, based largely on official sources, of American policy toward Cuba in the years mentioned. The author was a professor of history at Princeton. He had for many years been an official of the Department of State and had served our country in the Caribbean area. He is a happy combination of the academic and the diplomat. His book, which will, one hopes, be continued to cover the story of the twenties, is a model of objective historical writing.

Phillips, R. Hart. *Cuba: Island of Paradox.* New York: McDowell Obolensky, 1959.

———. *The Cuban Dilemma.* New York: Ivan Obolensky, 1962.
For the better part of three decades the author's Havana by-line was familiar to readers of the *New York Times.* An admirable re-

porter and a competent writer, she has condensed her Cuban experience in these two fascinating volumes. The political philosophy she expresses is not mine. For example, in the first of the two works cited, she attributes the United States's loss of prestige in Latin America "in no small measure to the failure of the United States government to protect United States citizens and their property" in the area. I disagree. I do not believe the United States can or should use the leverage of American political and economic power to secure a special position for its citizens and their property in these countries. Such an assertion has done much to create unnecessary frictions as well as to diminish the acceptability of the free-enterprise and private-property concepts in the hemisphere by identifying them with an "imperialism" repugnant to the aroused nationalism of the countries concerned.

Portell-Vilá, Herminio. *Historia de Cuba en Sus Relaciones con los Estados Unidos y España.* 4 vols. Havana: Jesús Montero, 1938–1941.
This work of over twenty-two hundred pages with some three thousand footnotes by a well-known and skillful Cuban writer should be a monument of definitive scholarship. But the author's passion and bias make most of his judgments suspect. He has two villains— the United States and Spain—and one hero—personified by the few Cubans of whom he approves. The author's presupposition that Americans in their dealings with Cuba will in every case be arrogant, rapacious, and stupid is reflected in the current approach of Castro and his propagandists. Portell-Vilá covers Cuban history from 1512 to about 1909 in his formal narrative, though he comments extensively and with characteristic acerbity on later events, particularly those of 1933. He was a public official in the first Grau government in that year. His work was aided by the Guggenheim Foundation.

Ruíz, Leovigildo. *Diario de una Traición.* Miami: Florida Typesetting, 1965.
Señor Ruíz has put together for the year 1959 an invaluable day-to-day chronicle of Castro's first year in power.

Schlesinger, Arthur M., Jr. *A Thousand Days: John F. Kennedy in the White House.* New York: Houghton Mifflin, 1965.
This is a valuable book especially because of the author's own participation in the handling of Cuban matters and because he worked closely with Adolf Berle on the President's Task Force for Latin America in 1961.

Semidei, Manuela. *Les États Unis et la Révolution Cubaine.* Cahiers de la Fondation Nationale des Sciences Politiques. Paris: Armand Colin, 1968.

The author, a young French researcher, has digested an enormous amount of material and has furnished a highly readable account of an episode concerning which European public opinion tends to take a superficial view.

Sierra, Angel J. *Azúcar Comunista*. Miami: Royal Palm Printers, 1967.
A useful contribution to an understanding of the sugar policies Castro has followed since 1960. It contains extracts from the Maximum Leader's pronouncements and much statistical material. The author was a lawyer in pre-Castro Cuba and had much experience representing the interests of the sugar planters ("*colonos*").

Smith, Earl E. T. *The Fourth Floor: An Account of the Castro Communist Revolution*. New York: Random House, 1962.
According to Ambassador Smith if the President and the Secretary of State had had time to listen to him, if the lower echelons of the State Department had not been pro-Castro, and if Batista had held the fair elections he had promised the Ambassador he would hold, Castro's coming to power would have been avoided. Not convincing to me! I believe the following: the Cuban politicians willing to play the electoral opposition game under Batista did not have the support of anything like a significant sector of Cuban public opinion, the Department of State was not pro-Castro, and Castro was not a Communist pre-1960. The chief element in Castro's achievement of total power in Cuba was the startling revelation of the total absence of influence over the Cuban people of the pre-Castro establishment—political, social, and business.

Sorensen, Theodore C. *Kennedy*. New York: Harper and Row, 1965.

Suárez, Andrés. *Cuba: Castroism and Communism, 1959–1966*. Cambridge, Mass.: M.I.T. Press, 1967.
The author is a Cuban lawyer who served as Under Secretary of the Treasury in the early months of the Castro regime. His is one of the most important books on Castro's relations with Communists at home and abroad. I believe it bears out my contention that Castro made Castroites of his local Communists before he became a Communist himself. This is a very carefully researched presentation of a complex subject.

Suárez-Rivas, Eduardo. *Un Pueblo Crucificado*. Coral Gables, Fla.: Service Offset Printers, 1964.
A political history of Cuba from 1923 to Castro's coming to power in 1959 by a Cuban politician who played a prominent role in that history from his student days to the end of the Batista dictatorship. The author was originally a Liberal. He became an Auténtico of the

electoralist rather than the abstentionist-insurrectionist segment of the party after Batista's coup in 1952. Nevertheless, in contrast to Márquez-Sterling, he held that in 1958 his party should have withdrawn rather than have participated in the elections of that year. He records that he was unsuccessful in persuading Grau to follow that course. His book contains much fascinating and probably controversial material about inside politics in Cuba during his day.

Szulc, Tad, and Meyer, Karl E. *The Cuban Invasion: The Chronicle of a Disaster.* New York: Praeger, 1962.
A good account by two able reporters who covered the Cuban story before and after the Bay of Pigs.

U.S. Congress. Senate. *Events in United States-Cuban Relations: A Chronology, 1957–1963.* Washington, D.C.: U.S. Government Printing Office, 1963.
Prepared by the Department of State for the Committee on Foreign Relations.

Weyl, Nathaniel. *Red Star Over Cuba.* Greenwich, Conn.: Devin-Adair, 1960.
A book for those who believe that were it not for the international Communist conspiracy directed from Moscow and Peking, we Americans would be living in a utopia without a care in the world. Endorsed by Spruille Braden.

Wood, Bryce. *The Making of the Good Neighbor Policy.* New York: Columbia University Press, 1961.
This is an admirable account of the genesis and the development of the philosophy of relations with the other American republics generated in the United States in the late twenties and the early thirties. Carefully researched, well organized, and attractively written, this seems to me a demonstration of how serious history should be written. The chapters on Cuba dealing with the period from 1930 through 1937 have been particularly enlightening and useful to me.

Index

ABC (Cuban political organization), 262
Agramonte, Roberto (Cuban Minister of Foreign Affairs), 10; as member of Castro's Cabinet, 25, 35, 49, 51–55 passim, 63, 66; dismissal of, 73, 88, 287
Alemán, José (Grau's Minister of Education), 282–84 passim
Alliance for Progress, 163, 178, 221
Almeida, Major Juan, 119
Álvarez-Díaz, José, 287, 303. See also Study on Cuba
American & Foreign Power group, 257. See also Electric light and power company
American Consular staff, 111, 142, 167
American Embassy staff, 38, 165; and closing of Embassy, 175
American investment in Cuba: and Batista, 11, 12, 16; in 1959, 41–46; and Castro, 74–75, 92–93, 160–61, 203–04; growth of, 255–57; influence of, 268–69. See also Compensation for nationalized property; Investment in Latin America, foreign; Nationalizations
American press: in Cuba, 82–83, 193, 201
Americans in Cuba, 84, 111, 167
American Society of Travel Agents (ASTA), 100–01, 106
Amnesty of 1955, 13
Amoedo, Julio (Argentine Ambassador to Cuba), 126–27, 139, 178
Anderson, Robert B. (U.S. Secretary of the Treasury), 149–50
Annexationist sentiment, 235–36
Anti-Castro Cubans, 95, 98, 111–13, 135, 141–43, 167, 169, 179–81, 190
Anticommunism in Cuba. See Communism in Cuba
Arbenz, Jacobo, 40, 87
ASTA. See American Society of Travel Agents
Auténtico party, 10, 11, 20, 76, 273, 277, 279; in power (1944–1952), 280–88

Banking: in Cuba, 256, 257

Barquín, Colonel Ramon, 15, 19
Baseball: and Castro, 95–97
Bat guano, 79
Batista, Fulgencio: 1952 coup of, 10; dictatorship of (1952–1958), 10–24; and break with Soviet Union, 11; and attempts to legitimize regime, 11–15, 19–23; and elections of 1954, 12–13; frees Castro, 13; and Ambassador Gardner, 13, 17, 47; rejects Civic Dialogue, 14–15; and United States, 17; and Ambassador Smith, 19–23 passim; and elections of 1958, 20, 22; flees Cuba, 23; Castro's view of U.S. policy toward, 31–33; and telephone rates, 46–47, 87, 90, 129, 146, 191; development program of, 243–44, 303
—early career, 262–65 passim, 272–75 passim, 277–79, 284, 286–88
Bay of Pigs, 135, 176, 179, 180, 181–86, 188, 192, 194, 196, 199–200, 222–23, 284
Berle, Dr. Adolf A., Jr., 177–79 passim
Betancourt, President Rómulo, 54, 161
Bissell, Richard, 182, 297n10
Bohemia, 17, 292n6
"Bombing of Havana," 104–07. See also Díaz-Lanz, Major Pedro
Bonsal, Mrs. Philip W., 38, 119, 136, 170
Bonsal, Philip W.: appointed Ambassador to Cuba, 25–26; diplomatic background of, 26–27; significance of appointment of, 27–28; early view of Castro regime of, 28–31; appraises his mission, 38–42; and telephone company "intervention," 46–48; at first meeting with Castro, 51–53; retrospective view of Castro of, 55–58; and meeting of American Ambassadors, 58–60; and Castro's trip to the United States, 62–66; speculation on Castro's thinking of, 66–67; and Land Reform Law, 70–76; and American news media, 82–83, 84, 85; and Foreign Minister Roa, 86–88; and interview with Castro, 89–91; and Washington consultations, 93–

311